MW01129009

"A true masterpiece that aggregates essential knowledge and insights to thrive within the forthcoming metaverse era."
Hwan Jin Choi, Professor, Hanshin University, South Korea

"An essential resource, and a refreshing and enlightening take on the metaverse as a canvas for creativity for people, business, and society."
Simon Cook, CEO, Cannes Lions

"We are in a new era of mass digital acceleration and significant industrial change. The lines are blurring in multiple ways across creative spaces, technology, behaviors, and society. It's easy to feel overwhelmed or unprepared. What we need is a modern companion to help us understand how we got here and what lies ahead, and that's exactly what *Decoding the Metaverse* offers readers. This is the perfect handbook for those designing the future, and it will help you navigate the crazy new era we find ourselves in."
Wayne Deakin, Global Principle, Creative, Wolff Olins, Omnicom Group

"Chris Duffey provides a valuable explanation of the building blocks for the metaverse, including its linkage to Web3 and blockchain. The practical examples featured throughout the book explain why and how the metaverse will trigger one of the most significant changes that we have experienced in the past few decades. This is a fantastic go-to resource for organizations developing their metaverse strategy."
Roberto Hernandez, US Customer Strategy and Experience Leader and Global metaverse Leader, PwC

"As businesses engage in the metaverse and Web3 technology, we must learn from history and make the conscious choice to use this technology to connect us, not separate us. Chris Duffey underscores this in *Decoding the Metaverse*, all of us need to be educated and informed on the metaverse and Web3 tech."

Jon Levy, behavioral scientist and *New York Times* bestselling author

"In *Decoding the Metaverse*, Chris Duffey provides insight into the commercial integration of emerging technology, business, and society. The book offers a much-needed technical overview and glossary that managers can use to think strategically about their involvement in the metaverse and Web3."

Matthew Quint, Director of the Center on Global Brand Leadership, Columbia Business School, and cohost of the *BRITE Ideas* podcast

Decoding the Metaverse

Expand Your Business Using Web3

Chris Duffey

KoganPage

Publisher's note

Every possible effort has been made to ensure that the information contained in this book is accurate at the time of going to press, and the publishers and authors cannot accept responsibility for any errors or omissions, however caused. No responsibility for loss or damage occasioned to any person acting, or refraining from action, as a result of the material in this publication can be accepted by the editor, the publisher or the author.

First published in Great Britain and the United States in 2023 by Kogan Page Limited

2nd Floor, 45 Gee Street
London
EC1V 3RS
United Kingdom
www.koganpage.com

8 W 38th Street, Suite 902
New York, NY 10018
USA

4737/23 Ansari Road
Daryaganj
New Delhi 110002
India

© Chris Duffey 2023

The right of Chris Duffey to be identified as the author of this work has been asserted by him in accordance with the Copyright, Designs and Patents Act 1988.

ISBNs

Hardback   9781398609068
Paperback   9781398609044
Ebook   9781398609051

British Library Cataloguing-in-Publication Data

A CIP record for this book is available from the British Library.

Library of Congress Control Number

2022951477

Typeset by Hong Kong FIVE Workshop
Print production managed by Jellyfish
Printed and bound by CPI Group (UK) Ltd, Croydon CR0 4YY

To my family who have made this experience we call life one filled with happiness, love, and purpose.

To my friend John D Seibert for being a shining example of strength, kindness, and success.

CONTENTS

ABOUT THE AUTHOR

Chris Duffey spearheads Adobe's strategic development design partnerships across the creative enterprise space.

Chris' keynotes have received over 50 million impressions, and his sessions have been reported around the world in Access Hollywood, Extra, OK, Hello, People, the Daily Mail, and Euro News. His work has been featured by more than 100 global media outlets, including The Wall Street Journal, The Economist, Inc., Adweek, Adage, Cheddar, The Guardian, The Mirror, The Drum, Campaign, CMO.com, the New York Post and Business Insider, and he has been profiled by Google, McKinsey and Wharton in their digital marketing book. Chris also serves on the Board of Directors for the Association of National Advertisers NY (ANA) and the Consumer Technology Association (CTA) Board of Industry Leaders.

Chris is author of the award-winning book Superhuman Innovation, the world's first book co-authored by AI about AI. It was named one of the best product innovation books of all time by BookAuthority. An award-winning executive creative director, noted speaker, author and leader in AI, Web3, metaverse, and experience design, Chris has been featured by Yahoo as one of "the industry's leaders on the top issues, challenges and opportunities in the fast-changing world of mobile marketing." He was selected by Qualcomm as one of the leading minds in AI and voted the #1 Boldest Digital Health Influencer Award by New York City Health Business Leaders. Chris has been a creative consultant for over 35 advertising agencies at WPP, IPG, Havas, Omnicom, Publicis, and MDC.

Chris has spoken around the world at the leading thought leadership conferences—CES, SXSW, Adobe MAX, Social Media Week, Dublin Tech Summit, the Irish Parliament, Cyprus Reflect Fest, London Book Fair, MAD Stars South Korea, Association of National Advertisers, Columbia University, Wonderland AI, WebXR, Swiss

Cognitive, Social Media Day, The Conference Board, Advertising Week NY, Seattle Interactive, CUTI Uruguay, The Next Web. And he is a ten-time Cannes Lions speaker, sharing the main stage with Kim Kardashian, speaking on mobile gaming.

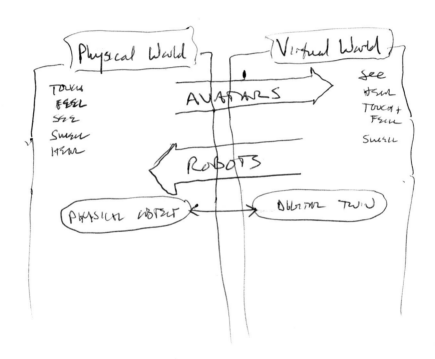

Introduction_

We are on the verge of the most significant expansion of societal and business potential in the history of humanity.

The metaverse is turning the business world on its head, flipping the script in every way. In the past, conventional business strategy models and shiny new technologies may have captured our collective minds, yet in the future the seminal advancement of the metaverse will unleash our collective minds. This audacious revolution will require a completely different way of thinking. One in which businesses must boldly leap into the next horizon of their growth: the metaverse—a pervasive expanse of 3D worlds in which humanity teleports across vast shared experiences.

In the metaverse paradigm, business growth is not about monetizing customers' time and attention. Instead, it's about rewarding their time and attention. It's no longer about...

- centralized authority—it's about decentralization.
- giving up ownership—it's about self-ownership.
- a singular economy—it's about a shared economy.
- giving up control—it's about autonomy.
- isolation—it's about interoperability.
- insecurity—it's about security.
- separation—it's about a shared economy.
- one-dimensional experiences—it's about immersive experiences.

Throughout this book, we will touch on these attributes to provide the next step into this new landscape. Upending traditional relationship building for businesses, products, brands, and consumers. Redefining creative excellence to create new ways to deliver both consumer and business value. Effectively empowering humankind to unleash their creative abilities and free their imaginations. Ultimately producing a byproduct of successful immersive experiences that evoke emotion and empathy at scale. The metaverse is ushering in a new world order—building businesses and brands from the bottom up and digitally inside out, through a soft bundle of not places but spaces.

We call this approach the Persistent Utility Loop—a future-forward business methodology that upends traditional marketing, product and sales strategies for entrepreneurs, small and midsize businesses, and Fortune 500 companies. It is a customer-first, product-market fit and flywheel-of-value method to catalyze business growth in the metaverse.

In physics, the theoretical concept of wormholes postulates that pathways through space-time could become highways for light-years' long journeys to other worlds in no time. Much like that, the metaverse will transport humanity to a universe of unlimited inventiveness, unhindered creativity, and unparalleled business expansion.

In this book, we will journey together through various dimensions of the metaverse, making sense of the business opportunities within it.

Part One
Decoding the Platform_

01 >Web 1.0, Web 2.0, Web 3.0_

The metaverse is a complex amalgamation of many diverse technologies working together to create an environment where people can work, play, and interact with each other. It begins with a grand vision to combine the physical and virtual worlds, often leveraging augmented and virtual reality. Conceptually, the metaverse is where people can enter virtual worlds as easily and as often as they currently use social media on their smartphones. In other words, the metaverse will continuously become an instrumental part of everyone's lives.

It's tempting to think about the metaverse in technical terms, but that is selling it short. Of course, technology is behind the metaverse, but it's not simply about technology: it's about making journeys, collaborating, communicating, and socializing. The central theme of the metaverse is to create an open and diverse society that is not controlled by a central authority. People will be free to unleash their full potential.

This potential includes creating new prospects for businesses previously thought impossible. Human creative abilities will be unfettered, leading to new and exciting value-creation breakthroughs. Businesses will no longer be tied to the physical world, creating unlimited expansion for new products, services, and offerings.

Before embarking on our journey into the metaverse, we must first examine the base technologies that make it possible.

Think of the metaverse as a layer cake: there are various technologies that fit together in layers. The bottom layer is the foundation. Nonetheless, no layer will operate unless the lower layers are in place.

Typically, specialists and computer engineers are familiar with the concept of the protocol or network stack, also known as the Open System Interconnection (OSI) model. This network stack consists of seven layers with hardware located at the bottom and applications at the top.[1]

In the ensuing sections, we'll illustrate the foundations of the metaverse using a layer cake analogy to clarify the concepts. The foundations of the metaverse are presented below.

No matter how we choose to illustrate the metaverse and its foundations, you must have hardware for anything to work at all, which is why it's the foundation of the layer cake. Moving upward, you have software, smart devices, the cloud, the internet, the Web (1, 2, and 3), as well as other supporting technologies and applications that work together to create the digital world.

Each layer is crucial in itself. You can't just remove a layer from the middle and expect the whole structure to work. Let's begin by discussing hardware, the cake's bottom layer.

Hardware

Preliminaries aside, the case can be made that computers are thousands of years old since the invention of the Abacus, but realistically computers came into use around World War II. For an army of that era to function, messages had to be sent back and forth over radio and phone lines. It was relatively easy for an enemy to intercept these messages, read them, and act.

To preclude enemies from reading confidential messages, combatants used primitive forms of data encryption, at least they were primitive by modern standards. Complex machines (for that time) enabled encryption and decryption of messages with the hope that the enemy would not figure out the mathematics behind the algorithms used. These primitive computing devices formed the backbone of message security, although it wasn't perfect because combatants on both sides could break the code and react to the messages. The Allies did a particularly decent job and used the information they gleaned from those secret messages to win battles on many occasions.

Notably, this trend toward inventing computers for military purposes continued after World War II and accelerated based on the need for guidance systems for rockets and satellites. As time passed, the uses for computers extended into the commercial world for accounting and other purposes. As computers tended to become more powerful and smaller, they found their way into consumers' hands in the form of personal computers and video games.

It's hard to imagine life without computers. Virtually everyone uses smartphones daily; many have video games consoles, tablets, and smart televisions. Consumers, the military, the government, and businesses are taking advantage of these smart devices throughout the homes and workplaces.

Today's hardware far outstrips the equipment from just a few years ago. You couldn't even dream of running today's gaming applications, artificial intelligence, augmented reality (AR)/ virtual reality (VR), and holographic glasses on the old 1990s desktop computers. The highly advanced supercomputers of those days would've had a challenging time running some of the applications that are common on today's smartphones.

The speed and size of disk space have increased exponentially. In 1956, 1 megabyte (MB) of disk space cost $10,000, required fifty 24-inch platters, and was housed in a cabinet the size of two refrigerators. In 1979, the price dropped to $233 per megabyte, and in 1983, a device was released that supported 10 MB for $2,700. Fast forward to 2011, and you'd find a 4 terabyte (TB) drive for $399.[2]

The proliferations in size and performance were not just limited to traditional disks. Memory and CPU power dramatically increased, and the size of devices dropped to the point where extraordinarily powerful computers, complete with memory and storage could be built into a smartwatch or smartphone. Furthermore, the price of computing power has dropped to such a low price point, spurring a proliferation of devices within homes, factories, and automobiles with seemingly no bounds.

Upon examining more closely, the uses of hardware by the internet are commonly known and include mobile computing devices, such as smartphones, tablets, or laptops; desktop computers; servers, memory, and disk drives in the cloud, and routers. To truly enable the metaverse requires a connection that supports 3D simulations, such as glasses, goggles, and sensory gloves. The wearable Internet of Things (i.e., sensors and other devices built into clothing) will enable tactile sensations (i.e., touch). The Department of Defense and other businesses are experimenting with direct brain implants, allowing the human brain to interface with computer technologies—and the metaverse directly.[3]

Hardware is the base of the layer cake. Without hardware, the metaverse simply cannot exist. Once hardware is in place, however, we can proceed to the next layer—software.

Software

We must recognize that hardware is just an inert pile of metal and rare earth elements without a connection to devices in isolation via software. Your disk drive would not know what to do unless software gave it directions. Think of software as a series of instructions that tells hardware or other software what to do. Generally, software is referred to as programs, although now people refer to them as applications.

Firmware is a type of software that exists within the hardware and manages the hardware itself. A disk drive, for instance, contains firmware that controls the spinning of the drives, the disk cache, and the motion of the read/write arms (among other things).

The operating system (also known as system software) controls a computer and its peripherals, including disk drives, monitors, and printers. Common examples include Windows, the Apple operating system, and Android.

The programs that most people deal with daily are known as applications. Applications allow users to perform games, payroll, and merchandising. Other applications run in the background, performing other tasks that don't require user inputs.

If you've used a smartphone, a desktop computer, a laptop, or even a personal assistant such as Alexa, you are familiar with software. Everything you do, from booting up a mobile phone to accessing your banking app, is accomplished with software designed for a specific purpose.

The metaverse necessitates much more advanced software, such as 3D graphics and human interface apps, banking apps that create 3D tellers that work just like real bank tellers, and countless applications to control your digital avatar and create simulations and experiences. Meanwhile, it goes much deeper than that—software operates the connections between such simulations, each of the digital worlds (i.e., silos), communications, and anything else you do after entering the digital universe of the metaverse.

Ultimately, software of all types is a prerequisite for the metaverse. The software can get complicated, but at its best it is nearly invisible to the user. Anyone who uses the metaverse can experience it through their digital avatar with all (or most) of their senses, and as we'll describe in more depth later, augmented reality (AR) is an emerging on-ramp into the metaverse in that digital images overlay real-world physical objects; in this case, no digital avatar exists. But first we must discuss the next layer of the cake, which is smart devices.

Smart Devices

Smart devices (using the Internet of Things or IoT) have exploded in their popularity. On the consumer side, it's common to see individuals equipping their homes with smart alarms, smart lightbulbs, smart electric sockets, and numerous other smart devices. Modern factories and manufacturing facilities depend on smart sensors and automated equipment, and even automobiles have become fully equipped platforms with a full range of entertainment, safety, and performance devices. The modern world is built upon ubiquitous smart devices that sense and control virtually everything.

We must also consider automated virtual assistants such as Alexa, Siri, and Google home, which serve as control centers for the homes and workplaces of consumers. These assistants allow consumers to use simple voice commands to control their television, home lighting, alarm system, and countless other tasks.

As of 2021, 46 billion smart devices exist worldwide. By 2030, that number is expected to increase to an astonishing 125 billion units, with the volume of data from all this equipment looming at 79.4 zettabytes (ZB).[4] Such significant numbers demonstrate just how useful these small, intelligent devices have become.

As their in-home usage increases, they control a wide variety of things like heating, air conditioning, lighting, televisions, and so on. In manufacturing, industrial-strength smart devices such as robots sense equipment failures, open and close valves, sort stock, and manage computer systems. It won't be long before smart cities use millions of intelligent devices to maintain traffic flows, monitor water levels, and even sense the appearance of potholes so maintenance workers can be automatically dispatched. IoT also extends to wearable smart devices, which can monitor blood pressure and blood sugar, change clothing colors, and sense when danger approaches.

In turn, the metaverse will link to many of these devices, enabling the physical and virtual world to interact. Imagine, visiting a virtual control center via your digital self to check the status of your home and control its temperature, alarm settings, and anything else you desire. From your virtual viewpoint, you can sit in your home's control room complete with dials and screens—a room that exists entirely within the metaverse and is connected to your home via smart devices.

The operation of such devices depends on the next layer of the layer cake—the cloud.

The Cloud

The consensus is that cloud computing is quickly becoming the bedrock underpinning modern society. Companies such as Amazon, IBM, Microsoft, and Google (among many others) offer near-unlimited disk space, memory, and central processing units (CPUs) at a highly reasonable cost. By leveraging its cloud, Microsoft, for instance, gives each home PC user a full TB of cloud storage connected to their computer. Consumers can then use this storage for backups, photo storage, or anything else they desire.

These public clouds are included in our definition of cloud computing. Decentralized databases and other assets don't require public cloud capabilities. Instead, they directly use the functionality from many different computers (e.g., smartphones and desktops), forming a distributed cloud-like environment, which we group into the definition of the cloud for convenience.

At any given time, public clouds have available pools of entitlements, such as discs, memory, and CPUs, offered to businesses and consumers on a pay-as-you-go basis. IoT devices, such as Amazon's Alexa, leverage the cloud to perform various functions such as voice translation. Companies then use these capabilities to eliminate the need for on-premise equipment and provide unlimited scaling. A significant advantage to using cloud competencies is that it's much simpler to design disaster recovery and high-performance solutions in applications because the cloud is a web of network-connected data centers. If one data center becomes unavailable or is destroyed, another data center simply can take over. These data centers can be located anywhere in the world.

Web 3 and the metaverse cannot function without the cloud and its associated mechanisms and services. The cloud enables smart devices, games, applications, and every other distributed technology possible by providing access to configurations. We could draft an entire book about the cloud but suffice to say, the "work" of the metaverse, Web 3, smart devices, and modern games are performed in the cloud. Your computer, smartphone, laptop, Alexa, smart device, and countless others offload much of their work to the cloud.

Keeping this in mind, the metaverse leverages the cloud. Your digital self must interface with digital worlds and people, and therefore must connect to cloud proficiencies. Every smart and, in the future, the metaverse-enabled device is considered "thin" to one degree, meaning the devices contain just enough hardware and software to work within the cloud. After all, people can't use their social media, internet banking, and multiplayer video games without an internet connection because those applications must use enablements outside of those local to the device.

In many ways, the cloud infrastructure and distributed computing are critical due to the need to transport substantial amounts of data very quickly to many users.

The traditional cloud model stipulates on-demand, metered access to components such as disk storage, memory, CPUs, and databases. These services are accessible over the internet and use virtualization technology to ensure security, privacy, and isolation. Cloud providers maintain cloud assets, meaning businesses, individuals, and devices don't need to access those facilities locally.

Conventional distributed cloud computing spreads the workload across different clouds. Hence, your application may simultaneously use compute resources from a cloud provider in Colorado, Houston, and New York. As far as the user is concerned, it is a single set of configurations.

The main advantage of cloud services is that users (i.e., businesses, devices, and mobile devices) don't need to create and maintain their servers or even server farms, enabling your applications to make the most efficient use of services as possible.

For example, look at your best-loved online video game and suppose it uses a distributed cloud system to operate. This game might run on the cloud of the game provider most of the time. However, suppose it's faster to access it on a different cloud in a different location. In that case, the video game might begin using more efficient cloud extendibility. It could use resources from other computers, smartphones, laptops, and desktops. None of this affects your gameplay. In fact, you won't even notice that you are now using a cloud in Denver instead of the one located in New York.

Relatively speaking, this can become complex. Your game might be stored on cloud storage at a cloud provider in Denver but use compute properties from a server in California and another in Nevada. It all depends on what is most efficient. Of course, rules are built to consider the cost of the different assets at each provider, and those costs are billed back to the game provider.

When you add decentralization to the equation, in addition to or in place of using cloud providers, storage on potentially thousands of computers all over the internet are accessed. The idea is that your game runs as quickly and efficiently as possible under the circumstances. For the metaverse, this kind of resource switching makes the implementation of synchronous virtual experiences much easier because supportability can be accessed when and where it is needed.

Without the cloud and decentralized computing, the metaverse can't exist—it requires public cloud functionality and decentralized resources. Therefore, the cloud and decentralized competence are indeed a critical layer in our layer cake.

The Internet

In the 1970s and 1980s, the US Department of Defense (DOD) funded the Advanced Research Projects Agency Network (ARPANET), the predecessor to the modern internet. The idea was to connect universities and government agencies in a network so they could communicate freely. In the 1990s, HyperText Markup Language (HTML) debuted, and the internet was officially born. Anyone from that time remembers services such as AOL and CompuServe, which connected homes in a communication network based on dial-up modems. Many remember the joy of finally receiving a superfast, 19,200 baud high-speed modem, the equivalent of 4,800 bits/600 bytes per second. Compare that to today's internet, where people believe it's sluggish when their home internet reaches 57,600 bits/second. Many homes even have gigabit lines, which is almost 1 billion bits per second.

Nonetheless in today's digital world, the internet's speed is of prime importance. It's increasingly common for people to work from home, watch streaming movies, and play video games over the same internet connection all at the same time. One of the basics behind the metaverse is high-speed communication between businesses, homes, storefronts, and everything else. Without high-speed communication, the metaverse would remain a dream that couldn't be realized.

The internet is far more than just fast, reliable bandwidth. It's a set of protocols and standards that all work together to create a unified cloth that enables people to shop at their favorite online stores, play games, converse on social media, read the news, watch streaming videos, in addition to an immense variety of other tasks.

Let's look at some of these protocols in more detail. The most basic protocol is known as Transmission Control Protocol/Internet Protocol (TCP/IP) and is the bedrock on which the internet rests. Every connected device is assigned an address, conceptually like a person's home address, uniquely identifying it to the outside world. The TCP/IP addresses enable those devices to be found. There are two versions of TCP/IP: IPv4 and IPv6. IPv4 is the original, shorter address, while IPv6 is the longer form and far superior because it supports more devices and various other functions.

As expected, humans don't find numeric addresses to be very user-friendly. Domain names were invented to convert TCP/IP addresses into more familiar words that can be typed into web browsers and other applications. They enable your average user to reference domains such as websites quickly and efficiently.

Alongside such protocols and addresses arrived the web, which is constructed on top of the internet layer in the layer cake. The invention of previously mentioned HTML, a markup language conceptually related to a proofreading markup language, enabled the creation of websites and other objects that present themselves in a structured and organized manner. One of the primary features of HTML is the ability to link from one object to another. To illustrate, a website contains links to graphics, documents, videos, and audio files. These then are combined and organized using HTML into storefronts, blogs, and whatever else is needed.

Bandwidth, TCP/IP, domain names, and HTML together meet the absolute minimum requirements to create a usable, dynamic web of interlinked information. Everything else then layers on top of these protocols, standards, software, and related hardware.

Moore's law states that the number of transistors in a dense integrated circuit will double every two years. The implication is that the hardware speed and memory density will increase simultaneously. The invention of faster hardware, denser and more capable memory, and disk drives with massive amounts of storage has followed Moore's law, which explains how people now carry the equivalent of a supercomputer from 20 years ago.

The internet is an additional layer on the layer cake. Notwithstanding, without an interface of some sort, the internet is not particularly useful to the average person. This brings us to our next layer—Web 1.0—or the Static Web.

Web 1.0—The Static Web

If you're like most people in the modern era, you take the web for granted. You know that you can jump on your computer or smartphone, use a web browser to find your preferred retailer, and spend some money to have products shipped directly to your doorstep. You probably also take advantage of search engines such as Google several times a day and spend hours communicating on social media.

Yet, this wasn't always the case. In the 1960s, the military funded, through Defense Advanced Research Projects Agency (DARPA), a project called the Advanced Research Projects Agency Network (ARPANET). Primarily, the intention was to link military sites to allow them to share information via email and other protocols. It wasn't long before educational institutions joined the ARPANET, expanding the number of nodes (i.e., systems) to over a thousand.

A huge ARPANET milestone was the creation of the three protocols:

- *Transmissions Control Protocol (TCP).* This protocol provided the means for two posts (i.e., three devices) to establish a connection and then exchange data. This protocol guaranteed data delivery and that packets would be received in the same order that they were sent.

- *Internet Protocol (IP).* This protocol defines how data is split up into packets and how they are addressed so they can be transmitted and received.

- *HyperText Transfer Protocol (HTTP).* This protocol is used to distribute information on the World Wide Web (WWW), which is simply referred to as the web.

ARPANET morphed into the internet and came into widespread use. While larger systems communicated with each other over permanent communication links, smaller computers used dial-up modems, allowing users to connect directly over phone lines. Services such as AOL and CompuServe sprung up quickly, serving as gateways for access via dial-up modems connected to phone lines, to provide access to various services including communications such as email. These services tended to use proprietary protocols with minimal capabilities.

In those early days, volunteers maintained the internet. These people strongly believed in the concept of open software and spent countless hours creating protocols and software, which they openly shared with others for no charge and without compensation. Their influence can still be felt today, because the results of their efforts form the basic building blocks of the web and the internet. Most of the major ideas, protocols, and concepts they designed and implemented are currently still in use to a greater or lesser degree.

Before the web, people communicated using UseNet newsgroups, which were dynamic bulletin boards consisting of groups, each covering a defining topic. People created and read messages, asked questions, and replied on these boards in response to messages. Newsgroups could be moderated or unmoderated. Such boards were extremely popular until the early 2000s, when blogs, websites, and social media newsgroups supplanted them.

Eventually, the internet changed forever in 1989 to 1990 when Tim Berners-Lee created the web. He designed a standard known as Hypertext Markup Language (HTML) that became the basis for displaying information and content. This standard led to the creation of websites and quickly coalesced into the World Wide Web.

At first, users connected directly to the systems of interest. Later, they connected to service providers who then granted them access to a network of computers in which to surf the net. During this era, AOL, Yahoo, AltaVista, and Netscape were born.

The following years became a period of incredible excitement, massive innovation, and tremendous investment. Described as a golden age of innovation, much of it was based on open-source services constructed by unpaid volunteers. Nevertheless, their creations tended to be limited to read-only with only a modicum of read-write capabilities.

You can think of the web's initial design as a quasi-online magazine. Publishers produced content, and then users read that content. The trajectory of social media, dynamic websites, and personalization didn't appear until much later during Web 2. At that time, dynamic content existed in message boards, guestbooks, and shipping carts, but relatively lacked the fully dynamic web of today.

This early edition of the web orientation centered around supplying information, communications, and transactions. Its primary output was a one-way publishing method and only supported transactions with minimal user interaction. Web 1 is thus often referred to as the *read-only web*.

Open protocols dominated Web 1. We've already discussed HTTP and TCP/IP, but there were many others. Here are a few examples:

- SMTP, POP3, and IMAP—Email. Sending mail is performed by Simple Mail Transfer Protocol (SMTP), while the receiving of mail is handled by Post Office Protocol 3 (POP3) and Internet Messaging App Protocol (IMAP).

- USENET—Newsgroups. Largely obsolete today, think of newsgroups as threaded group messages.

- FTP and SFTP—File Transfer Protocol (FTP) and Secure File Transfer Protocol transferred files.

- TELNET—Application protocol for remote terminal support.

Believe it or not, these protocols are still currently the foundation of the web and internet, although they have grown over time to include layers of security amongst other features.

In the 1990s, Tim Berners-Lee laid out some of the critical concepts of the web:[5]

- *Decentralization.* Permission is not needed from a central authority to post something on the web. The web is designed to operate without a central controlling system, so there is no single point of failure. The original concept stated that the web shouldn't have a "kill switch," it was to be free from censorship surveillance. The web, as currently implemented, meets some of these goals: it is decentralized and without a single point of failure. Yet, because of the lack of an integrated security model, surveillance is difficult to prevent (i.e., several mechanisms have been designed to add layers of security to the web with mixed results). Further, it's believed that some countries have built "kill switches" to isolate their parts of the web and internet from the World Wide Web, which goes against decentralization.

- *Bottom-up design.* The web was initially intended to be open source, meaning that its development and coding were *not* designed to be controlled by a corporation or group. The web's code, specifications, and design were openly developed for all to see, change, and work on. This design philosophy is still followed with some exceptions.

- *Net neutrality.* Everyone can access the web at the same level, based on their connections to the internet. If you pay for 100 MB of service, you should be able to communicate at that speed regardless of the content or whom you are communicating with, as long as they are paying for the same or greater access.

- *Universal.* Every computer or system involved must speak the same universal "language," meaning they all must use the same underlying protocols to communicate (i.e., HTTP, TCP/IP).

- *Consensus.* Everyone must agree to use the same web standards, or the entire web concept ceases to work. The transparent process presented at the World Wide Web Consortium W3C that designed new standards in which anyone can participate is how this occurs.

Building upon these concepts, businesses, governments, and people began expanding into the new world of Web 1.0, also known as the World Wide Web. Primitive by today's standards, Web 1.0 was so valuable that it became the basis of a revolution in how people communicate, do business, and socialize that continues to this day.

Historically at that time, businesses created mostly static websites where they presented information that users could search for and read. Their minimal interaction consisted of guest books, ordering forms, and message boards. Emphasis was centered on searching and directory services instead of dynamic ways for users and businesses to interact. You can think of the early web as a one-to-many communication model.

The services for this early web stage were designed for a presentation orientation with primarily static web pages. In those early days, HTML pages were hand-coded for the most part and didn't provide for much user interaction.

When you combine all these protocols, you get the foundations of Web 1.0 (i.e., the early internet). Static web pages and limited e-commerce might sound primitive today, but at the time, they were exciting and allowed for incredible innovation.

At first, volunteers crafted vast handmade directories consisting of hand-coded HTML files categorizing an expansive number of websites. Tim Berners-Lee generated the World Wide Web Virtual Library—the oldest online directory—thereupon he began early attempts to organize and make sense of the early web.

Formed in 1998 by two Sun Microsoft engineers, the multilingual DMOZ (i.e., an open-directory project) quickly became the standard way people found information on the web. Moderators manually added, modified, and deleted websites from the directory, which at its peak, contained over 5 million uniform resource locators (URLs).

Arguably directories were great for finding content, but they couldn't even come close to indexing the entire web. Search engines then appeared to fill this niche. In 1993, the W3Catalog (also known as Jughead) was launched to index the existing directories.

A similar example known as WebCrawler, launched in 1994, was the first real search engine designed to index the web page content on websites all over the World Wide Web. Lycos, a web search engine/ portal, established itself. In 1995, several new search engines appeared for commercial purposes, including Excite, Altavista, and Yahoo.

In 1997, Larry Page and Sergey Brin, with a $100,000 investment by Sun Microsystems, raised $1 million and launched Google. Other search engines suffered from spammy results, however, as people attempted to use tricks to move their websites to the top of the rankings. To combat this, Google introduced technologies to detect these attempts. In 1999, Google again changed the web forever by introducing AdWords to its search engine, introducing commercial possibilities into the world of search. In 2005, Microsoft released its search engine called Bing.

Over the years people found Web 1.0 useful and it changed the world. Still, the technology was limited in its commercial possibilities. People wanted more; businesses wanted to provide more dynamic, user-centric experiences; and the static nature of Web 1.0 didn't fulfill those desires. The time was right for a new web experience—Web 2.0.

Web 2.0—The Dynamic Web

Darcy DuNucci, an information architecture consultant, published an article in January 1999 titled *Fragmented Future* that described Web 2.0 and defined the term. In it she said:

> The web, as we know it now, is a fleeting thing, Web 1.0. The relationship of Web 1.0 to the web of tomorrow is roughly the equivalence of Pong to *The Matrix*. Today's web is essentially a prototype—a proof of concept. This concept of interactive content universally accessible through a standard interface has proven so successful that a new industry is set on transforming it, capitalizing on all its power possibilities. The web we know now, which loads into a browser window in static screenfuls, is only an embryo of the web to come.[6]

In 2004, O'Reilly Media and MediaLive hosted the first Web 2.0 conference where John Battelle and Tim O'Reilly delivered a speech and described their vision of the future web. They spoke about building applications that run on the web, not the desktop, which was a revolutionary concept at the time.

They equated Netscape to the new vision. Netscape focused on building a web browser that produced a market for server-based products, by creating a "webtop" that replaced the typical desktop. Advantageously, Netscape created software and gave it to users so they could populate the webtop with applications.

Google, on the other hand, sold services built upon data. They indexed the web, creating a database of links to websites and user-generated content. Their database was constantly updated to add, delete, and modify website links.

These concepts detached the applications from the user's computer. Instead, the applications moved to the web, and the user accessed them from their browser webtop. They found websites through dynamically assembled indexes instead of hand-coded directories.

In 2006, the official choice for *Time Magazine's* Person of the Year was "You", meaning the countless people who contributed anonymous user generated content. In that issue's cover story, Lev Grossman explained:

> It's a story about community and collaboration on a scale never seen before. It's about the cosmic compendium of knowledge Wikipedia and the million-channel people's network YouTube and the online metropolis Myspace. It's about the many wresting power from the few and helping one another for nothing and how that will not only change the world but also change the way the world changes.[7]

When we talk about Web 2.0, we are referring to social media and e-commerce websites. Sites with personalization capabilities that can change their look and feel based on their internal datasets of products and services. In other words, Web 2.0 was viewed as a new era of "read and write".

The key qualities of Web 2.0 are summarized by WebAppRater. Com as:[8]

- Free classification of information (also called *Folksonomy*)
- Web-based applications

- A provision of rich user experiences using tools such as Ajax and HTML5
- User-contributed information such as product reviews and posts on social media
- Services offered on demand and charged on a pay-as-you-use-it basis
- Crowdsourcing
- Sharable content
- Omnichannel content distribution

Even so, there are some downsides to Web 2.0, including the following:

- Trust is malleable, such as when a platform removes a feature unexpectedly.
- Platforms are siloed, which makes it difficult to move assets between them.
- Sometimes, financial exclusion can occur when content creators are excluded from the value they've created.

Web 2.0 was a dramatic step up from the earlier Web 1.0. Furthermore, as internet use exploded, it became apparent that changes needed to be made, especially centering around ownership, privacy, security, and commerce. Irrespectively, the idea of another version of the web, which came to be known as Web3, began to be introduced. Later, the creation of a *blockchain*, which is a database that stores information in an electronic format, enabled a new paradigm to be designed: one more decentralized, secure, private, and safe; one central to the metaverse.

Web3—The Decentralized Web

Web 2.0 is the web that most of us know, use, and love today. Its original intent was that data was to be generally kept in centralized silos; however, this intent has evolved as time goes on.

In his discussion with CMSWire, a cloud-based web development platform provider, Matt Biilmann, CEO of Netlify, explains:

> The web started out as a decentralized system based on DNS and the ability for anyone to buy, own, and manage their own domain name and move it from one host to another as they see fit with full control and ownership over all the underlying data. Consequently, as the web grew up, our online presence has become increasingly centralized on corporate platforms. For instance, when someone registers an Instagram handle, they can't just move that handle with all of their content and followers somewhere else because they're tied to that network.[9]

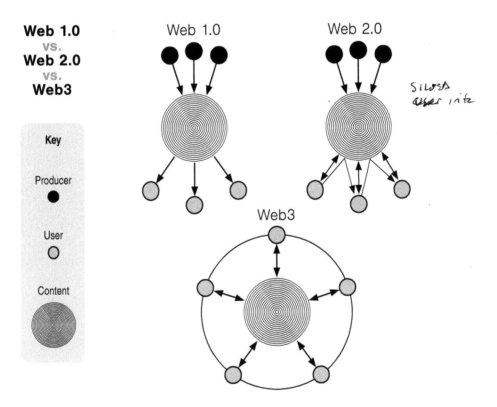

Web 1.0
vs.
Web 2.0
vs.
Web3

Key

Producer

User

Content

Web 1.0

Web 2.0

Web3

Web3 envisioned to solve this problem by creating a peer-to-peer decentralized network owned by users. In this paradigm, your internet-connected devices store your data, run your applications, and host your websites. All this gets distributed over dozens, hundreds, or even thousands of computers.

So, how do you get people to coordinate and work together when no one knows each other? And if no one knows each other, how can they trust one another? Designers of Web3 set out to solve this fundamental problem. Since the earliest days of the internet, trust has always been an issue. It's been addressed with a multifarious series of protocols, best practices, and security layers. Social networks and other businesses then came about and enforced their version of trust upon anyone who wanted to use their services.

In many ways, it all comes down to the question of how strangers come to trust one another. Web3 sets out to resolve this issue of trust, among others.

Note, Web 3.0 and Web3 are not the same thing. Tim Berners-Lee defined Web3 as the Semantic Web, meaning that internet data is machine-readable, structured data. According to Jacob Ansari, Web3 conceptually is more about decentralized technologies such as blockchain, cryptocurrencies, non-fungible tokens (NFTs), etc. The term *Web3* was coined by Gavin Wood, founder of Polkadot and co-founder of Ethereum, and he referred to Web3 as "decentralized online ecosystems based on blockchain."[10] This book aligns with this Web3 definition because of its importance to the metaverse.

The Byzantine Generals Problem

Think about a situation where several generals oversee a group of armies that they are using to protect a fortress. They have two options: to attack or retreat. Some generals prefer one option, while others prefer the other. All generals must vote to agree on the same option and carry it out with vigor because a disorganized strategy would most likely fail or cause the war to be lost.

One complication is that some of these votes may be false or cast by generals with bad intentions. To make this even more involved, their votes are sent by messengers, which could be intercepted, resulting in their messages being deleted or altered. This analogy illustrates the problem of trust when no one knows each other. How do they coordinate effectively without trust?

Byzantine fault tolerance is designed to defend against failures of components to reach agreement among themselves. Any component that doesn't succeed in delivering a message doesn't get a vote. A default value can be used if these unsuccessful attempts are in the majority. In the previous analogy, any general who doesn't do the work (i.e., succeed in getting their message through) doesn't get a vote.

In computers, the generals are the computers, and the messages are the communications between those systems. In electronics, this solution is used to filter out components that are misbehaving or non-functional. It allows multiple CPUs to operate even if one or more of them "goes bad."

This solution can also be applied to people and solve the problem of getting individuals to coordinate when no one knows each other and, therefore, cannot trust one another. People must do the work to submit a credible vote. Anyone who hasn't done the work doesn't get a vote.

Web3 makes it possible to replace centralized controls with a system where those who use the system get a credible vote if they participate fairly. In other words, they honestly do the work and are not cheating the system.

Hashcash

Hashcash is a Proof-of-Work system constructed to reduce email spam and denial-of-service attacks, and is now part of the mining algorithm for bitcoin and other cryptocurrencies. Hashcash requires that a certain amount of verifiable work be computed. In email, a Hashcash stamp is applied to a message to prove that the sender expended the effort (i.e., CPU resources) to calculate the stamp, indicating they are likely sending a valid (non-spam) message. The theory is that spammers rely on the ability to send millions of emails at little-to-no cost. Adding the overhead of creating a Hashcash stamp to each message raises the cost of generating spam and subsequently, in theory, discourages spammers.

Web3 expands upon this concept by requiring those who run the network to invest money, equipment, or Proof-of-Work, which provides a robust way for it to operate while being decentralized.

 The definition for Web3 is a decentralized internet based on blockchain (we'll investigate blockchain later) and token-based economics. It's important to understand that Web3 differs from Web 1.0 and even Web 2.0. It is not based on centralized platforms and regulated financial services. Instead, Web3 is decentralized and centers on users and their ownership of their data and wealth.

The Design of Web 3

Web3's design includes the following features of decentralization, blockchains, decentralized finance (DeFi), decentralized applications (dapps), smart contracts, distributed autonomous organizations (DAOs), and non-fungible tokens (NFTs). You'll likely recognize many of these from Tim Berners-Lee's original concepts discussed earlier. Note that Web3 builds on Web 1.0 and Web 2.0, and all three can and do exist simultaneously on the World Wide Web.

We'll go into these concepts in greater detail throughout this book, as they are the building blocks of Web3 and help enable the metaverse. However, for now, let's break them down a bit.

1. DECENTRALIZATION

In Web3, data can be stored in a distributed network of hundreds, thousands, or even millions of computing systems (i.e., smartphones, desktops, and so forth). This storage network builds in redundancy because the resources are not stored in a central location; redundancy protects against network failure and attacks.

Decentralization is essential to Web3. In contrast, in Web 2.0/1.0, information is stored in a single, fixed location, often a single server, and is located based on its TCP/IP address (and domain name). In Web3, data is typically distributed across many systems in multiple locations simultaneously.

2. BLOCKCHAIN

Cryptocurrencies form the basis for financial transactions on Web3. These currencies are built on blockchain, decentralized, and are self-sufficient entities. As of this writing, the market capitalization of cryptocurrency is estimated to be at $2 trillion.

Blockchains are a method to maintain a decentralized and secure transaction record, guaranteeing the fidelity and security of the information it contains. Within a blockchain, data is collected into groups known as *blocks*. When these blocks are filled to capacity, new blocks are created. These blocks then are linked together, much like the links on a chain, hence the term *blockchain*. The blocks are chained in chronological order and the data within each cannot be changed (i.e., it's immutable).

In addition to cryptocurrencies, blockchains are useful for just about any other kind of data. They can hold medical records, family trees, and contracts, just to name a few. Due to their flexible and decentralized nature, blockchains are a foundational structure of both Web3 and the metaverse.

For example, medical records can be stored in a blockchain. When a child is born, a blockchain about that child is generated. A new link is then added to the blockchain for each of the child's medical exams, tests, vaccinations, prescribed drugs, and physical condition entries. Records about their medical conditions will accumulate throughout their life. These records cannot be changed, are highly secure, and are owned by the child. Said child could assign permissions to allow access to any part of their medical blockchain or even the whole thing. They could also revoke consent, set time limits, and even specify what kind of information could be added (e.g., their eye doctor could only add information about their eyes).

Blockchain is one of the primary technologic enablers of the metaverse because it allows information to be stored safely and securely, while granting the owner the ability to set security limitations and rules that determine how the data can be used and accessed.

3. DECENTRALIZED FINANCE

Decentralized Finance (DeFi) is a digital infrastructure designed to eliminate the requirement for a central authority to regulate finances. It is based on blockchain and, at its core, removes the need for any single entity to control transaction ledgers.

4. DECENTRALIZED APPLICATIONS

Decentralized applications (dapps), which is an application on blockchain, run on smartphones, laptops, and other computers. They use blockchain to store data and maintain its privacy. The creators of these applications do not control how the application is used. dapps make use of smart contracts, discussed in the following section. The creation of dapps is easy and is one of the main goals of blockchains like Ethereum, which serves as a host for these digital applications.

A dapp is simply an application that is decentralized, meaning its backend code runs on a decentralized network. The backend of "normal" applications typically runs on a central server. The dapps have the following characteristics:

- They are decentralized; they run on a public platform without centralized control.
- They can perform any action if they have access to the necessary resources.
- They are isolated and run in a virtual environment to prevent bugs in the dapp code from affecting anything else.
- They are deterministic, which means they will work the same in any environment.

The dapps have the following advantages:

- Because they are decentralized, they are not subject to downtime.
- Because they are based on smart contracts, they are considered to be private.
- Because they are based on blockchain, the data in a dapp cannot be modified.

- They do not depend on trusting a central authority.
- They are resistant to censorship.
- They are infinitely scalable.
- They are fault-tolerant.

Examples of some dapps that currently exist include:

- Bitcoin (which was technically the first dapp)
- Ethereum
- EtherTweet
- Melonport

5. SMART CONTRACTS

Smart contracts are applications that run as part of a blockchain to record and enforce the rules of a contract. For example, an author could create a smart contract that gives her a royalty for each electronic book sold and increases the royalty amount after a specific number of books were bought. The smart contract could also set the terms for copyright—how the contents of the book could be used by others and the rights to derivative works such as movie scripts based on the book. All of this work is done automatically by the code of the smart contract.

Vitalik Buterin, the founder of Ethereum, talked about smart contracts in his blog article titled *DAOs, DACs, DAs and More: An Incomplete Terminology Guide*:

> A smart contract is a mechanism involving digital assets and two or more parties, where some or all of the parties put assets in, and assets are automatically redistributed among those parties according to a formula based on certain data that is not known at the time the contract is initiated.[11]

Smart contracts function on a predetermined condition that automates agreements, meaning they don't need an intermediary to enforce or engage the contract. Smart contracts can also automate workflows when certain conditions are met.

Internally, a smart contract consists of "if/then" statements written into a blockchain. The actions could be anything, such as selling a car, purchasing an event ticket, transferring money to people, and so on. Once created, a smart contract may not be changed. Only those people with permission can see the results of the contract's execution.

Smart contracts can include as many "if/then" clauses as needed. These define the rules (i.e., terms) of the agreement. In addition, any exception conditions must be specified. This establishes the framework for how disputes are resolved.

Smart contracts are becoming progressively easier to create with modern web interfaces. They are fast, efficient, and accurate. They are also transparent in that all parties involved can see and understand all the terms. There is no need for intermediaries—smart contracts don't require lawyers, judges, or anyone else to decipher. They simply operate as they are programmed. Note that smart contracts are not yet recognized by many courts as valid, although that could change over time.

They are, however, very secure because they are encrypted and because they exist in blockchains, which are inherently secure, and they cannot be modified once the contract is executed.

6. DAOS ~~Modern~~ [The] Mutual Insurer of The future ?!

Based on dapp technology, a decentralized autonomous organization (DAO) creates an organizational board and eliminates hierarchies by setting the policies using a weighted voting system. Voting power is based on tokens; whoever has more tokens has more voting rights. Thus, those who have invested more time, effort, or investment into the organization will have more say.

DAOs allow people and digital entities to operate together. They define the rules of governance for how to make decisions, jointly own things, take part in the economy, and get together in groups, among other things. Anything involving people or entities interfacing with one another could be governed by the rules defined in a DAO.

In a DAO, decisions are completed from the bottom up, meaning the group members (i.e., community) govern based on rules defined and enforced by a blockchain. People gain voting rights based on how much they invest into the DAO, and because of that, they have influence over the DAO. DAOs have the following characteristics:

- They are managed by their members and not a central authority.
- DAOs have a built-in treasury, and the funds may only be accessed with approval by the members of the DAO.
- They don't use a hierarchical management structure.
- They are owned by a group of members.
- They are entirely autonomous.
- They are transparent.
- They are based on open-source blockchains.

DAOs solve the trust problem amongst parties; members of a DAO don't need to trust anyone else in the DAO, because the rules are fully defined (and viewable) in a smart contract.

Stakeholders, those who invest tokens into the DAO, can vote to use funds from the treasury and to change the rules.

The bitcoin network (BTC) is the earliest example of a DAO. bitcoin miners and nodes within this network are the stakeholders who vote on what to support.

7. NFTS

Cryptocurrencies are fungible—they can be exchanged. bitcoin, one of the first cryptocurrencies, is an example of a fungible asset—a single bitcoin has the same value as any other bitcoin. This is a fundamental truth of cryptocurrencies; they are like money, in that one dollar can permanently be changed for another dollar, and those dollars have the same value.

NFTs, on the other hand, are non-fungible. Each unit, or non-fungible token (NFT) is unique, and any one non-fungible asset is *not* equal to any other one. Every token is uniquely identified and contains ownership information. NFTs are often compared to passports—they may appear to be similar, but each passport uniquely identifies the passport's owner and differs from any other. NFTs can be extended, which means an NFT can be combined with another NFT to create a unique, third NFT from the first two.

NFTs are vital to Web3 and the metaverse because they support the representation of physical assets as digital assets. This support enables NFTs to be referenced, used, traded, sold, owned, and represented in the digital universe. NFTs are discussed more in-depth later in this book.

An NFT is a unique item that can't be replaced by anything else. For example, a dollar bill is fungible—you can trade one dollar for another dollar and they are the same. However, a one-of-a-kind antique vase is non-fungible, because if you traded it for another antique vase, you'd gain a different object with distinctive characteristics and a different value.

The purpose of an NFT is to digitally represent objects such as music, art, videos, books, and other content and items. Owners are associated with an NFT, creating the concept of ownership in the digital world. NFTs thus create the ability for ownership and value of physical items in the metaverse.

Say you and your band record a new song. If you simply released it on the internet, listeners may be able to download and copy it. In the past, Distributed Rights Management (DRM) and other similar technologies attempted to add a layer of encryption and ownership, but they can unfortunately be defeated and cracked. In some instances, applications can be found that remove DRM entirely.

Now you can associate the song with an NFT, thus granting ownership—in fact, an NFT can only have one owner (but that ownership can be transferred). This allows content owners and artists to make income from their creations. They no longer need to rely on someone else, say a store or auction house, to sell their item. Instead, they can sell their song (or whatever item/content they want) directly to the public. In many ways, NFTs will streamline go-to-market processes for content creators.

NFTs define the asset's ownership, giving the owner the right to define the rules for what can be done with that song. An NFT can also be programmed to provide the owner a royalty every time the item is used or even viewed, giving them a percentage of the price every time the object is sold to another owner.

Let's look closer at how that works. Suppose an artist produced a piece of art and now wants to sell it. She would first create an NFT for the artwork, and then program in the purchase price and a royalty amount. If someone purchases the art, she is paid the price she set. If someone resells her art, such as a store or a download site, she is paid a royalty amount. Her payment is automatic and is built into the design of her art's NFT.

Built on blockchain technology, NFTs can be both tangible and intangible items. For instance, an NFT can be any of the following:

- A song
- A work of art
- An image
- A collectible item
- A phone ringtone
- A dress
- A dress pattern
- Dance choreography
- Posts on social media (yes, even a single post)
- Items in a video game
- A video game

Summary

We'll talk more about the technologies of non-fungible tokens (NFTs), decentralized autonomous organizations (DAOs), blockchain, and the economic system Decentralized Finance (DeFi) throughout the upcoming chapters. These technologies are the central blocks of Web3 and enable elements of the metaverse to deliver consumer and business experiences.

Web3 (and the metaverse) changes the paradigm of Web 1.0 and Web 2.0 by decentralizing finance, governance, organizations, and even applications and databases. Web3 is based on blockchain and redistributes control and rights to individuals in many ways. Individuals own data in Web3, applications can run anywhere, and smart contracts and NFTs govern finance.

The metaverse is the next advancement: it adds virtual 3D worlds on top of Web 1.0, 2.0, and 3.0. In the metaverse, users interact with each other. Their exploits are immersive—users can experience them using their senses of at least sight and sound and, likely down the road, other senses.[12]

The metaverse pulls together everything that came before it—the internet, Web 1.0, 2.0, and 3.0—and adds an interface on top, making it useful and accessible to everyone. You can consider the metaverse as the glue that holds together all the technologies and concepts that originated before it.

Now that you grasp the foundations, let's move into the next chapter and define the metaverse. What is it? Why is it needed? What problems does it solve?

Notes

1   G Lee. Welcome to Cloud Networking, 2014, www.sciencedirect.com/topics/computer-science/networking-stack (archived at https://perma.cc/PA7V-VPH6)

2   The Cost of Data Storage Through the Years, visual.ly/community/Infographics/technology/cost-data-storage-through-years (archived at https://perma.cc/45TJ-27HZ)

3   L Threat. How Brain-Computer-Technology Will Facilitate Human Integration in the Metaverse, 15 December 2021, peacockplume.fr/opinion/future-metaverse (archived at https://perma.cc/H64T-DUX6)

4   N G. How Many IoT Devices Are There in 2022? [All You Need To Know], 14 March 2022. techjury.net/blog/how-many-iot-devices-are-there/ (archived at https://perma.cc/QF7G-8CWK)

5   World Wide Web Foundation. History of the Web: Sir Tim Berners-Lee, webfoundation.org/about/vision/history-of-the-web/ (archived at https://perma.cc/W8J2-2NST)

6   D DiNucci. Fragmented Future, January 1999. darcyd.com/fragmented_future. pdf (archived at https://perma.cc/H4G3-VG49)

7   You, yes, you, are TIME's Person of the Year, *Time Magazine*, 25 December 2006

8   7 Key Features of Web 2.0, 29 June 2010. webapprater.com/general/7-key-features-of-web-2-0.html (archived at https://perma.cc/ARD9-4XBD)

9   S Clark. How Is Web3 Decentralized?, 2 February 2022. www.cmswire.com/information-management/how-is-web3-decentralized/ (archived at https://perma.cc/W57M-L3YZ) (archived at https://perma.cc/CF5N-5PNE)

10 S Fagan. Why Web3 and Web 3.0 Are Not the Same, 24 March 2022, www.reworked.co/information-management/why-web3-and-web-30-are-not-the-same/ (archived at https://perma.cc/AEX5-L7YM)

11 V Buterin. DAOs, DACs, DAs and More: An Incomplete Terminology Guide, 6 May 2014, blog.ethereum.org/2014/05/06/daos-dacs-das-and-more-an-incomplete-terminology-guide/ (archived at https://perma.cc/TV8T-LU2P)

12 B Marr. The Important Difference between Web3 and the Metaverse, 22 February 2022, www.forbes.com/sites/bernardmarr/2022/02/22/the-important-difference-between-web3-and-the-metaverse/?sh=9d8a26a5af33 (archived at https://perma.cc/4YDF-QK6Z)

02 >The Metaverse_

The metaverse is coming to fruition, yet there is much debate on precisely what the metaverse will become. (In its current state, the metaverse is still in the alpha stage, a proof of concept for a new reality that merges the physical and digital worlds together. Fundamentally, the metaverse is the successor of the internet, building upon the foundational technologies that came before: hardware, software, smart devices, the cloud and web 1.0, Web 2.0, and Web3.

In many ways, the metaverse is an expected evolution, as we as a civilization have come to crave more immersive experiences. This heightened desire for immersive experiences is significantly driven by the vision of moving beyond the screen.

In this chapter, we will dig through the hype and noise by describing the metaverse and analyzing it through two lenses: The Conceptual and The Practical.

The metaverse can be described as: The convergence of the physical and digital worlds enabling immersive experiences to increase business expansion and consumer value with persistent utility, creating new-era needs for creative, technical, and soft skills.

Conceptually, the metaverse pulls from the constructs of social media, entertainment, gaming, and e-commerce, to create new value propositions in the form of Communities, Commerce, and Co-Journeys.

From a practical standpoint, the metaverse will be based on several elemental traits: Immersive 3D, Real-Time, Ownership, Interoperable, Shared Experience, Shared Economy, and Persistent. These are built upon predecessor technologies as well as leveraging Web3 capabilities.

Using this description and this conceptual and practical framework, the metaverse will be composed from the ground up before our very eyes. Enabling all of us to be creators of the metaverse to reimagine optimal experiences from both a user-first and technical standpoint. We, the builders of the metaverse, will need to come together to help create the future. A future centered around collaboratively solving problems, asking questions, overcoming challenges, and ultimately sparking inspiration. All done responsibly and respectfully. The metaverse will change our world as we know it.

Here is a glimpse of just a few capabilities of the metaverse before delving deeper into the Conceptual Value Propositions and Practical Elements of the metaverse.

Capabilities of the Metaverse

Immersive Meetings

It is undeniable that we're all joining virtual meetings on an increased basis to connect with others through our mobile devices, laptops, and desktop computers. Just a few years ago, these meetings were somewhat one-dimensional gatherings, with a moderate sense of all the textures of human interaction. Virtual meeting platforms attempt to present information intuitively, given the limited space on the screen and bandwidth. But attending one can still be fatiguing since participants are not entirely socializing with people to the full extent.

Imagine that you are now in a more immersive meeting room, full of people interacting, more akin to physical life. You can see everyone at the same time, perhaps seated around a gravity-defying floating table or in lounge chairs surrounded by a serene vista. Attendees can be represented as a customized 3D digital avatar; you hear others speak with spacial and directional cues, perceive their emotional reactions, and eventually shake hands with them with haptic feedback. All as the meeting occurs entirely in a virtual world.

Meta-Vacations

Speculatively speaking, you could purchase "meta-vacations" to exotic locations by taking advantage of the metaverse. You may choose to travel to India and climb the Himalayas through a riveting experience, ride a surfboard in Hawaii, or climb to the top of one of the pyramids in Egypt. Or, if you prefer, you could visit the fictional Mars of Edgar Rice Burroughs, fly with space aliens from *Starship Troopers*, or sit beside Neil Armstrong as he lands on the moon. All without leaving the comfort of your home.

Medical

The possibilities go well beyond mere vacations and advanced conferencing. The metaverse will also be able to assist doctors in performing complex surgeries from a virtual viewpoint within their patient's body. Robotic microsurgery supported by the multi-sensory perceptions of the metaverse will unleash medical discoveries, leading to much more precise diagnoses and cures. Exploratory surgery, for instance, won't consist of randomly cutting away the tissues of a person's body. Instead, your doctor can move through a simulation of your organs, checking each for obstructions that may need to be treated.

Manufacturing

The prospects for manufacturing are equally as transformative. Imagine fully robotic factories, building complex machinery at scale. Sensors, all part of the Internet of Things, are strategically placed around the factory floor, allowing technicians to monitor each robot and machine in real time throughout the factory. Alternatively, imagine an airplane with engine trouble. Sensors, also connected with the Internet of Things, will allow air traffic controllers to see and feel what the pilots and passengers experience in real-time – or even later when investigating a crash or accident.

Real World Metaverse

Augmented reality delivers yet another glimpse of what is to come with the metaverse. Imagine walking down a street in Paris and seeing small popup messages appear over local landmarks as you pass. Each display provides personalized and contextual information that is of specific interest to you. Next, you stop at a shop and look at the clothing in the window. You see a shirt you like, and with a simple voice command, a virtual mirror shows you wearing that shirt. This is an instance of the mixed-reality world of augmented reality, where virtual images are superimposed and mapped over the top of the actual world.

If you've ever played Pokémon or accessed an app on your smartphone to preview furniture in your home before you make a purchase, you've used early iterations of augmented reality. In many warehouses, workers already wear augmented reality goggles. They see digital arrows on the floor leading to products, and a digital heads-up display (HUD) interface appears over the shipping crates with information about the contents.

These examples are not flights of fantasy coming from a science fiction novel or movie; they are extrapolations of the here-and-now potential of the metaverse. The metaverse is ushering in a new reality.

Points of Differentiation

The metaverse pulls together all the technologies, from the hardware to the software to artificial intelligence to virtual reality to the Internet of Things, into a coherent virtual representation.

And yet, the influence of video games in the metaverse should not be underestimated. Video games' very advanced appearance, thanks to 3D graphics, artificial intelligence, and other technologies, allows players to fully immerse themselves into a virtual world that often seems real with goals, tools, finance, and the different characteristics you'd expect to see in the near future from the metaverse. Undoubtedly, the metaverse will take advantage of many of the concepts used in modern video games, and the metaverse will certainly allow for rich and powerful gaming capabilities. However, it should be noted that video games are not the metaverse in themselves.

Overall, many technologies and different types of experiences will help make up the metaverse, individually many of these components are predecessors to the metaverse. Even so, the metaverse is something entirely new that will forever transform human society and the world. People will directly experience the metaverse through a series of 3D interconnected simulations, with the goal that platforms and businesses will create unique worlds that interconnect inorder to create an expansive, open and accessible metaverse.

Let's now unpack the Conceptual metaverse Value Proposition in more detail.

Conceptual: The Metaverse Value Proposition

Cultivated Communities

The metaverse will be, for all intents and purposes, a virtual functioning world where it's not dependent on location to build a sense of community. The metaverse will include video games, education, remote meetings, cultural experiences, and sports, many aspects of which are impossible in the material world because of the limitations of space, time, and the laws of physics. The metaverse is the new wave of digital interaction. These mesmerizing experiences will be rich, persistent, shared interactions with collaboration and co-creation at their core. Tim Sweeny, CEO of Epic Games, has said:

> This metaverse is going to be far more pervasive and powerful than anything else. If one central company gains control of this, they will become more powerful than any government and be a god on Earth.

TIM SWEENEY

COMMUNITY BUILDING

Communities in the metaverse will center around shared interests and activities, resulting in shared influence. The metaverse's spectrum of abilities, from education to entertainment, will create a vast landscape of communities. From a business perspective, there will be an increased need for community builders and managers to develop new forms of authentic connections with like-minded community members. These shared communal experiences will increase loyalty, stickiness and make the metaverse an increasingly important platform for up-leveled experiences with businesses and brands.

FANDOM

One emerging byproduct of cultivated communities in the metaverse is the notion of Fandom. Communities that form deep bonds around shared interests are giving rise to "super fans". These super fans can serve as growth drivers for businesses, large and small. The shared influence of the community cannot be overlooked. When Fandoms are adequately unlocked, it encourages co-creation and opens up shared equity opportunities for fans and brands. This is the Creative Economy in action; customers and fans are invited to build worlds together in the metaverse. This is ushering in a new reward and loyalty system where the capabilities of Web3 and the metaverse allow for co-ownership and collaboration. When communities co-create with brands in the metaverse, there is now a shared monetization model with use cases such as NFTs, Gaming, Entertainment, and Digital Fashion. Fandom in the metaverse offers a window into the business and revenue generation opportunities of Web3 and the metaverse. Tapping into Fandom businesses will amplify equity-driven participation and encourage world-building for shared mutual benefit.

Co-Journeys

The metaverse is, in essence, an interface that connects the physical and virtual world, revealing the opportunity to be transported to an immersive experience reminiscent of the *Matrix*. Today's video games offer a glimpse of what the future of the metaverse may look and act like; moreover, in the metaverse, fully functioning virtual civilizations will exist. You'll be able to shop in digital shopping malls, visit a library to read books, and travel to far-off lands.

Digital worlds in the metaverse, in many cases, will overlay upon the physical world, using augmented reality and AI to merge the two worlds, creating several new dynamics. As an evolution of the Web 2.0 concept of Customer Journeys (all the interactions a customer has with a brand, product or service across purchase, consumption, and post-purchase stage) in the metaverse the Co-Journey will be co-created and co-owned with the consumer.

EMERGING FORMS OF ENGAGEMENT

These new immersive co-journeys will allow businesses to connect with their audiences in completely new ways. As customer expectations and attention evolve, it will drive the metaverse space forward. Quickly requiring companies and brands to act and show up in innovative ways to allow and encourage co-creation and co-ownership. The metaverse will enable businesses and consumers to seize the opportunity to create meaningful ongoing forms of engagement.

STORYTELLING BEYOND THE PHYSICAL

Within the metaverse, brands will get more imaginative, significantly fueled by the fact that previous physical and digital limitations are eliminated. This chance to deepen connections will drive businesses forward when authenticity is at the core. Recently there has been much discussion on UGC (user-generated content); in the metaverse, UGS (user-generated storytelling) will be the new norm. Allowing people to build a brand's story together. By activating communities in new ways in the metaverse, brands will co-create immersive, memorable, and valuable journeys.

A NEW PLAYGROUND

These new forms of immersive Journeys in the metaverse are an incredible opportunity for unleashing creativity as an economic multiplier, meeting communities in unexpected ways to drive and scale loyalty.

New Commerce systems

The metaverse leveraging the principles of Web3 is more than just captivating 3D graphics, augmented reality, and special effects. People will have a greater sense of control and ownership in the metaverse. Similarly, businesses and entrepreneurs will have access to new modes of commerce.

NEW WAYS TO COMMERCE

With the emergence of the metaverse, new commerce models will also come to be —revolutionary new ways to buy, own and use assets in entirely novel and inventive ways. The concept of owning our time has a new meaning in the metaverse. In the metaverse, consumers can monetize their time and be rewarded for their attention and actions. The infrastructure of the metaverse x Web3 will enable the ability for brands to enact new tools and technologies to create co-ownership of assets and IP with their consumers and communities.

VALUE CHAINS

Layer one blockchains will activate and support smart contracts as forms of compensation. For instance, as metaverse Community members share and contribute to a brand's IP, such world-building members not only have the opportunity to tap into their creativity but also have an opportunity to be monetized. This activates the very core of Web3 capabilities to fuel the creative economy in the metaverse. These new value chains are well beyond just buying and selling assets but enable being rewarded for making assets and contributions within metaverse Communities. Brands that create environments that enable value vs. just trying to sell authentically will be the winners of tomorrow.

METAVERSE WALLETS

The metaverse and Web3 create new forms of reward systems by leveraging concepts such as tokens and digital wallets. In some ways, digital wallets may act as the evolution of the cookie did in Web 2. Similar to a cookie, a wallet can be a unique identifier. As the wallet transcribes purchase history, it will enable persona building and modeling based on personalization affinities.

The Relationship of Web3 to the Metaverse

To underscore, the metaverse is not to be conflated with Web3; they are distinctly different and meet different needs. However, Web3 is a core enabler that unlocks the fullest potential of the metaverse.

Mark Minevich, Global Digital Cognitive Strategist, wrote, "Web3 is the third generation of the internet, and it's built on the philosophy that the internet should be a decentralized network of computers rather than a centralized one. This means there is no single point of failure and no central authority controlling the flow of information."[1]

Web3 is the successor to Web 1.0 and Web 2.0, while the metaverse provides enticing interaction by leveraging internet and web technologies into 3D worlds. Web3, on the other hand, implements concepts such as blockchain, smart contracts, decentralized applications, and digital identity. The metaverse can (and should) take advantage of the powerful features of Web3.

Now, let's dive in and talk about the practical elements of the metaverse.

The Practical Elements of the Metaverse

The metaverse is comprised of several mission-critical elements. Without these practical elements, full implementation of the metaverse simply won't work and won't meet evolving user expectations. The metaverse becomes existent and usable with each of these elements fully defined and implemented. These depend on the foundational technologies of the internet and Web 1, 2, and 3. What are these elements?

1 Immersive 3D
2 Real-Time
3 Ownership
4 Interoperable
5 Shared Experience

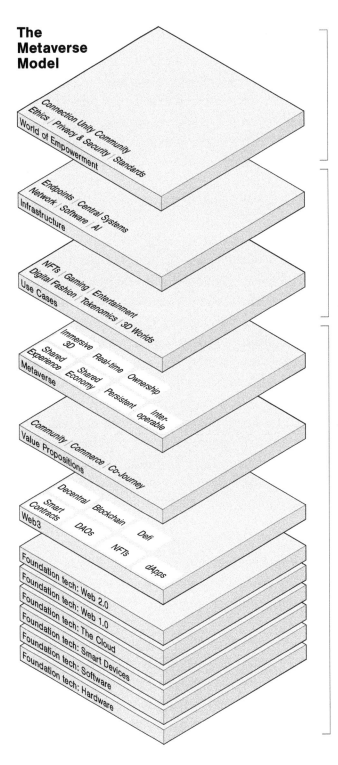

**The
Metaverse
Model**

Connection Unity Community
Ethics / Privacy & Security / Standards
World of Empowerment

Endpoints / Central Systems
Network / Software / AI
Infrastructure

NFTs / Gaming / Entertainment
Digital Fashion / Tokenomics / 3D Worlds
Use Cases

Immersive
3D   Real-time   Ownership
Shared
Experience   Shared
Metaverse   Economy   Persistent   Inter-
operable

Community / Commerce / Co-Journey
Value Propositions

Decentral   Blockchain
Smart
Contracts   Defi
Web3   DAOs   NFTs   dApps

Foundation tech: Web 3
Foundation tech: Web 2.0
Foundation tech: Web 1.0
Foundation tech: The Cloud
Foundation tech: Smart Devices
Foundation tech: Software
Foundation tech: Hardware

**Decoding
the
Imperative**

Part Three
of the book

**Decoding
the
Experience**

Part Two
of the book

**Decoding
the
Platform**

Part One
of the book

6 Shared Economy

7 Persistent

These elements differentiate the metaverse from anything that's come before it. With each of these elements in place, a fully functional meta-universe can be created. A complete universe that simulates and expands upon the real world composed of digital identities, experiences, economies, systems of governing, and full collaborative capabilities.

Let's go over each of the elements of the metaverse briefly.

1. Immersive 3D

An immersive 3D experience creates a world in which an individual or group perceives being physically present in a virtual world as a digital entity. Users can use their senses to experience the world around them and manipulate (and sense) objects and their environment. They can also interact with other real-world people and digital people (think of non-player characters (NPCs) in video games).

Users can perceive the world around them using sight, sound, touch, and even taste and smell. When you're in the metaverse in its ultimate configuration, it will appear to be a multi-dimensional 3D world to all intents and purposes. You'll be able to feel objects, pick them up, put them down, smell flowers, taste food, walk around the city, browse shelves at a library, or wander around a virtual national park.

Richly integrated augmented and virtual reality, artificial intelligence and machine learning, and other advanced technologies will amplify and personalize your experience as you enter infinite virtual worlds. You can engage with each world's content on a contextual and real-time basis.

The dissimilarity between a Web 2.0 e-commerce and a metaverse experience is that the metaverse store will be more immersive and experiential. In the metaverse, an e-commerce business could build an entire digital store personalized for you and your affinities. A store where you can browse the aisles, select items you want, and add them to your virtual shopping cart. Once you're finished shopping, you push your cart to the checkout, and your credit/debit card or digital currency wallet is automatically charged for your purchases.

This might sound familiar if you've ever used an Oculus headset to experience your favorite digital world and play a video game. I'm sure you noticed that the experience described above sounds like playing a game - and you'd be right. Many gamification concepts developed for video games directly apply to the metaverse.

2. Real-Time

In the metaverse, events will happen in real time, as they occur, as opposed to a recording played later. Essentially, what users experience happens as it unfolds in a non-linear format.

Events in the metaverse take place in real-time, meaning they happen live and simultaneously for all its users. The play in a video game co-occurs (at the same time) for all players, and the action moves forward without delays. Contrast this with a traditional chess game example: players take turns one at a time, and each wait for the other to take their turn. This is a linear reactionary-based approach, not simultaneous. These complexities associated with the need for speed and scale of real-time experiences in the metaverse will significantly depend on cloud and distributed infrastructure to support fully real-time immersive experiences.

3. Ownership

The concept of self-custody in the metaverse is anchored on the belief that individuals own the rights to their digital assets. It's a similar concept to ownership in the physical world. A person who owns their house or car has the right to live in and use their house and car as they please, and they also have the legal title proving and demonstrating their possession.

In the metaverse, people will have the ability to own their possessions and assets and own rights to use them as granted by digital contracts such as NFTs (which we will talk about shortly). Ownership is a core principle of the metaverse and Web3.

Possession and asset custody is a compelling concept for both the metaverse and Web3 because it allows people to own digital assets without needing a complex bureaucratic system or being granted authority by an individual. For example, a prospective buyer doesn't gain ownership with a specific person's permission when they purchase a cryptocurrency like bitcoin. They buy the bitcoin and obtain its possession.

This matters in the metaverse because it permits ownership rights without a central authority. You can own assets and be free to do with them as you desire. You can keep them, sell them, or transfer them to someone else. It's up to you because you are the owner.

In other words, self-custody is a decentralized way of owning assets. Self-custody is related to NFTs because NFTs authorize self-custody; it's all based on blockchain technology. Users control their private keys, giving them entitlement and control over their finances, assets, records, and anything else they own.

4. Interoperable

One of the core beliefs of the metaverse is interoperability, which will allow a range of transportability of assets such as avatars between virtual worlds – people will have the option to be represented with a digital version of themselves, known as an avatar. These avatars embody the appearance, possessions, and everything else about a digital version of the person, empowering metaverse users to function frictionlessly across virtual worlds.

To be interoperable, avatars and assets must be able to move between the worlds of the metaverse. In other words, they need to be able to seamlessly move between different platforms (worlds), similar to how people do in the physical space. For instance, an avatar could walk along a digital street from the bank to a shopping mall. They could "teleport" there if they desire and, after making some purchases, stroll over to another virtual world for their daily social media interaction. When finished, they could see a comedy show or watch a live real-world soccer game.

Note that avatars are not limited to only representing real-life humans. Avatars will also be created for digital entities (AI Synths). Powered by artificial intelligence's and machine learning's advanced capabilities, AI Avatars will be interacted with in many of the exact intricate ways we relate with real people. For instance, a company could hire "digital employees" to perform routine tasks such as a first response customer service representative. These digital employees could work alongside physical employees as assistants on more complex tasks. *Consultant, legal advisor, project coach*

TUTORING, TRAINING, EDUCATION

5. Shared Experience

A shared experience in the metaverse means that people simultaneously see, feel, and hear the same things.

A critical enabler of shared experiences is an immersive environment, created via 3D renderings of the surroundings to add a greater sense of reality. A virtual 3D store complete with a cashier is not necessarily essential for shopping in the virtual world, but it may make the experience seem more real and engaging by providing a relatable visual shorthand. World-building creates opportunities to build new and interesting environments that immerse people in full-sensory experiences and interrelate with each other in meaningful ways. This exposes areas for collaboration and co-creation with brands and customers to interact through shared experiences.

Video game players have long been aware of the importance of in-game surroundings, such as the design of caves, tunnels, roads, lakes, and rivers, as players intermingle in the virtual world. The environment (background scenery) enhances shared experiences since people can see and hear the same things at the same time.

The movie *Ralph Breaks the Internet* illustrates this point. Ralph and Vanellope live in video games. One day they are forced to visit the internet to find a replacement part for one of their games. Together, they share a journey through various virtual worlds of the internet and have some interesting adventures. The two visit real-life businesses. Vanellope, for starters, interacts with all the Disney princesses in a grand circular room complete with furniture, curtains, and a ceiling, yet this room exists only in the virtual world.

Shared experiences will allow us to identify with others and create a greater sense of closeness as we are transported throughout metaverse environments.

6. Shared Economy

The metaverse requires a functional economic system supported ubiquitously in the virtual world. Without a shared economy, the worlds of the metaverse simply aren't as valuable as they could be.

To enable this, Web3 provides an economic system complete with currencies (cryptocurrencies) and products and services that can be bought, sold, and traded in the metaverse. You can put your digital money into a crypto bank or fintech firm for safekeeping, invest in the stock market (or a digital version of it), and do many things you can do with the money in the physical world.

Equally, the money that you earn and save in the digital world, depending on how it's defined, may be used in the physical world (and vice versa). These currencies may be valid anywhere, both inside and outside metaverse platforms.

A fully functional economic system is far more than cybercurrency, just as the physical world's economy is far more than just dollars or other currencies. Some aspects of a comprehensive economy include:

- Trust that the currency will retain its value, whether it's a paper dollar or a cryptocurrency.
- People must be able to use it for trade – buying and selling.
- The currency must be universally (or at least locally) accepted.
- One currency unit is the same as another unit (a dollar equals a dollar).
- The currency can be saved or spent.

These economic features will be described further in the chapter about Tokenomics. Tokenomics refers to the qualities of a crypto token that make it useful and valuable.

7. Persistent (*virtual world doesn't pause or stop when you gone*)

One of the core concepts of the metaverse is persistence, which means extending the existence of the experience beyond the time when it is being experienced, giving a lasting "persistent" place in the world. In other words, experiences continue forward in time even when users are not experiencing them. Think of persistence as continuity rather than a reset, a pause, or an end, just as time is experienced in the real world.

The Problems that the Metaverse is Solving

The metaverse's fundamental promise is to enable humanity's capacity to access infinite opportunities. For instance, the ability to collaborate virtually with coworkers at a conference, go on an adventure with friends in the caves of Carlsbad Caverns, hike the highest mountains, or swim in an ocean clear across the planet.

This vision sounds intriguing, but you may be asking yourself: Why not just do these things in the physical world? What is the value *Adds to* of doing them in the metaverse? And these questions get to the very *doesn't* heart of the mind shift needed to understand the metaverse – it is not *replace* necessarily one or the other, physical vs. digital; they are not adversarial. Instead, the metaverse amplifies the physical and digital worlds – a blending of the two. Let's explore three examples of how The metaverse, merging the physical and digital, can help resolve several pressing issues.

The Problem of Classroom Sizes and Student Engagement

To begin with, let's look at education. During the lockdowns because of the COVID pandemic, students were required to take classes from their homes using web conferencing tools. Students and teachers took time to adapt to the solution because, in many ways, it removed much of the social interaction and sense of presence that makes education valuable.

This could be addressed with the metaverse. In addition to speaking in person to a few dozen students over web conferencing platforms, students could put on 3D goggles and find themselves sitting in a chair in a virtual classroom, surrounded by other students. These students could listen to the lecturers, collaborate within study groups, and break into rooms to chat socially 1:1 with friends.

Additionally, AI in the metaverse can enhance lectures, allowing an AI-enabled lecturer to personalize interaction with students and answer questions. Teachers could have digital assistants to assist students who needed more one-on-one attention. These advances mean classroom sizes would cease to be an issue; lectures attended by thousands of students will become routine.

The Possibilities for Entertainment are Endless

The tools provided by the metaverse allow for the creation of fully functional, entertaining worlds that will facilitate entertainment to be more self-determined without being carefully scripted. Artificial Intelligence and machine learning add new levels of depth to enjoyment. Where the characters in a game or movie appear to come alive, respond off-script in the moment, and perform actions that were not considered by the movie or game creator. Video games and movies will likely merge into an interactive type of movie. One where the viewers are in the scene and can view it from all viewpoints and directions, ask questions of the "actors," and get more information as the movie progresses.

The potential for documentaries is immense. Today, a documentary is a carefully scripted event with a narrator and materials such as videos and images that work together to tell the story. A metaverse-enabled documentary brings the viewer into the show, allowing them to feel like they are in the land of dinosaurs, the African jungle, or a beehive. Instead of seeing a flat 2D image of a dinosaur, the viewer can walk up to the virtual rendition of the creature, look up and get a feel for its immense height and strength, and seemingly touch the skin.

The metaverse will create a revolution in entertainment that alters the industry forever by providing thoroughly engaging participation at a much cheaper cost.

The Metaverse Changes the Online World into an Immersive Experience

The metaverse opens new opportunities for social interaction by creating virtual worlds filled with people's avatars. Someone attending a concert, city hall meeting, or classroom via the metaverse will experience a full 3D rendition of the event, complete with a sense of community with other people who are also attending. You will be able to relate with them, socialize and have experiences in a much less one-dimensional experience.

Let's Summarize It All

Now that you have been properly introduced to the metaverse, you can envision what the metaverse can do and how it operates. As we've seen, people can engage in endless new interactions in the virtual world, for instance, in the form of an avatar. These avatars begin as blank slates, waiting for someone to give them life, granting people the flexibility to express all facets of their identity and personality freely. The immeasurable value of the metaverse is that it's not about spending more time online; instead, it's about offering more meaningful ways to connect and build communities with others.

From a business perspective, the metaverse will deliver new long-term revenue streams, inventive business models, and ground-breaking commerce opportunities. These advancements are already happening, and the future of business expansion has never been brighter. Yet it mustn't be overlooked that metaverse strategies must work in synergy with the overarching business strategy for maximum outcomes.

The one sure thing is that the metaverse will revolutionize our world forever.

The following chapter will examine blockchain in greater depth. We'll then explore several metaverse use cases.

Notes

1 M Minevich. The Metaverse And Web3 Creating Value In The Future Digital Economy. *Forbes*. 17 June 2022. www.forbes.com/sites/markminevich/2022/ 06/17/the-metaverse-and-web3-creating-value-in-the-future-digital-economy/ (archived at https://perma.cc/6UBA-5MPP)

03 >Blockchain: The Basic Building Block of the Metaverse_

In this chapter, you'll learn about blockchain—what it is, its purpose, and how it works—and its relation to the metaverse and cryptocurrencies. You might find the content and specifics discussed in this chapter to be initially academic sounding and detailed. Rest assured, you need a deep understanding of blockchain and cryptocurrency because these are foundational to Web3 and the metaverse. (If you are eager to discover use cases in the metaverse, feel free to advance ahead to the next chapter on non-fungible tokens (NFTs) and return to blockchain at another time.) Make no mistake about it, blockchain has the potential to transform our world, as noted by William Mougayar in his book *The Business Blockchain*, "The blockchain cannot be described just as a revolution. It is a tsunami-like phenomenon, slowly advancing and gradually enveloping everything along its way by the force of its progression."[1]

Blockchain is a distributed database of ordered data blocks designed to work as a digital ledger with support for securing and transferring assets without the need for a central authority. The blocks are encrypted, linked, and cannot be changed (i.e., they are immutable). They contain ownership information and can be used to represent many data types, including currency, medical records, and even genealogical material. Blockchain is a foundational technology for the metaverse because it supports ownership, interoperability, and is infinitely scalable.

The following describes a blockchain:

- Is a single source of truth
- Is a distributed ledger
- Is immutable (i.e., cannot be changed)

- Contains smart contracts
- Is decentralized
- Is peer-to-peer
- Is open (i.e., permissionless)

How did blockchain get started? Why did it come into existence? Let's delve further in!

What are the Origins of Blockchain Technology?

Blockchain is often misunderstood, and the term is incorrectly used interchangeably with cryptocurrency and shrouded in mystery. But simply put, as Anthony Scaramucci described and noted in the book *Engineering and Operations of System of Systems*:

> The blockchain concept was pioneered within the context of crypto-currency bitcoin, but engineers have imagined many other ways for distributed ledger technology to streamline the world. Stock exchanges and big banks, for example, are looking at blockchain-type systems as trading settlement platforms.[2]

In 2008, Satoshi Nakamoto (a pseudonym) released a whitepaper describing bitcoin in technical detail and the motivations behind the concept. This paper argued for the invention of an entirely new online payment system and deliberated the methods for performing transactions, rewarding individuals, and how to use the network.[3]

Nevertheless, there is a differing opinion if Satoshi invented block-chains because evidence suggests that blockchains existed before bitcoin, albeit under a different name. Thus, there is some debate about when and how the idea for blockchain began. The Satoshi whitepaper references cryptographer Stuart Haber's whitepapers about timestamping. In his whitepaper, Haber claims to have created the first blockchain known as Surety. He further speculates that Satoshi cited his work (including three out of nine citations in the bitcoin whitepaper) for blockchain technology. Haber stated that his blockchain version was centralized, while bitcoin's version is decentralized. The point here is that there is some disagreement about the blockchain's origins.

In 2009, soon after the great recession, the peer-to-peer system of currency known as bitcoin was created. It first began as an experiment, but then it quickly took off; as this book is being written, it has a market cap of $758,761,533,328.66. Bitcoin requires a secure, scalable, private method to store data and uses blockchain for this purpose.

The term *blockchain* was first used on a forum called bitcoin Talk a full year after bitcoin was released. Whichever came first, bitcoin and blockchain cycled through several iterations. Blockchain began as a scalable, secure, distributed database designed specifically for bitcoin. It wasn't long before people realized blockchain could be separated from bitcoin. Accordingly, it could be used to store an infinite variety of other information.[4]

Later, smart contracts were created using a new (at the time) blockchain system called Ethereum. This innovative technology embedded computer programs directly into the blockchain to support concepts such as loans, bonds, and legal contracts without the requirement of a central authority.

Following came the concept of "Proof-of-Work," a consensus mechanism that verifies new cryptocurrency transactions. This verification is important because centralized authorities do not control blockchains. Proof-of-Work provides a means to guarantee the pedigree of the data contained within the blockchain.

The use of blockchain continues to grow, but there are still limitations to the current technology. It is challenging to scale blockchain due to the large amount of data needed to store information from origination to the most recent block on the chain. Other challenges, such as processing fees, block size, and response time, also currently limit the scalability of blockchain. As of this book's writing, this problem has not been resolved, but many researchers are working on solutions.

Although, blockchain does attempt to solve one of the most fundamental problems of the internet: it is difficult, if not impossible, to embed trust in the digital sphere.

Electronic Systems and Trust

As reflected throughout this book, trust was not inherently built to the internet and Web 1.0 initially because they were primarily designed for military, educational, and trusted organizations. As the internet caught on and expanded to include home users, businesses, and e-commerce, it became essential to establish the foundations for security and trust.

An extended description of trust is the belief that someone (or something) is the foundation for every relationship. Without trust, a relationship cannot exist to begin with. Yet, how do people trust one another when they are strangers? This is one of the problems that blockchain set out to solve—to create a completely decentralized "trustless" framework. In the case of blockchain, "trustless" means there is no need to put your trust in a third-party like a bank. Thus, blockchain reduces the likelihood of deception while increasing the possibilities for trustworthiness. *As LONG AS ITS TRUSTED*

As of this writing, e-commerce and other platforms already enforce trust using a centralized, trusted organization. These platforms are entrusted, and each organization collects a fee to bring together two or more individuals in that trusted environment. E-commerce is an instance of one type of trust relationship. The internet works similarly in that a business (i.e., a central authority) creates a platform that lets people socialize with one another, make purchases, or form communities.

As we'll review, this situation is still not completely ideal. It would arguably be better instead, if connections and relationships could form without a third party to enforce the trust. Blockchain solves this problem because it is:

- Immutable
- Organized in chains
- Transparent
- Decentralized
- Trustless by design

Blocks are created whenever anything occurs to the chain. For example, if a blockchain was created to record a sales process, an initial block is made at the time of purchase (or even when the product is manufactured). Additional blocks are then added as needed for the transaction ledger. These blocks could record the final payment, the product's shipping, and the product's receipt.

Blocks are never deleted or modified. They are kept in perpetuity. Any changes to the chain cause every computer in the entire network to validate the operation in the blockchain by solving complex mathematical problems (i.e., Proof-of-Work) or in some other manner (which we'll delve into later in this chapter). The blockchain is considered valid if there is a majority consensus among all the computers involved. Because blocks are encrypted and decentralized and the community validates the blockchain, it becomes exceedingly difficult, if not impossible, for the system to be hacked. In summary, the whole community enforces trust. No central authority or single party is involved.

Ownership and Assets

Trust is fundamental to the design of blockchain, enabling the ownership of assets. A *blockchain asset* is a digital representation of a physical or virtual item. These assets can be anything, including cybercurrency, legal documents, medical data, non-fungible tokens (NFTs), or anything else that can be represented digitally.

As we've discussed, decentralization is one of the key concepts for public blockchains; no computer or organization owns or hosts the chain. Instead, the chain is distributed to all the nodes (i.e., computers) in the network. Nonetheless, the assets represented by the blocks in the chain are owned by someone—one and only one entity. The block's ownership records are kept within the blockchain in an electronic ledger. Once an asset is created on the blockchain, an owner is applied to the block. This cannot be changed unless the owner verifies that the change is acceptable.

Suppose you created a digital representation of an original painting using a blockchain. (This would be an NFT, which we discuss in the next chapter.) The identity of the owner of this painting is stored in a blockchain. If the owner wanted to sell the painting, she'd be required to verify the new owner of the blockchain. Each procedure is recorded on the blockchain, meaning there is a complete digital record of every change of ownership (and any other change).

Let's look at the case of supply chain records. Many organizations record the movement of products through and from the source to destination (i.e., from the factory, to shipping company, cargo ship, and receiving port). The recorded data is not easily accessible by anyone who wants to see the whole picture because the individual transactions are kept in databases at the various businesses.

If supply chain records were stored in a blockchain, they would be owned by the entity that manufactured the product, which would authorize people (i.e., businesses) to view or add to the chain. The product's complete journey would always be available to the manufacturer and authorized entities in a single, all-encompassing, secure ledger. In this fashion, blockchain is useful for anything requiring a ledger to record transitions in status or ownership, from supply chains to store inventories to copyrights.

A significant use for blockchain (in fact, the first use case) is to create a digital currency.

Physical and Digital Money

Money is a medium of exchange, serving as legal tender to support the trade of goods and services. The US dollar is an example of a currency, which is a monetary system. In general, governments produce their currency, and in the past, it was backed by gold or other precious materials. Today, the issuing authority, usually a government, guarantees the value of the money.

Going back in history, people exchanged goods and services by bartering. If you needed to get dinner, you would trade something of value for the meal—perhaps by working for a few days or giving them an item in exchange. The Mesopotamian shekel was the first known instance of currency in roughly 3000 BC. Coins began to be minted around 1250 BC. It's theorized that governments created money for trade and taxation.

Money represents value and is vital for the establishment of commerce. It's challenging to create an economic system based on the barter system—coinage and money make it much easier to accomplish. In historical times, money or coins had actual value on their merit. For example, coins were minted in gold and silver, which could be melted down and sold in their rights.

As economies were established and expanded, paper money was introduced. These exchange units were backed by gold or other precious metals, meaning you could demand the government exchange the paper bills for their value in the metal. So, the basic trust of money was that it was backed by physical objects that had value in their own right.

Today, money is generally not backed by a commodity. Instead, they are backed by trust in the central government authority or bank. Money is only as valuable as it is trusted. In other words, you can no longer get a dollar's worth of gold in exchange for a paper dollar; without trust, paper dollars are worthless.

The monetary system is a highly complex system backed by a central authority. Until recently, each country defined its own money as bills and coins. Since World War II, the US dollar can be used just about anywhere on the planet, and the European Union (EU) created its bills and coins, which may be used throughout Europe. In the EU, individual countries do not mint their currency.

To many, however, cryptocurrencies are a new method of exchange. Trust is decentralized and does not depend on an issuing authority. Trust is enforced as part of cryptocurrencies' digital design and blockchain base.

Cryptocurrencies are money, even though they do not exist in a physical form. Because they are a valid method of exchange, each monetary unit has identical value to other monetary units (thus, a dollar always equals a dollar), and in this way they form the basis of an economic system consisting of banking, stocks, and bonds.

Advocates of cryptocurrencies postulate the advantages are:

- They are self-governed and managed.
- They are decentralized.
- They are secure and private.
- Transferring funds is optimal and extremely fast.
- Currency exchanges are efficient.
- Transaction costs are low.
- They are accessible to everyone.
- They are transparent.
- They offer protection against inflation.

Let's take a closer look at how blockchains are secured.

Origins of Cryptography

Militaries throughout history faced a communal problem of communicating with their troops, generals, and other leaders. Additionally, spies needed to convey their information, and bankers (or those who held large fortunes) were often required to obscure the size and location of their fortune. There were undoubtedly other reasons why messages needed to be kept secret as well.

Several thousand years ago, people began attempting to encrypt their information to make it more difficult for their secrets to become known. Julius Caesar encrypted secret messages to his generals by substituting characters with other characters or symbols. This primitive means of encrypting messages worked well enough for that time. Caesar used a three-shift cipher, meaning each character was shifted by three places. The letter A might be represented as D, B as E, and so on. In substitution ciphers, the security of the message is preserved in the knowledge of the formula used.

During the sixteenth century, the first cipher that used an encryption key was invented; the key to decrypt the message was repeated multiple times within the message. In this method, the security of the message depended on keeping the encryption key secret.

As militaries became more powerful and electric devices appeared, machines were designed to use one or more rotors to encrypt and decrypt messages. The key was stored on a rotating disc within the machine. The first used a substitution method, where the character substitution depended on notches within the rotating disc.

This led to the Enigma machine, which Arthur Scherbius invented near the end of World War I. This machine used several (three to four) rotors, rotating at different rates to determine how characters were encrypted. Poland broke this code and sent it to the British, who were able to design countermeasures. This enabled the allies to crack the code and read German encrypted messages throughout the war.

In the 1970s, IBM sponsored the creation of a cryptography group that designed a cipher called Lucifer, which later was accepted and renamed Data Encryption Standard (DES). An exhaustive search attack broke this cipher due to the size of the encryption key. In response, a new standard was created called Advanced Encryption Standard (AES).

By this time, e-commerce had appeared on the internet, and encryption was required to keep customer and payment information safe. Secure Sockets Layer (SSL), more commonly known as HyperText Transfer Protocol Secure (HTTPS), was invented to build encryption into the web protocol.

Claude Shannon is known as the father of mathematical cryptography. He authored an article titled *A mathematical theory of cryptography* while working at Bell Labs. Written in 1945 and published in the *Bell System Technical Journal* in 1949, this article is considered to note the beginning of modern cryptography. In it, he defined the standards that form the basis of cryptography today.

In the late 1970s, the invention of public key encryption changed cryptography by defining two keys: the private key, which remains confidential, and a public key, which can be shared. These two keys form the foundation of modern cryptography systems.

Now that you have a basic understanding of the origin of cryptography, let's move forward by further defining a blockchain.

What is Blockchain?

As we have mentioned, a blockchain is a distributed database that stores information shared on all the nodes in a computer network. More specifically, it is a peer-to-peer, encrypted distributed ledger updated only by consensus; new blocks can only be appended (i.e., never deleted or modified). Data is collected in blocks, each containing information. When a block is filled, it is closed, and a new block is added, thus creating the blockchain. These data chains form into a distributed ledger that records not just information but the owner, date/time, and other meta-information about the data in the block.

The purpose of a blockchain is to provide a way to securely store information that cannot be edited, is infinitely expandable (i.e., scalable), decentralized, and doesn't need a centralized control mechanism. Blockchains are an immutable record of an asset and are fully transparent. By design, blockchains reduce risk, virtually eliminate fraud, and have various uses.

Every block in a blockchain contains the following components:

- Data.
- A nonce that is a 32-bit randomly generated number. The nonce is created simultaneously as the block and used to create a block header hash (which is described later in this chapter).
- A 256-bit number known as a *hash* is combined with the nonce. It's an extremely small number.

At the time of the creation of the first block in a chain, the nonce is generated and this, in turn, generates the hash. The data, nonce, and hash, therefore, remain linked forever.

Blockchain is a method whereby information can be stored in an organized format. Every block in a blockchain summarizes all transactions in the block. They use a data structure known as a Merkle Tree (named after their inventor and also known as a Binary Hash Tree) because this is an efficient method to summarize and verify large datasets.

There are an infinite number of applications for blockchain technology. In addition to cryptocurrency, some of the blockchain applications incorporate:

- Royalty tracking for music, books, movies
- Voting
- Real-estate processing and record keeping
- Medical information
- Personal identity information
- Internet of Things (IoT) data
- Portfolio management
- Trading and settlement
- Budgeting
- Smart contracts
- Wills

Several steps are needed to add a transaction to a blockchain. These steps apply regardless of the application. Typically, these embrace the following:

1 A transaction is requested via a wallet.
2 This transaction is sent to all computers in the specific blockchain network.
3 Each of these computers uses rules to validate the transaction.
4 Once validated, the transaction is stored in a lock and sealed with a hash.
5 The block is added to a blockchain.
6 The transaction is finished.
7 From this point forward, the block cannot be modified.

When people are talking about blockchain, they are referencing public chains. There are several other types of blockchains as well:

- *Private.* In this blockchain, users must be invited to private blockchains and typically use the Proof-of-Authority consensus model. A PoA is a consensus algorithm that delivers an efficient solution for vetting blockchains, specifically private ones, by approved accounts.

- *Public.* Blockchains where the consensus is decentralized, and its code is open source. This blockchain is available to anyone, everyone can validate transactions, and there is no central authority.
- *Consortium.* In this blockchain type, known participants are preapproved by a central authority, allowing them to participate in consensus. These blockchains are typically used by entities such as banks.

Blockchain technology is beneficial for many applications. Further, before we proceed with an application based on them, let's consider the pros and cons of the technology. Pros for blockchain include the following:

- The data is high quality, durable, and secure.
- The blockchain is immutable and transparent.
- A blockchain has longevity and is reliable.
- The ecosystem is simple.
- Transactions are traceable.

Some cons involve:

- There are privacy concerns.
- The cost of resources for supporting the blockchain is high.
- Regulations are in flux.
- They are difficult to scale.
- The cost of supporting the blockchain is high.
- Blockchains do not integrate well into legacy systems.
- Blockchains are inefficient.
- The blockchain's performance is redundant.

Given that you now understand the concept of blockchain, let's briefly examine how ownership is recorded.

Documenting Ownership

It's fundamental to the blockchain design that once a block is placed on the chain, it cannot be modified or counterfeited. The data within each block can also include a record of the ownership of the data. Using a paper ledger, data can easily be changed; even traditional computer records can be modified without much trouble. The blockchain is different, however, and by including ownership data people can ensure that any goods they purchase, including cryptocurrency, belong to the individual recorded in the blockchain.

To summarize, when data is published on a blockchain, it is signed with the digital signature of the person who created it. Ownership (including every previous owner) is viewable by anyone at any time. Each block is identified by a nonce (as previously discussed) combined with a hash.

Hashing Data

When you create a copy of data or a file, how do you know it wasn't changed from the source? *Hashing* is a technique that is often used on the internet and by applications. In this technique, information is translated into a code, which can be used to compare versions to ensure they are identical. A hash is simply a method to verify that the contents of a block of data or a file are valid.

In a blockchain, an algorithm converts any length of input data into a fixed-length string. Bitcoin uses SHA-256 (Secure Hashing Algorithm, 256-bits). Hashing operates one way—the input data cannot be decrypted based on the hash code. If the input data changes, the hash also changes. Consistency of the blocks in a chain is maintained, because the new hashes are linked to previous hash codes.

Blockchain hashing accepts the bits in the data (any number of them), performs the necessary calculations (determined by the hashing algorithm), and outputs a fixed-length series of bits. This output is known as the hash.

A unique number is assigned to each block to identify it and to ensure that the blockchain is not modifiable. The following information is stored in the header of each block:

- Version number
- UNIX timestamp
- Hash pointers
- The nonce
- A hash of a Merkle root

A *blockhash* is the reference number for a block within a blockchain. Blocks are linked together and form digital ledgers, which we discuss next.

What is a Distributed Ledger?

A ledger describes or catalogs transactions. In accounting, a general ledger lists money spent and money received as income, along with identifying information about each transaction. Ledgers can record just about any type of data that must be organized and retrievable.

A distributed ledger is simply a database where each entry (or, in the case of blockchain, each block) is held and updated by every network participant. These records are built and stored by every node, instead of being managed by a central authority. This means that every network node receives, stores, makes conclusions, and votes on each block in a blockchain.

In real-world terms, an accountant enters debit and credit information into a ledger. If there is a centralized copy of this information, it is known as a centralized ledger. It would become decentralized if the ledger was copied to every office in the company, and if every copy was updated with every new transaction.

There are numerous advantages to a distributed ledger:

- Every node verifies every block, which reduces the chances of fraud.
- Every node votes, which eliminates the need for a central authority.
- If a node fails, the blockchain continues to be available.

Though, there are some disadvantages:

- Proof-of-Work requires heavy use of system and network resources.

- There are security concerns due to the complexity of decentralization.

Network Topology

As we've mentioned, a blockchain is comprised of Merkle trees, a data structure that relies on hashing. This composition method was chosen for blockchain because it's an efficient and secure data structure. Data on a blockchain can be quickly verified and moved from one computer to another in a peer-to-peer network. The data can also be distilled into a single hash value known as the Merkle root, which allows you to prove that the information which produced the hash didn't change.

A Merkle tree consolidates the data, hashes them together two at a time, and merges them into the Merkle root at the top. Blocks use the root of the previous block as a leaf (this also includes the data in the block).

A blockchain is a Merkle structure, consisting of linked trees. The topology of a blockchain is determined by the order in which they were connected. The blockchain topology is invariant by combining blocks to the right blocks in the chain.

Identifying and Protecting User Accounts

Wallets are the equivalent of user accounts for cryptocurrency and blockchain. You can think of crypto wallets as the digital version of your physical wallet. It's where you store your private keys (equivalent to the passwords that grant you access to your blockchains and cryptocurrencies) and cryptocurrency, which you can then use for transactions. You can use crypto wallets to send, receive, and spend cryptocurrencies.

Crypto wallets contain sensitive data much the same as the activities in your bank account. You must follow the highest security practices when dealing with your crypto wallets to ensure your safety and to prevent malicious individuals from breaking into your account. Some best practices include:

- Use complex passwords. (You should store your passwords in a password manager such as LastPass, so you don't have to write them down.)
- Set your account to two-factor authentication (TFA).
- Ensure that all your accounts have unique passwords—don't share passwords between accounts.
- Don't access your crypto wallet or other accounts over public Wi-Fi.
- Use anti-virus/anti-malware software.
- Use the highest security on your home router.
- Keep your operating system patched on your home computer, laptops, and mobile devices.

A crypto wallet can be a hardware device such as a USB stick (supported by Ledger) or a mobile app such as Coinbase.

Once you have your crypto wallet, you can begin authorizing interactions.

Authorizing Transactions

Initially, blockchain designers created it so that it didn't need a central authority. After all, there is still the need to authorize transactions by authenticating them. Blockchain uses public and private key encryption and digital wallets to perform this authorization. Users agree on a matter, which is then approved via consensus (which is considered later in this chapter). The design of blockchain includes a decentralized method to store operational data.

Storing Transaction Data

Blockchain is designed to store information in a decentralized network. The data is stored on unused disk space on hard drives, which can be located anywhere in the world. This is intended to be an alternative to the traditional, centralized data storage, as with the cloud or legacy computers. Files are split up into parts in a process called sharding, and each shard is copied and encrypted. This activity is recorded in the blockchain ledger, which allows the data to be synchronized between nodes. This is the same protocol that BitTorrent uses.

Assume a supermarket created a blockchain to record every step of an individual throughout the customer journey. The chain's root would consist of the first identifiable contact, perhaps their creation of an account for the web store or the purchase of a product from a brick-and-mortar establishment. Each contact with the customer— visiting the web store, making a purchase, leaving a review, and so forth— adds another block to the blockchain.

Upon creation, each of these blocks is split into smaller pieces (sharding), and the data is sent to every node within the network. Retail establishments would probably set up their private block-chains and maintain centralized control over them to address security and privacy concerns. Given this explanation, how is a decentralized database used?

Using the Data Store

A concept known as Distributed Ledger Technology (DLT) is at the foundation of blockchain. DLT is how a database is created, tracked, and maintained across many computer systems. Every block in the blockchain is duplicated on multiple nodes in the computer network. The DLT system is then responsible for verifying and synchronizing the transactions to all the various nodes.

Because of the replication to all nodes, blockchain uses a large amount of storage and bandwidth to transfer and store the data. Because blockchains are never changed or deleted, the volume of data moving around and being stored could quickly overwhelm systems. Therefore, this vital data must be managed.

On the other hand, a blockchain is not suitable for storing metadata (which we will contend with later) for information such as images, videos, and parameters. So, what is done with that material?

Distributing a Data Store among Peers

A decentralized data store for blockchain technology is *not* a great solution for regular data storage. Transactional information is stored in the blockchain (i.e., on-chain) while related data, such as videos and photos, is stored elsewhere (i.e., off-chain). This dramatically reduces the volume of data that is copied to every node.

Many solutions are available to relate the off-chain data to the on-chain data (i.e., transactions). Chainlink is an Oracle decentralized network technology whose purpose is to maintain the connections (and is the glue) between the on- and off-chain data.

Choosing the correct data storage that is fast, efficient and scalable is important when adding and verifying transactions.

Verifying and Adding Transactions

Transactions are encrypted using public/private keys. Users each have their private keys, which provides them with the means to create a secure digital identity. These keys are used to create digital signatures, which, in turn, can unlock transactions.

The following is the sequence for verifying and adding transactions:

- Users agree on a transaction. They each maintain a secure digital identity with digital signatures to authenticate their wallets and interactions.

- Public blockchains then use the consensus method to decide to add a transaction to a blockchain. In the Proof-of-Work consensus (which will be described later), computer resources are used to solve complex math problems. This process is known as mining, which we'll cover later in this book. Miners are rewarded for their work by earning digital currency as an exchange for developing a newly minted block. This method determines which nodes can add a block to the blockchain.

- Based on consensus, the winning nodes add the block to the blockchain.

The original whitepaper, known as the Satoshi whitepaper, described the concepts behind blockchain in detail.

Satoshi Whitepaper

As we highlighted earlier, an anonymous programmer (or a group of them) released a whitepaper in 2009 under the pseudonym Satoshi Nakamoto, describing a new type of digital currency known as bitcoin. This whitepaper described blockchain technology, Proof-of-Work, and a record-keeping system where data could not be changed. Hence, bitcoin was born, and it grew into a peer-to-peer electronic cash system.

The Satoshi whitepaper was released after the great recession of 2008, with the intention of decentralizing the control of the money, hoping to avoid similar economic situations in the future.

The first block, known as the genesis block, was mined on January 3, 2009, and the initial transaction occurred a week later. For the first year, bitcoins (BTCs) didn't have any real value. Then, on May 22, 2010, a Florida man bought two Papa John's pizzas, which were delivered for 10,000 BTC. In 2010, bitcoin became available on exchanges to purchase, sell, and trade. In 2011, other networks like Ethereum were created.

By February 2011, the price of bitcoin reached $1. In April 2013, it was worth $200, and by November 2013, its worth grew to $1,000. By November 2017, the value rose to $10,000; in November 2021, the value peaked at $68,990.

Bitcoin is the first (or one of the first) cryptocurrencies, and it continues to grow in value and utility today.

What is Cryptocurrency?

Cryptocurrency is money (i.e., currency) that exists in a digital format. It uses cryptography to authenticate transactions and secure the supply. The funds are used to purchase products and services.

Cryptocurrencies were designed around decentralization. Their data is stored in unused space on disk drives worldwide. Additionally, calculations are performed on computers based anywhere on the planet.

You access cryptocurrencies using crypto wallets protected by private/public keys to store, receive, and spend your cryptocurrency. Your crypto wallet is identified by a unique address, which is its virtual location. Transfers to and from said wallet are called *transactions*. You can buy and sell your cryptocurrencies at exchanges, which are online digital marketplaces.

Online Trading on Cryptocurrencies

Cryptocurrency is popular among traders, partially because their prices change, which introduces opportunities to purchase them at a low price and sell at a higher price, making a profit.

Before you can trade in the cryptocurrency market, there are a few steps that you need to perform:

1 Create a cryptocurrency brokerage account.

2 Put funds into that account by connecting it to your bank account. You can use a debit card or a wire transfer to move your funds.

3 Decide which cryptocurrency you want to invest in. Note, you are not limited to just one. You can choose from several types, including bitcoin, Ether (from Ethereum), Tether, Binance coin, in addition to many others.

4 Define the strategy you want to use to make your trade.

5 If you'd like, you can automate your cryptocurrency trading.

6 Your funds will be stored on the exchange using your digital crypto wallet.

You can engage in a Contract for Difference (CFD), which means sellers and buyers agree to exchange the difference between the opening and closing of a financial asset contract. Investors in CFDs don't own the assets—their revenue is based on the asset price change. As in the stock market, you can buy long (you believe the value will rise) or short (you think the value will fall).

You can use CFDs to trade in cryptocurrencies, or you can use an exchange. In the latter case, you purchase crypto coins by creating an exchange account, buying the cryptocurrency you want and storing them in your wallet (i.e., account), and then selling them. If you want someone to do this for you, you can engage a crypto trading broker to act as an intermediary. It's important to remember that when you invest in cryptocurrency, you are not investing in a physical or tangible asset—the assets are entirely virtual.

Bitcoin Predecessors

While bitcoin is the best known of the digital currencies, other attempts have been made to create electronic money. Here are a few:

- *DigiCash:* In 1989, David Chaum founded DigiCash, an electronic currency. He couldn't get banks to use the technology, so the business only lasted a decade.
- *E-gold:* This was an investment opportunity created by the National Spot Exchange Limited (NSEL). This currency allowed for the purchase of gold in digital form.
- *Hashcash:* In the mid-1990s, Hashcash was developed and became highly successful. Its design was like bitcoin in many ways. While there was quite a bit of interest in the currency, the processing power requirements caused it to fall by the wayside.
- *B-money:* A developer named Wei Dai proposed an "anonymous, distributed electronic cash system" called B-Money, and the design was quite different from bitcoin. Yet, his concept didn't gain any traction and was unable to launch.
- *Bit Gold:* Nick Szabo proposed a decentralized model like bitcoin. It was not successful but was the inspiration for several digital currencies.

At this point, thousands of cryptocurrencies are available for trading. Each currency has its unique advantages and disadvantages. Some are lucrative, while others start up only to disappear. The cryptocurrency market is relatively new, and some want to expand on the basic bitcoin paradigm. Be that as it may, bitcoin remains the most significant cryptocurrency because it has many advantages over other choices.

Bitcoin and Its Advantages

Because bitcoin is the first and best-known cryptocurrency, people naturally are interested in investing and seeing it prosper. Also, remember that no one owns the bitcoin technology, so anyone is free to start their cryptocurrency whenever they want.

As you've learnt, bitcoin runs on a decentralized, trustless, peer-to-peer network. It has the following advantages:

- Permissionless
- Resists censorship
- Decentralized
- Open source
- Anonymous
- Transparent
- Immune to seizure
- Anyone with an internet connection can participate

To manage your bitcoins, you need:

- to acquire a digital crypto wallet linked to a payment method
- to pick and join an exchange
- to manage your assets

Bitcoin uses blockchain to manage and store bitcoin data. Every block is encrypted with public and private keys to ensure the data's security.

Public and Private Keys and Custody

Encryption protects the blockchain, and public/private keys are used to decrypt and encrypt data. Both of these keys are large prime numbers related to each other but are different. The public key is used to decrypt data that has been encrypted using the private key. Note, you cannot infer the private key from the contents of the public key. The public key is used to encrypt the data. People are then given a private key to decrypt the data.

Custody refers to holding assets and keeping them safe. In the blockchain, custody refers to the cryptographic keys that unlock wallets.

The Unspent Transaction Output Model

The Unspent Transaction Output (UTXO) model refers to the "change" left after a cryptocurrency transaction. This model tracks the ownership of all the parts of cryptocurrency. If you spent .005 of the .010 that you owned, .005 is left, and the .005 that went to someone else would be tracked. Bitcoin uses UTXO, but Ethereum does not.

A CAUTIONARY TALE

In 2017, Sam Bankman-Fried, who was 25 years old, founded Alameda Research, a small trading firm to in essence purchase cryptocurrency in one country and then sell it at a higher amount in another, keeping the difference as profit (this is known as arbitrage trading). In 2019, he went on to found FTX, a cryptocurrency exchange to allow investors to buy, sell, and store cryptocurrencies and digital assets such as NFTs, in part to provide additional funds for further Alameda investments. To generate even more revenue for investment, he launched a new token, known as FTT, on FTX. FTT token ownership was intended to allow access to FTX capabilities and services, as well as give owners discounts on fees.

Alameda in turn invested in the FTT tokens and as such, because Alameda was a major trader, began to influence the price of the tokens.

This interconnected business model gave the appearance of financial strength for each of the companies, when in reality they were in many ways propping one another other up. Investors had minimal visibility into this scheme because Alameda and FTX were privately held. Simultaneously, the two companies began funding billions of dollars of investments to expand their influence and reputation into at least 246 early-stage crypto companies.

This house of cards collapsed when the value of cryptocurrencies unexpectedly fell in the spring of 2022. The worth of FTT tokens dropped drastically, lenders asked for their loans to be repaid, and FTX reportedly began using customer funds to pay back lenders. The two companies consequently filed for bankruptcy on November 11, 2022, affecting more than a million creditors and investors and potentially losing tens of billions of dollars.

This cautionary tale underscores the need for even greater education on the fundamental concepts of cryptocurrencies and blockchain technology. Furthermore, while many investors believe crypto assets are an entirely new and alternate form of investment, the reality must not be forgotten: they also follow and must be evaluated using standard accounting and investing best practices. The FTX/Alameda calamity was a combination of current crypto marketplace volatility, a lack of traditional financial controls, minimal transparency, and little to no corporate governance.

As Web3, crypto, and blockchain become more prevalent, it is incumbent upon future investors to educate themselves about not only investment assets but also the organizations offering them.

Security Fundamentals

The data structures of blockchain are inherently secure by nature of their design. The model is based on consensus, cryptography, and decentralization, and the blocks are connected such that they are virtually tamperproof. The consensus model guarantees that every transaction is true. Additionally, throughput records may not be changed.

Protecting blockchain requires that systems and the network follow security best practices. Breaches by malicious actors can allow them to destroy, modify, or view blockchain data, especially if system security is so weak that they have time to hack the encryption.

There are several vulnerabilities inherent to blockchains:

- *Routing attacks.* This is a man-in-the-middle attack where data is intercepted and rerouted en route to an internet service provider (ISP).

- *Sybil attacks.* These are attacks where the target network is flooded with false identities, which crashes the system.

- *Phishing attacks.* In these attacks, users are convinced to open their digital wallets through standard phishing emails.

- *51% attacks.* In these attacks, malicious miners can acquire more than 50 percent of the resources in a blockchain and consequently gain control over ledgers.

Crypto wallets are protected by encryption; if the encryption key or password is lost, all the data may be lost. However, you can recover the data using a recovery seed or recovery phrase, which is a list of words (12, 18, or 24) that can be used to recover a wallet.

Consensus

The Consensus Protocol is the core component of a blockchain network. It is where all the peers in a blockchain network use these same procedures to agree on the present state of a distributed ledger. Consensus protocol is vital in establishing trust between peers who don't know each other. Consensus ensures that each block added to a blockchain is the only version of the truth.

There are diverse ways to form consensus:

- *Proof-of-Work.* This works by solving a complex math puzzle to a solution. Solving this puzzle requires resources, and the first node to solve the puzzle is assigned as the miner for the next block.

- *Proof-of-Stake.* Coins are invested as a stake. It's like placing a bet that the miner can discover a block they believe will be added to the blockchain. Rewards are then given out to validators based on their bets, which increases their stakes accordingly. The idea is that validators are chosen based on economic incentives.

- *Proof-of-Burn.* Coins are sent on a one-way journey to an address. Those who "burn" or use more coins have a greater chance of becoming validators.

- *Proof-of-Elapsed-Time.* This method generates a random time value to decide who wins the mining rights. Miners wait for a randomly selected time, and the one with the smallest time value is the winner.

These are only a few of the methods used to form a consensus. There are several additional ones, and more are always being developed.

Next, we'll further discuss smart contracts, a fundamental component of blockchain.

Smart Contracts

A smart contract is simply an application stored on a blockchain. This application is run when specified conditions are met. One use of smart contracts is to automate agreements so that an intermediary, such as a lawyer, is not needed. Smart contracts can be used to automate workflows. In this case, the next action is set into motion after previous conditions are met.

On Ethereum, smart contracts are generally written in a programming language called Solidity. This code is compiled so that the Ethereum virtual machine can execute it.

Despite the name, smart contracts are not generally legal agreements. Instead, they provide an automated means to perform a series of pre-determined actions.

As you know, buying a home is a complex process involving inspectors, lawyers, real estate agents, numerous fees, permitting, and paperwork. Smart contracts can be designed to automate many of these steps, thus eliminating or reducing the need for third parties to coordinate the steps. This makes it much less likely that an action or process will be forgotten or done improperly.

What Blockchain Solves for and Its Utility

The utility of blockchain goes far beyond just cryptocurrency. Because a blockchain is a ledger of information and is secure and cannot be modified, it can be used to solve many problems in the real world. Blockchain is a solution for any application that:

1 Needs excellent security

2 Maintains a ledger of transactions or data

3 Needs transparency

Because blockchains are decentralized, it's difficult for dishonest actors to break the security or overwhelm the network. The consensus system encourages honest nodes and discourages dishonest nodes. It is what makes the democratic system operate without a central authority.

Some of the usages for blockchain include:

- Improving supply chain management
- Enforcing copyrights and royalties
- Automating real estate transactions
- Sharing government resources within agencies
- Crowdfunding
- Sports loyalty programs
- Dealing with customer transactions

Mining

The mining of blockchains refers to the work (or other types of proof) that nodes must do to earn new tokens and gain the right to create new blocks on the blockchain. It is the method that blockchain uses to verify the integrity of transactions.

In the Proof-of-Work consensus model, math problems are set to a difficulty level where a block is mined every 10 minutes. Other consensus models use different methods to regulate mining.

Despite the name, mining has nothing to do with real-world digging for coins or shifting sand for bits of gold. Instead, a consensus model, such as solving complex math problems, controls the process. Whoever wins gains the right to publish a new block; their reward is the transaction fee and, in the case of bitcoin, a newly "minted" coin.

Mining is a concept central to blockchain and exists in each of the variants in one form or another. Because Ethereum and bitcoin are open sources, anyone can create a new currency or even a new blockchain implementation anytime. These altered versions are known as *forks*.

Forks, Altcoins, and Sidechains

Because blockchain is open source, it's open for change. Anyone can create a new and different version that performs unique functions or works differently. If you wanted a different encryption model, you'd create an alternate version known as a fork and modify your version.

Creating custom modifications to the software core is known as forking, which is not to be confused with forking the blockchain, which means creating a split in a ledger. These terms are two different concepts that use the same word, so be careful to understand their varying context.

Here are some of the terms and their meanings:

Altcoins. This is a forked version with different consensus rules. Examples include Litecoin and Dogecoin. Ethereum, even though it was built from the ground up, is also referred to as an altcoin. Solana is another instance of a competitor to Ethereum.

Sidechain. This is a blockchain tied to the main chain. An example is the US Dollar Tether (USDT), which is pegged to the US dollar. The purpose is to provide visibility to the value of US dollars they have on hand as a backup to their tokens.

Multichain. A multichain is an ecosystem that interconnects several blockchains to create a better user experience and a more efficient system. Multichains allow data to be moved between different blockchains. Composability provides the means to combine various system components for specific requirements, effectively eliminating the barriers between blockchains.

Parachain. A parachain is a single layer-one blockchain functioning in the Polkadot and Kasama multichain networks. Parachains are very flexible and can be implemented differently with various features.

Ethereum is a popular blockchain that includes features not present in bitcoin. Ethereum is not a fork of bitcoin; instead, it was designed and implemented from the ground up.

The Evolution of Ethereum

Bitcoin is currently the most popular cryptocurrency, but it's quickly being challenged by a younger, open-source, public upstart known as Ethereum. It's a programmable blockchain designed to support smart contracts, DeFi (reviewed later on), and other functionality.

Vitalik Buterin became intrigued by bitcoin in 2011 when he was only 17 years old. In 2013, he wrote and released a whitepaper explaining Ethereum. The new platform uses a general scripting language and is designed to support more functionality than cryptocurrency. Ethereum was crowdfunded in 2014 and raised over $18 million. The result was Frontier, the name of the first release, which became popular and proliferated.

Digital tokens that are based on bitcoin are known as colored coins. These coin types represent assets outside of the bitcoin block-chain. Mastercoin (now OMNI) is a predecessor to Ethereum based on bitcoin. Ethereum's design took the concepts of Mastercoin to the next level.

Any user who wants to perform a function on the Ethereum block-chain must pay a fee known as a gas fee. Gas is the amount of ether (ETH), the Ethereum cryptocurrency, that must be used to get anything done within the Ethereum network.

A dapp is a decentralized application that uses Ethereum to get work done. These apps are stored within and run on the blockchain. They are not under the control of a central authority and can be used for applications such as gaming, finance, messaging (think Twitter), and so forth. Tools to create dapps for blockchains using Ethereum are included in what is known as the Truffle Framework—a development environment which provides boilerplates and code generators.

But what if you want to launch a cryptocurrency of your own? In that case, you'd issue an initial coin offering (ICO).

Bitcoin ICOs

An ICO refers to the launching of a new cryptocurrency, which is like an IPO (initial public offering) except for cryptocurrency. This is essentially (when legitimate) a way to raise funding for creating a new cryptocurrency. Here are ICO's steps:

1 Document how the system will work (via a whitepaper).
2 Create a website.
3 Explain the pros and cons of the ICO.
4 Pitch to investors.
5 Send investors coins with the goal that they will become popular and valuable.

Blockchain Platforms

According to Liquid, "Rather than having multiple websites where people need to input data to authenticate their identity (and expose themselves to identity theft), blockchain platforms enable the individual to own their authentication and use it as they want."[5] By doing this, users can avoid the risks associated with using different websites for authentication.

The Hyperledger Foundation supports blockchain advancement by hosting infrastructure and resources. They state:

> Blockchain solves a core problem: many organizations want to share data in a distributed database, but every user will trust no single owner. Blockchain technologies enable direct transactions in a secure, transparent way, baking trust into systems that operate with the efficiency of a peer-to-peer network.[6]

To aid in developing applications and solutions, Hyperledger Fabric is designed to offer services such as consensus as plug-and-play, which makes it easier to work with because it's modular, scalable, versatile, and performs well. Hyperledger Fabric may be optimized for different use cases like financial services and insurance.

Blockchain has the potential to impact many industries in a variety of ways.

Industry Impacts

Because blockchain implements a virtual ledger with many capabilities (as seen throughout this chapter), many industries are finding uses for the technology. These include:

- Financial services, such as banks, investments, and stocks
- Healthcare, which can use blockchain for the patient and other medical data
- Agriculture, to document crop rates, failures, and problems
- Supply chains, to remove paper-based recordkeeping
- Real estate, to record, track, and transfer land titles

In fact, any industry you can think of can use the technology to improve its capabilities and workflow.

Blockchain Projects

Numerous projects are in the works that depend on blockchain technology. These include:

- *The R3 Consortium.* Enabling digital collaboration using DLT platforms. They have one of the largest DLT production ecosystems in the world
- *T Zero.* Overstocking the Stock market. Overstock.com's cryptocurrency
- *Blockstream Distributed Systems.* Enhancing the bitcoin ecosystem

- *Decentraland.* A digital world that allows people to create, explore, and trade
- *Lighting Networks.* A network designed for bitcoin and blockchain transactions

Of course, there are many hundreds, if not thousands, more projects related to the blockchain and bitcoin.

Now that you know about blockchain and cryptocurrency, let's discuss how governments and financial services use the technology.

How Governments and Financial Services Respond to Blockchain

Blockchain and cryptocurrency are improving the transparency of payments, enhancing trust and security, increasing efficiency, and reducing costs. Because the financial industry handles trillions of dollars daily, even minor changes can result in massive disruption.

Financial industries are responding to blockchain by using the technology to improve their operations, increase their efficiencies, and increase their staff's productivity. Additionally, they are focused on improving customer service, which makes them more competitive, and they view blockchain and cryptocurrencies as a way to accomplish this task. Their speed of implementation is essential, as there are impressive competitive advantages to those who are first to do so.

Governments also see the advantages of blockchain and are moving forward to aid in areas such as law enforcement, controlling money laundering, and anti-terrorism efforts, in addition to taking advantage of its uses for record-keeping, documentation, and streamlining operations. The US government has even explored the idea of creating a complimentary cryptocurrency for the dollar, and El Salvador was the first to adopt bitcoin as its national currency.

One advantage governments see in blockchain is that its transparent ledgers provide a complete transactional record that cannot be changed. Moreover, blockchain supports anonymity.

Using Blockchain to Stay Anonymous

By design, blockchains are not anonymous. Your blockchain address is your public address and doesn't contain any information that could identify you. Blockchains are public ledgers, and you or anyone else can view transaction histories about the cryptocurrency in each crypto wallet. This enables law enforcement and governments to examine and use these ledgers in criminal and terrorist investigations—theoretically, any time they want.

There are several ways to remain anonymous, however:

- *Coin mixing.* Think of this as a form of money laundering. Mixers take your cryptocurrency and mix it with that of others. They then return someone else's coins to you.
- *CoinJoin.* This service receives multiple payments and joins them together, making the payments more difficult to trace.

Even a technology as powerful and useful as blockchain has its limitations. Let's consider those now.

Blockchain's Limitations and Considerations

You might come away from this chapter believing blockchain is the perfect solution to many problems. It indeed has many advantages, but there are some limitations as follows:

- It's still an emerging technology, and people generally do not understand its value to them and their organizations.
- Records may not be changed (i.e., they are immutable). Yet, this can limit the value when changes or revisions are needed.
- Someone could lose access to their private key, which means the data is irretrievable.
- Because blockchain keeps copies of literally everything on every system in the network, it can demand enormous amounts of resources.

- Obtaining consensus can be a timely and resource-intensive process.

- Because data on a blockchain can never be deleted, they technically violate General Data Protection Regulation (GDPR) standards, which require that consumers can order their data to be deleted.

- It might be possible to trace public keys and addresses to a specific individual, thus providing access to the user's transaction history.

- Because no central authority exists to enforce and validate security, malicious actors may be able to break into blockchains with impunity.

The Future of Blockchain

The pace of development and implementation of blockchain technology is moving forward rapidly. Businesses are finding ways to use it to improve their operations, provide better customer service, and increase their privacy and security. The result for these organizations will be an improved bottom line, and they will be able to compete better in their marketplace.

The possibilities for blockchain are, for all practical purposes, infinite. The combination of blockchain, Web 3.0, and the metaverse promise to give the world a decentralized, trustless internet that's fully transparent, far more secure, and much more useful than the current one.

Unfortunately, the blockchain's scaling problem is significant and threatens to slow down the use of the technology. Currently, Visa processes 1,700 transactions per second, while blockchain merely crawls at 7. This speed differential is caused because blockchain transactions are copied to every node in the network and then again when it is mined, which consumes substantial disk, CPU, and bandwidth resources.

Practical solutions include the following:

- Better consensus mechanisms could help resolve this issue by using fewer resources.

- Sharding breaks down transactions into shards, which are then processed in parallel, allowing several transactions to be worked on at once.
- Nested blockchain could use the main blockchain to set parameters for the blockchain network.
- zk-STARKs and zk-SNARK—zero-knowledge proof technologies—can improve performance because they are high-performing proof systems.
- The Directed Acyclic Graph (DAG) model could mean miners won't have to compete for new blocks to add to a chain—DAG networks contain no blocks of transactions.
- Sidechains create a multi-branched blockchain. The rules are configurable, allowing several branches to propagating simultaneously.

Other issues to resolve with the blockchain and cryptocurrency include privacy concerns, performance, and security.

Nonetheless, it's important to understand that blockchain is a recent technology and is still being developed and implemented. As with all emerging technologies, its performance will improve, security will be enhanced, efficiency will be increased, and resource usage will decrease. The technology is instrumental, and, before long, it will power governments and industries worldwide.

Summary

As we've shown throughout this chapter, there is a common theme of duality when unpacking the metaverse. For instance, the metaverse creates transformative advantages by merging the physical and virtual universes. Additionally, when the metaverse is coupled with blockchain, it facilitates inventive new business models.

Blockchain will allow digital information to be recorded and distributed to deliver efficiencies and cost advantages, ultimately increasing the capacity to reinvent how people and businesses converge. Individuals will benefit with greater control and access to use, sell, and trade their assets in the metaverse. Therefore, blockchain is central to the foundation of the metaverse.

This new digital reality of the metaverse will build upon blockchain by incorporating and enabling the following:

- Emergence
- Authenticity
- Traceability
- Consensus
- Composability
- Interoperability
- Ownership
- Creativity
- Immutability
- Decentralization
- Decentralized identity (DID)

The blockchain creates the technical basis for shared experiences in the metaverse and technologies. As we'll soon see, non-fungible tokens (NFTs), which are analyzed in depth in the next chapter, use blockchain as their datastore.

Notes

1 W Mougayar (2016) *The Business Blockchain: Promise, Practice, and Application of the Next Internet Technology*, John Wiley & Sons, Inc.
2 R B John Mo (2019) *Engineering and Operations of System of Systems*, CRC Press Taylor & Francis Group
3 S Nakamoto. Bitcoin: A Peer-to-Peer Electronic Cash System, bitcoin.org/bitcoin.pdf (archived at https://perma.cc/5MAT-F56B)
4 A Hertig. Bitcoin and Blockchain: The Tangled History of Two Tech Buzzwords, 13 September 2021. www.coindesk.com/markets/2019/05/19/bitcoin-and-blockchain-the-tangled-history-of-two-tech-buzzwords/ (archived at https://perma.cc/AF5A-4SZA)

5 How Do Blockchain Platforms Work, blog.liquid.com/how-do-blockchain-platforms-work (archived at https://perma.cc/5F3F-NHG6)

6 Hyperledger Foundation, www.hyperledger.org/ (archived at https://perma.cc/Y238-N98G)

Part Two
Decoding the Experience_

04 >Non-Fungible Tokens_

Even though CryptoKitties, one of the first breakthrough non-fungible token (NFT) projects, has been around since 2017, many people still don't understand the full ramifications that NFTs offer. NFTs, by their nature, eliminate the need for the central operational control that computer, internet, and web technologies have required until now. This new paradigm places the asset owners in charge of their destiny and provides much more freedom and openness than the closed systems that dominate much of computing today.

NFTs generate much conversation; some believe they are a great solution to many problems, and others look more at their disadvantages. Whatever you know or think about NFTs, they are a core aspect of the metaverse. They are powerful tools not just for investments but also for many other uses. But what are they? Why should anyone except for crypto investors care? To begin, we'll explain the concept of fungibility—an interesting word describing several powerful concepts.

What is Fungibility?

A *fungible asset* can be exchanged with other assets of the same type. Money is an example of a fungible asset; you can exchange a dollar for another dollar, and they are treated equally for all intents and purposes. You can also split a dollar down into its parts—pennies, nickels, and dimes—and trade those in any combination. Any dime is worth the same as any other dime. In other words, in the application, they are identical. Even if one dime is corroded and discolored and the other is pristine new, they are the same in value.

Non-fungible assets differ from other assets, even if they look and feel the same. An original piece of artwork is different from another original artwork. Everyday stamps used for postage are fungible. Even so, postage stamps may be non-fungible in that they may have markings and other characteristics making them unique. Note, the postage stamps you buy at the post office are fungible because one stamp is considered the same as any other. One or more of them become non-fungible only when they become unique collectors' items.

Houses are not considered fungible because each home is in a slightly different environment, even if built precisely the same. Perhaps the crime rating for the house down the street is higher, it's closer to the school, or it's made of slightly varied materials.

Adding a unique identifier, such as a number, might turn something that could be considered fungible into a non-fungible asset. A limited edition print might include a serial number on each print. Those numbers make them unique, and the lower numbers might be more desirable to collectors, and accordingly, be worth more.

Cryptocurrency is a fungible asset because one unit (a bitcoin, for instance) is the same as another. Wheat, oil, and other commodities are fungible. A print of a piece of artwork is fungible (if the prints are not unique in any way), but the original artwork piece is not.

Non-fungible assets are the basis for NFTs, which we cover in the next section.

What are NFTs?

An NFT is a *non-fungible token*, which means it is a token that represents a unique asset. An NFT can be digital, physical, or even a combination thereof. This is because (and this is important) an NFT is *not* the object itself (whether physical or virtual). Instead, it is a digital representation of the object.

NFTs are currently mostly part of the Ethereum blockchain. They are intended to allow creators and collectors to mint tokens representing their unique creations, to use smart contracts to protect them and set their value, to define royalties and commissions, and so on.

Any digital asset can be copied, even if protected via an NFT. The ownership rights to the asset are defined by the NFT, which is a unique digital identifier, and by design, you cannot copy them, subdivide them, or substitute something else for them. The NFT certifies the ownership and the authenticity of a unique asset.

Anything unique can be represented by an NFT, and this includes actual artwork, real estate, virtual artwork, a movie, or any other unique asset. To illustrate, the original version of an electronic book is a unique asset. You could copy the eBook if that's allowed by the smart contract, which we'll review later. The NFT specifies who owns the original version (and guarantees its authenticity) and the rules under which copies may be made.

The History of NFTs

On May 3, 2014, Kevin McCoy created the first NFT on the Ethereum blockchain. He minted a non-fungible token known as Quantum, which was a pixilated image of an octagon filled with oscillating shapes—a one-of-a-kind piece of digital art. Additional NFTs were made for various original artworks during the next few years.

In 2017, the first decentralized exchange and marketplace that allowed the buying and selling of digital collectibles (represented by NFTs) opened. It wasn't until 2018 that the first artist produced an NFT contract. In addition, several NFT marketplaces opened at that time, and by 2020 the world of NFTs expanded to include all forms of creativity (i.e., music, art, and physical objects). People continue to build on NFT technology and constantly find new ways to use them for their creations.

Before NFTs, colored keys were small units of bitcoin. Appearing in 2012, these keys were identified by colors, each of which specified specific attributes of the coin. These attributes were defined by bitcoin's scripting language and allowed for units as small as one Satoshi (i.e., 0.00000001 BTC) to represent assets. This was a powerful concept but didn't gain wide acceptance because:

- Bitcoin never officially adopted them.
- Bitcoin's minimum transaction size (at the time) of 5,430 Satoshi (i.e., 0.000543 BTC) was too large for colored coins to be useful.
- The concept of NFTs (which appeared in 2015) made colored coins obsolete.

A few notable NFTs projects are listed below:

- *Cryptopunks*. These are unique digital avatars.
- *CryptoKitties*. These are collectible digital kitties.
- *Bored Ape Club*. These are limited edition NFTs giving you membership to an ape swamp club.
- *Beeple*. An artist who sells his digital artwork as NFTs.
- *VeeFriends*. A Gary Vaynerchuk NFT project involving meaningful intellectual property and an extraordinary community.

Let's talk about the mechanics and utility of NFTs and how they can be used to support business, Web3, and the metaverse.

The Value of NFTs

Non-fungible digital assets are not new to the internet or the computing field. A domain name, consequently, is non-fungible because it is a unique asset. Other items like virtual items purchased in a game, digital avatars, event tickets, and even individual tweets are a case in point of non-fungible assets.

Undoubted, the pace of digitalization throughout society generated a demand for a solution to ownership rights and certifying authenticity. Let's look at an example of a movie star's autograph. In the physical world, you could obtain a certificate of authenticity proving the autograph was genuine, and you establish ownership by possessing the signature. In the digital realm, such concepts were difficult to establish and enforce, although attempts have been made (such as with Distributed Rights Management). Non-fungible tokens (NFTs) were designed to solve these issues.

Most NFTs reside in the Ethereum blockchain and consist of individual tokens storing valuable information. They can be treated just like other works of art (or other collectibles); in other words, they can be bought and sold. Because the data is unique, they can be validated and their ownership established.

NFTs contain information on their blockchains that record the ownership of the virtual or physical item that the NFT represents. This information includes a complete ledger documenting any changes of ownership.

An NFT's value is based on the type of artwork and its popularity, the artist, the amount of effort it took to craft, the creative story, and other criteria. The most crucial factor is its rarity, and the second is its utility (i.e., usefulness).

There are many novel terms to describe various features and the technology of NFTs. Several of these are described in the succeeding section.

NFT Terminology and Buzzwords

A few of the standard terms regarding NFTs are as follows:

- *Alpha.* Future announcements are kept secret to avoid manipulation of prices.
- *Blue-chip NFTs.* Collections of investments that perform well in the long term.
- *Consensus models.* The methods that are used to guarantee trust.
- *Cross-chain interoperability.* It allows bridging between blockchains.
- *Crypto wallets.* Wallets where the cryptographic private keys are held.
- *Decentralized applications (dapps).* Apps that are produced and run on decentralized blockchains.
- *Degan.* It's a high-risk investment style.
- *Digital wallets.* Money storage systems that are hosted by providers such as banks and trading platforms.

- *ERC-20 tokens.* Smart contracts that are simple and interoperable.
- *Ethereum.* Open-source blockchain that supports smart contracts and blockchain.
- *Flipping.* Buying assets and selling them for a higher price in a quick time frame (days, weeks, or hours).
- *Gas fee.* Fees that pay for smart contract activations.
- *Generative art.* A technology used to build extensive collections of NFTs.
- *Initial Game Offering* (IGO), like IPOs.
- *Layer-1* blockchains. Basic blockchain functionality.
- *Layer-2* blockchains. Another type of blockchain functionality that is built on the Layer-1 blockchain to improve the functionality.
- *Minting.* The act of buying an NFT as the first owner.
- *Not Financial Advice* (NFA).
- *Original (OG).* Slang term meaning "Original Gangster".
- *OpenSea (OS).* OpenSea is one of the largest Ethereum NFT marketplaces.
- *Profile pictures* (PFP).
- *Play-to-earn games* (P2E).
- *Pump-and-Dump.* A type of price manipulation.
- *Rug pull.* Various NFT scams.
- *Shilling.* Encouraging people to purchase an NFT for more than it was paid for. As with any business, selling for higher than the purchase price is desirable. This term simply means you are marketing or advertising your NFT.
- *To the moon.* A coin that will increase immensely in price.
- *Traits.* These are the properties of an NFT that make it unique.
- *Whitelist.* A way to sell NFTs to selected people where they are guaranteed a spot in the line to purchase.

The NFT sector is growing rapidly due to its usefulness and utility.

How Big are the NFT Sector/Sales of NFTs?

In 2021, NFTs reached $17.6 billion in sales, a 20-fold increase over 2020. This is split up as follows:[1]

- $2.8 billion in art
- $523 million in utilities
- $513 million in the metaverse
- $8.47 billion for collectibles
- $5.18 billion for gaming

A few of the prices paid for NFTs follow:

- Mike Winkelmann, known as Beeple, designed a collage of 5,000 digital images. The NFT associated with this sold for $69.3 million.
- Cryptopunks #3100 sold for $7.67 million.
- Cryptopunks #7804 sold for $7.6 million.
- The first tweet sold for $2.9 million.
- Cryptopunk #4156 sold for $10 million.
- Not Forgotten, But Gone, sold for $1 million.

Until now, we've canvassed how NFTs are related to investments. Yet, they have other uses as well that make them far more powerful than just another investment opportunity.

Uses and Types of NFTs

NFTs have taken off with video games because they solve many problems faced by gaming creators. Unique assets, such as swords, skins, clothing, and even land, can now be purchased inside the game. An NFT represents each of these items, meaning that the asset can be traded, bought, or sold and, in theory at least, can be transported to other games and virtual worlds.

If you play multiple games, one friction point is that each game requires you to make and maintain a digital avatar just for that game (or a limited number of games by one vendor). Conceptually, NFTs enable the creation of digital avatars that can transverse from game to game (and to other virtual worlds). They can also be used as digital passports.

NFTs can even be used to fund game development. Because players often purchase assets while playing games (using real currency), they quickly introduce others to play. This word-of-mouth advertising provides more game players and, as a result, brings in more income to the gaming companies, who can use that income as a funding source.

Finally, play to earn is becoming a popular way for players to earn money from their time playing the game. It's an incentive designed to increase the time people spend within the gaming world. NFTs are awarded for meeting gaming objectives, achieving results, reaching a new level, and achieving other various goals.

A few notable games that have pioneered NFT ownership of items and other things in the gaming world include:

- Axie Infinity: Buy in-game items that can be used in many games.
- Cometh: A DeFi-powered game where you can own yield-generating NFTs.
- Gods Unchained: A game that gives you ownership of your in-game items.

Other uses for NFTs include the following:

Artwork. Today, most NFTs are works of art because artists have quickly understood the value of NFTs for their medium. A few types of art involving NFTs include:

- Static art
- Gifs/video
- Photography

Virtual fashion. This fashion type includes fashion items for digital avatars (i.e., characters), typically in gaming. Using NFTs, you could buy a prom dress or a suit of armor (both unique) for your character or avatar to wear in game.

Access. An NFT that you can purchase can give you access to an event or venue. These NTFs are programmed into smart contracts. One example is VeeCon 2022, a conference that requires the purchase of a VeeFriend NFT to attend.

Virtual assets. You can use NFTs that allow you to purchase/own a virtual asset and give you proof of ownership of it.

Music. Albums, songs, lyrics, and even sound bites can all be represented by NFTs. Specific examples of NFT music include:

- The song *Death of the Old Grimes*
- The instrumental One-*Hundredth Streams*
- The album *When You See Yourself* by Kings of Leon
- *Jenny* by Steve Aoki and 3LAU
- *BeatBoxes* by Zebblocks

Redeemable. NFTs are redeemed for actual, physical products. One example is Fridgits, an NFT collection consisting of 20 unique characters with hand-drawn assets.

Identity. An NFT designed to provide an identity recognized across platforms.

Collectibles. NFTs may be virtual or physical collectibles. Some examples include:

- Cryptopunks
- Hashmasks
- Bored Ape Yacht Club (BAYC)
- Measuring Rarity

Sports. These NFTs are digital collectibles and trading cards for any sport. Examples include:

- NBA Top Shot
- Sorare
- Chiliz

Digital property. These NFTs allow for the ownership of digital property rights in games and virtual worlds. Examples involve:

- Decentraland
- The Sandbox
- Cryptovoxels
- Somnium Space

Now, let's look at the problems that NFTs solve.

What Do NFTs Solve?

Ownership is a significant problem that digital creators have faced since the dawn of the computer age. When you form a digital image, an electronic book, a song, or an avatar in a game, how do you maintain your rights of ownership over the item? Until NFTs arrived on the scene, awkward attempts, such as Digital Rights Management, attempted to fill this need with mixed success.

NFTs were designed to verify that a digital creation exists and to establish its ownership. They let you claim ownership and, with the addition of smart contracts, they let you define the rules others must follow to use or copy your own. You can specify royalties or commissions on sales or restrict the usage of digital creation.

Physical creations can also be represented by NFTs, allowing the same rights management as virtual objects.

When combined with smart contracts, NFTs solve many of the problems associated with the current copyright system, which, in the age of the internet, provides limited support to content creators. Copyright provides legal protection for your creations for a certain number of years, but because these laws were on the books many years before NFTs, they don't offer any physical means to restrict or profit from copies. NFTs and smart contracts fill this void with an ownership mechanism combined with an enforcement policy.

The following section reviews a few of the core properties of NFTs.

Core Properties of NFTs

Physical objects in the real world are characterized by properties that define them. In fact, you can specify an object by its state (i.e., solid, liquid, or gaseous), weight, size, and hardness. NFTs have the same kind of properties. Let's quickly summarize the main properties of NFTs here:

Indivisible. An NFT may not be divided into parts. You can't sell table pieces and still sell them as a table; in the same way, you cannot cut up an NFT for a digital video or graphic.

Peer-to-peer. NFTs do not need platforms in which to operate. They are transferred directly from one node (i.e., peer) to another.

Programmable. Because NFTs are designed with smart contract blockchains, they are programmable and can define the rules that apply to their usage.

Rare. NFTs are scarce, which ensures that they are valued.

Secure. NFTs are encrypted and designed so that their ownership information may not be manipulated or changed when a transaction is confirmed. This means an NFT cannot be stolen because the current (and all other) owner is maintained within the NFT blockchain.

Traceable. Because they are built on blockchain, NFTs contain a complete record of ownership, which helps to prevent counterfeiting and fraud. It also makes it difficult to steal and resell NFTs, because the NFT will not identify the thief as the owner.

Transferable. Because their design follows standard and established protocols, NFTs can be moved between applications without difficulty. Therefore, if you purchase an avatar in one game, you can transfer it to another if both games support NFTs.

Unique. An NFT contains information to describe its properties, making it different than any other NFT.

Verifiable ownership. Ownership cannot be modified and NFTs are designed so they cannot just be copied. In particular, suppose you own the NFT for a digital painting. Your ownership is recorded in the NFT forever. Any attempts to create copies must follow the rules of the NFT using the built-in smart contract. Your rules could specify that anyone can refashion copies, but you will receive a small royalty or that copies are not allowed at all.

With this understanding of the core properties, let's take a look at an overview of the technical components of NFTs.

Overview of Technical Components

As illustrated previously, NFTs are designed to use blockchain networks, which means they take advantage of the properties of blockchain to maintain a ledger and certify that they are unique and non-interchangeable. Because blockchain is encrypted, security is ensured, and changes are not allowed.

The address of the blockchain, consisting of a unique ID associated with the NFT, is used for transactions such as the buying and selling of digital art. The identifier is used to identify the NFT when it is transmitted or received.

Additionally, NFTs can support built-in smart contracts that define the rules by which the NFT is created, ownership is transferred, or other actions are taken, such as copying or displaying the digital image. These contracts specify price ranges, royalties, and other criteria, and because smart contracts are programming code, their usage is almost limitless.

The properties of an NFT are described by its metadata, which is stored within the NFT. The actual data represented by the NFT is stored outside the NFT, possibly in the cloud. In fact, the NFT for a digital painting links to the source image of the painting stored on a cloud service. This is necessary because the blockchain upon which the NFT is based is decentralized, which means the entire blockchain is copied to every node. The overhead would be tremendous if the actual data (i.e., a video, image, or something else) were included in the blockchain (and the NFT).

What is metadata? The following section answers this question.

NFT Metadata

Metadata is information that records information about other details. For a phone call, the metadata includes the calling and receiving phone numbers, time and date, and the call's length. Metadata does *not* contain the actual data itself. In our example, the phone call is *not* part of the metadata.

NFTs use metadata to describe the NFT and its associated information. This may include the type of data, its size, the name of the artist(s), and the scarcity. Note that the metadata within an NFT generally only identifies the asset and a few other essentials.

For instance, if your NFT were a video clip, the NFT would note your clip's location (probably on a cloud service). NFTs usually use InterPlanetary File System (IPFS) hashes or an HTTP URL. Internally, ERC-721s, uses a standard JavaScript Object Notation (JSON) to notate the location. Nonetheless, because the JSON is relatively large, the Ethereum contract includes a Universal Resource Identifier (URI) to record the external site for the JSON definition. In other words, the metadata is stored off-chain (described later in this section).

Metadata is assigned when the token is minted, which means the data cannot be changed. Because of this, if the asset (i.e., the actual data) is moved or deleted, the token will no longer be valid, and *it cannot be changed*.

NFT metadata may be stored in two ways:

- *On-chain*. The metadata is stored in the blockchain and contains the location of the actual data associated with an NFT.

- *Off-chain*. Because of the volume of information in metadata, for most NFTs, it's stored outside the blockchain (hence the term "off-chain") to reduce the amount of expensive, decentralized storage needed.

How NFTs Work

Before an NFT can be sold or used, the virtual or physical item must be created or acquired. The process varies depending on the blockchain, but generally it follows these steps:

1 A product, such as a graphic or video, is developed.

2 Next, you choose a blockchain for your NFT. Most people use Ethereum, but there are other options such as Tezos and Cosmos.

3 You set up your digital wallet, which you use to buy the currency you will need to pay fees to the marketplace, which is required to fund the initial investment.

4 You then select an NFT marketplace. You'll need to pick one that works best for you and your asset.

5 Next, you upload your digital file to your chosen marketplace.

6 You then connect your digital wallet to the chosen marketplace.

7 Your digital object is minted. During this process, an NFT is developed, and the object's ownership data is included in the NFT. The marketplace will have instructions about how to mint it in their environment.

8 Finally, the NFT is listed for sale on a marketplace if desired. The marketplace will have instructions about the methods you can use to sell your NFT. You usually have options such as a fixed price or an auction (i.e., a timed or unlimited sale).

Let's briefly review how NFTs are verified during the creation process.

Creating NFTs: Verification

When an NFT is generated, it must be confirmed as an asset on a blockchain. If you just added NFTs without verifying their validity, you'd make the perfect situation for fraud and counterfeiting, which would defeat the purpose of creating NFTs in the first place.

Transactions confirm that an NFT was built and added to a block, which is then added to the blockchain. The marketplace must update the account's balance to account for that asset. Once this happens, the NFT can be traded or verified as owned.

Finally, every system on the network must be informed that the newly minted block is correct.

It's the miners' job to notify every system on the network about your NFT and its ownership. This explains why mining includes proofs by performing highly complex mathematical equations. If this didn't happen, it would be a simple matter for anyone to take over your NFT and claim ownership. Accordingly, the job of mining must be performed by trusted entities. After minting, miners are also responsible for verifying the properties of the block.

NFT Standards/Databases

Modern technology is based on standards. You could say standards rule the world, because we would be in chaos without them. To illustrate, all televisions of the same model use the same parts, voltages, sizes, and components. The same manufacturer may use those same parts in all their television models to make them more easily serviceable and to standardize their supply chains. Television manufacturers have agreed on a standard for HDMI cables so people could connect the devices without single-purpose cables.

Standards in software are designed to simplify development and enable compatibility with other software and hardware. Application Programming Interfaces (APIs) are a standard method for software developers to easily access complex tools without writing them. Multiple standards fit together in a vast quilt, all working together in harmony to achieve the goals of the software designers.

NFTs are also based on a series of standards to ensure they work together and with other items in predictable ways. The Ethereum ERC-721 standard defines the basic structure and operations of NFTs. Different standards, such as Solana and Tezos, extend the ERC-721 standard with new features.

Specific examples of NFT-related standards include:

- ERC-20. The standard for fungible tokens includes smart contracts (only usable within Ethereum).
- ERC-223. Allows approval of fungible tokens for use by on-chain third parties.
- ERC-721. Non-fungible tokens.
- ERC-777. An improved version of ERC-20.
- ERC-865. Smart contract to allow payment in tokens instead of gas.
- ERC-875. Smart contract for transferring several NFTs in one transaction.
- ERC-998. Smart contract for merging NFTs into one NFT.

- ERC-1155. Smart contract to allow management of Ethereum tokens.
- ERC-1137. Recurring payments.
- Ethereum Name Services (ENS). A naming system for the Ethereum blockchain.
- Proof of Attendance Protocol (POAP). Protocol that proves that people attended a virtual or in-person event.

Many other standards are available, with some being proprietary to specific blockchain platforms and others that are open to anyone.

Remember, though, that there is a difference between an NFT you've designed and one you own.

Creating and Owning NFTs

When you own an NFT, the NFT records your ownership. This becomes an immutable record (meaning it cannot be changed). Because you own it, you can sell it, and if you include the correct code, you can receive resale royalties.

On the other hand, when you construct an NFT, you have more power over it. First, the fact that you made the NFT is recorded in the blockchain. You can code in royalties that you'll receive whenever it's sold (or not, if you wish), and you can sell it anywhere you want without an agent. You have control over setting the scarcity of your NFT.

Once you have created or owned an NFT, you have many options that you can pursue in NFT marketplaces.

NFT Bidding Marketplaces and Auction Platforms

To buy and sell NFTs, you must find and form an account at a marketplace. These platforms offer a secure environment with the tools you need to examine, purchase, and sell NFTs. Many marketplaces also allow you to generate your own NFTs as well.

The largest marketplace is called OpenSea, which allows you to find, collect, and sell NFTs. It was the first NFT marketplace and included all the tools you'll need, including digital wallets; and instructions on setting up collections, adding (i.e., creating) NFTs, and listing them for sale.

While OpenSea is easily suitable for most purposes, you may have unique requirements indicating that other marketplaces must have features of which you can take advantage. So, which marketplace should you use? It depends on what you are trying to achieve.

Other marketplaces include the following. While there are many more of them, this list should give you a starting point:

- AAvegotchi
- Async
- Axie Infinity
- Bounce
- Cargo
- Decentraland
- Foundation
- KnownOrigin
- Makersplace
- Mintbase
- Mintable.app
- Mythmarket
- NBA Top Shot
- Nifty Gateway
- OpenBazaar
- Solanart
- Solsea
- SuperRare
- Rariable
- The Nifty Gateway

Once you've settled on a marketplace, you are ready to buy an NFT.

What is Needed to Buy NFTs

So far you've learnt about NFTs, and you're now at the point where you want to invest in them. Perhaps you've found digital artwork that seems like a sound investment or an excellent video, or maybe you want to try one out as social currency.

Ready to jump in? Well, here's how to go about buying one or more NFTs.

First, ensure everything needed is ready to go. This way, there won't be a scramble to gather up something in the middle of the process.

DIGITAL WALLET

You'll need a digital wallet to perform any kind of transaction. As noted previously, your digital wallet is an application that lets you conduct financial transactions. It's the digital version of your wallet or purse. It stores money in all its forms (i.e., credit or debit cards, EFT information, and so on). Money is added to your digital wallet when something is sold and removed when a purchase is made.

A digital wallet can also store other things, such as:

- Coupons
- Your driver's license
- Gift cards
- Loyalty cards
- Membership cards
- Tickets

Digital wallets also track your payment history, so you will have a permanent record of everything you purchased.

Importantly, digital wallets are highly secure and encrypted. You must authenticate your identity to log into them.

CURRENCY

You'll need money, and in most marketplaces, this means an accepted form of cryptocurrency, although "normal" money (i.e., fiat currencies) can sometimes be used. It's essential to understand the conditions of currency allowed by your marketplace. OpenSea and SuperRare only accept cryptocurrencies, while Nifty Gateway and NBA Top Shot also accept fiat currencies.

There are some challenges to using fiat currencies because marketplaces must build on-ramps and off-ramps for their applications. Accepting fiat currencies can make the application development process more complex, while just accepting cryptocurrency simplifies them.

Today, many payment processors (such as PayPal) don't support NFT transactions, and if the marketplace doesn't support fiat currencies, you must purchase cryptocurrency to purchase an NFT.

Fraud is a big concern, and regulators do believe criminals can take advantage of NFTs for money laundering and other criminal activities. Because of this, platforms for NFT trading must implement various standards to detect or avoid these illegal activities. These include Know Your Customer (KYC), Anti-Money Laundering (AML), and Counter Terrorist and Proliferation Financing (CTF/PF).

A MARKETPLACE USER ACCOUNT

Once you've chosen a marketplace that meets your needs, you'll need to establish a user account, which gives you access to the features of the market.

Crypto wallets are tools that store NFTs and cryptocurrencies. These wallets interact directly with blockchains to perform their tasks. There are two types of crypto wallets: custodial and non-custodial:

- *Custodial.* For a custodial wallet, the service owns the private key that you use for your wallet. They maintain security and operate the customer service teams to help you with issues that you might experience. Suppose that you forget your password: you can call customer service, and they will help you reset it. Custodial wallets include Coinbase, Gemini, Free Wallet, Binance, BitNex, Blockchain.com, and BitGo.

- *Non-custodial.* Non-custodial wallets are owned and operated by users who control their digital assets and the wallet. One downside is that everything in the wallet is lost if passwords (or other login criteria) are lost. Examples of non-custodial wallets include Electrum, Exodus, Zengo, and Wasabi.

Next, you must follow these steps to continue buying your NFTs:

1 Buy some ETH (Ethereum or another blockchain that supports NFTs) from an exchange and send it to your digital wallet.

2 Follow the instructions, which are unique to the marketplace.

Once you own (or have created) an NFT, you are free to sell it.

How to Sell NFTs

At some point, you may want to sell an NFT. You'll either need to make a new NFT for a digital asset or buy one that's already been made. We'll discuss how to design NFTs later in this chapter, so let's assume you have an NFT in hand (whether you built it or bought it from someone else).

You'll need to select a marketplace, ensure that you have the funds within your crypto wallet, and then list it for sale. This is a simple matter of clicking on the "Sell" button and setting a few parameters and the auction type. Here are the common auction types:

- *Fixed price.* In this form of auction, you simply list the price, which is the price that a buyer will pay for the NFT.

- *Regular auction* (ascending bid). If you've ever bought or sold anything on eBay using their auction feature, then you know how this works. The seller can set a reserve (i.e., minimum) price and a few other parameters, including how long the auction lasts. Buyers then place their bids that go higher and higher, and when the time is up, the highest bidder wins the auction.

- *Dutch auction.* Dutch auctions work oppositely. The seller sets a high price that drops at regular intervals (i.e., a few minutes) until someone makes a bid at the current price. They win the auction. This is commonly used to sell a collection of NFTs.

- *Dutch auction* (sealed bid). Buyers submit their bids for the NFT over a set period. The offers are then unsealed at the end of that time, and the highest bidder wins.

- *Vickery auction.* This auction type works the same as the sealed-bid Dutch Auction, but the winner pays the second highest price.

After all, NFTs offer many more capabilities than just trading, including the ability to set up a complete, working financial system.

The following steps are used to sell an NFT, whether you are the owner or creator:

1 Select the marketplace from which you want to sell your NFT.

2 Create or buy the NFT.

3 List the NFT for sale.

4 Promote the NFT's listing.

5 Accept bids.

6 Once a bid is finalized, collect the amount offered and transfer the ownership of the NFT to the winner.

Note, there are many possibilities for using NFTs for branding and marketing, as described in the following section.

Business/Brand Strategy for NFTs

The uses for NFTs far exceed their role in just gaming and investing. Businesses and brands can release NFTs for use in their marketing efforts. Say a soda company could launch unique NFT artwork to give away in sweepstakes. Companies can use this NFT artwork to secure their domain names, and fast-food restaurants can make a collectible line of NFT products, one per meal purchased.

NFTs can enhance brand awareness by creating unique digital assets that include digital collectibles or even unique digital representations of experiences—or even representations of physical objects. For instance, if a rock climber scaled a particularly tough cliff, she could receive NFT videos, photos, and sound clips of her ascent to the top. She could then receive royalties if her fans purchased digital copies of her unique experiences using smart contracts. The contract could specify that her video-editing team, photographer, and sound personnel also receive compensation for such sales.

Consider someone purchasing a pair of real-world sneakers, which came with an NFT for a digital representation of those shoes. This could allow those same shoes to be worn in video games and other immersive experiences, albeit digitally. This service can easily be used as part of a social media campaign or other marketing and advertising techniques. A person could use NFTs to implement an entire wardrobe in an immersive experience, from gaming to sporting events to conferences.

It's even possible to assign a unique identifier to each product sold, which enables their use as NFTs. To demonstrate, a consumer purchases a new hat represented by an NFT. From here, sensors in both the physical and digital world could detect the hat and tie immersive experiences around it. Advertisements could be designed to respond to the hat, suggesting accessories. There are many possibilities for converting a simple sale into an engaging, long-term experience.[2]

There are many uses for NFTs in business and brands. A few of these include the following:

- Digital certifications of authenticity for physical world items
- Badges and prizes for participating in social media campaigns
- Using the same products in digital and virtual worlds
- Creating marketing campaigns centered around collecting NFTs artwork, stamps, avatars, videos, or other collectibles
- Creating luxury versions of products
- Creating unique versions of everyday products to provide an experience for consumers

Many possibilities exist for brands to use NFTs to form a connection with consumers by offering immersive, unique digital and physical products. Making these connections tends to increase consumer loyalty and provide additional ways for businesses to gain customers' attention and enduring customer value and experiences.

On top of this marketing potential, NFTs and Decentralized Finance (DeFi) have the promise to offer better ways to allow your customers to perform transactions.

NFTs and DeFi

Decentralized finance (DeFi) implements a financial system based on blockchains. The idea is to achieve a fully working economic system without a central authority (like everything considered in this book). Many concepts that apply to the real-world financial system also apply to DeFi, with the obvious caveat that any single entity does not control the system. Instead, DeFi is specifically designed to operate without that central authority. In other words, no central bank or government can set the value, make regulations, or decide what can and can't be done.

NFTs provide an additional type of asset that applies to the DeFi ecosystem. Because you can combine NFTs with smart contracts, you have many new, engaging, and promising options (and control). Let's look at a few samples of these new financial models:

- *NFT-backed loans.* Because NFTs represent assets (albeit digital assets for the most part) with real value, they can be used as collateral for loans. Hence, if you wanted to obtain credit, you could use one or more of your NFTs to secure the loan. This works like the physical world, except the collateral is an NFT.

- *Fractional ownership.* Let's say you wanted to buy a car but didn't have the money. What if you could ask three friends to become co-owners? In other words, the four of you each own one-fourth of the car. Fractional NFTs allow you to do this for any asset represented by an NFT. You could gather together a group to combine resources to purchase that million-dollar digital asset, and each of you would own part of that asset (how big a part depends on how much you invest). You can purchase fractionalized NFTs on Niftex, Unicly, NFTX, and other marketplaces.

- *Automated market maker.* This handy feature lets you purchase NFTs (and other digital assets) automatically by using liquidity pools, or, as it is often called, an autonomous trading mechanism. The concept is to eliminate the requirement of any central authority, including financial institutions and even marketplaces. In other words, you don't need to get an intermediary to engage in a transaction.

Smart contracts are another feature of NFTs that define a series of rules to be followed under specific conditions.

NFT Smart Contracts

In the physical world, you often need the services of a lawyer to write and enforce contracts. Negotiating can be laborious and time-consuming, and ensuring that the agreement is adequately executed requires even more time and effort. Lawyers might need to get involved at any contract stage, from execution to final termination when everything is done. The possibility of anything going wrong is high because the contract terms are open to interpretation.

Smart contracts attempt to solve the problem of governance. They do this by embedding small programs within a blockchain. These programs are run when one or more predetermined conditions are met.

A smart contract is used to automate the execution of the terms of agreements without requiring the services of a lawyer or other inter-mediary. This saves time and money, although it still takes time (and a coder might be required) to write the code and double-check it to ensure it's correct. Smart contracts can also be used to automate workflows.

Let's take the example of an NFT created for an electronic book. Without smart contracts, booksellers collect royalties that flow through to publishers, who eventually pay out a percentage of sales to the author.

This workflow changes with the advent of smart contracts. The contract is coded into the blockchain for the book NFT with conditions determining the amount and type of royalties paid. If the book is purchased outright, the smart contract executes and pays out a royalty directly to the author (and the bookseller is also paid). But if the book winds up in a library, the smart contract could specify that the author receives a commission from the library every time the book is borrowed.

Smart contracts may be used for other applications, including NFT lending and NFT loans. You can also build crypto art NFTs as well.

Dynamic NFTS

Dynamic NFTs (dNFTs) are a new type of NFT; they can adapt and change based on criteria such as data and events. For example, a background can be dynamically updated depending on weather events or the outcome of sporting events.

Crypto Art and How to Create NFTs

Did you know you can integrate your crypto art and associated NFT? As we've explained earlier, image files, videos, and other digital art forms have sold for tens or hundreds of thousands of dollars. A few even breached the million-dollar level. If you are creative, returns like this may make it worthwhile to enter this new emerging space to see what you can create and sell.

In 2014, Kevin McCoy and Anil Dash launched the first NFT artwork while giving a presentation at Seven on Seven at the New Museum in New York City. In front of a live audience, they linked a work of art to an NFT. Namecoin enabled this feat. Also, in 2014, Robert Dermody, Adam Krellenstein, and Evan Wagner founded a startup called Counterparty, designed to allow people to produce assets and link them to NFTs.

In 2015, the game Spells of Genesis let players purchase and use in-game assets (NFTs), and in 2016, another game called Force Of Will was released with similar support. NFT avatars appeared in 2016 on Counterpart, and in 2017 Peperium was founded as a marketplace for NFT memes and trading cards. In 2017, John

Watkinson and Matt Hall launched Cryptopunks, a company called Axiom Zen that released CryptoKitties as well. The world of crypto art took off in 2021 with the sale of The First 5000 Days by Beeple for $69.3 million.

You can produce an NFT for just about anything, including digital art (i.e., GIFs, PNGs), movies, memes, recipes, music... you name it, and you can probably find a way to make an NFT for it. There are few, if any, restrictions on what can be tokenized and made into an NFT. One significant exception is that you should avoid using copyrighted material because you don't own their rights.

Because we're talking about the virtual world, you'll find you have some exciting options not available to traditional art in the physical world. Such options include:

- *Programmable art.* You can define a series of instructions to determine how the media should be rendered, viewed, listened to, and so forth. You generate layers of tokens that represent movement and color changes.

- *Secondary sales.* In the physical world, you depend on contracts and the honesty of others (i.e., booksellers, art galleries, publishers, and so forth) to pay royalties and commissions. With NFTs (as we previously considered), you can define how you should be paid each time the artwork is sold, loaned, or rented. Art marketplaces include KnownOrigin, which provides an online venue for selling and purchasing digital art.

- *Virtual galleries.* Artists can display their artwork in virtual galleries. Anyone can view the artwork—these are online albums, except the art is in the form of an NFT.

Creating NFT artwork requires a few steps:

1 First, produce your digital artwork.
2 You'll need to set up an Ethereum wallet for the transaction.
3 Next, buy some Ethereum. You'll need this to pay the fees associated with creating your digital artwork (i.e., gas fees).

4 Finally, connect to an NFT marketplace.

5 Form an account (if you don't already have one).

6 Follow their instructions (which can differ from marketplace to marketplace) to upload your art and build your NFT.

7 Place your NFT artwork up for sale.

8 Wait for bids or for your auction to close.

You won't have trouble finding tools and utilities to help you design your artwork. Adobe Creative Cloud includes a suite of applications such as Photoshop and Substance, designed to make it possible for anyone to create their digital masterpieces. It is one of the most complete and feature-filled creation platforms available.

Oasis Digital Studios has designed an environment where artists share in the revenue of the initial sale and royalties for their work. Their program includes offerings to support digital artwork, trading cards, limited editions, series, and even physical products.

Autonomous (i.e., non-human) systems can also invent artwork. This is known as generative art, and it is designed to generate artwork without guidance from humans. It's also known as algorithmic art or synthetic media.

There is a bright future for digital artwork (i.e., NFT artwork). It would be a mistake to think of digital artwork as superior; it provides an additional way for artists to express their creativity. Digital art adds new features (3D, in particular), a broader audience (the entire internet), a superior copyright system, and a well-defined method for compensating all parties involved.

The most exciting use for digital art is with immersive technologies. Imagine looking at a painting in a museum and finding yourself in the painting, being able to see what's happening around the subject. The upshot is that digital art allows viewers to experience and interact with the artwork.

When an NFT is crafted, it must be minted. This is described in the following section.

What Minting is and How to Mint

The process when a government in the physical world forges coins is known as *minting*, which consists of making money from metal sheets. These coins are then released to the public and become the currency used for transactions.

Conceptually, the term minting has a similar meaning for NFTs. If you need to build an NFT, you must mint the NFTs after they are made. The process adds an asset, such as a piece of digital art or a video, onto a blockchain, which means it becomes a digital asset that can be traded, bought, and sold in a digital marketplace. When you mint an NFT, you can define its royalty conditions, schedules, and other parameters used during transactions.

Uploading the file containing your digital asset is the easy part of the process, and it's similar in concept and form to uploading to any other website, such as your online photo album or favorite video site. Once you've uploaded the asset and defined its title, subtitle, description, and other attributes, you can launch the associated NFT.

The process of minting on the Ethereum blockchain (the most popular one for NFTs) is not free. You must pay a cost, known as a gas fee or more simply gas, of $50 or more. This price depends on the resources required to produce and store the NFT. You can also choose different blockchain networks, including OpenSea and others.

Minting an NFT consists of several steps:

1 Select an NFT marketplace and connect your wallet to it.
2 Upload the file containing your digital art or video and define the parameters such as the title, subtitle, and so on.
3 Click the button to mint the NFT or to place your digital asset up for sale.
4 When the marketplace asks you to approve the gas fee, indicate your acceptance.
5 Sit back and wait for your NFT to be minted.

Currently, minting uses numerous computer resources to perform "work" as Proof-of-Work. So many resources are required that the energy consumption for all the blockchains and NFTs in the world is roughly 1,000th of the world's energy consumption. It uses so much energy that it contributes significantly to global warming.

Ethereum is the most common blockchain, but depending on your needs, you might want to look at the features of others.

Which Blockchain Should You Choose?

Not all blockchains are the same, and your choice of which to use for your NFTs will depend on the features and characteristics that are important to you. Think of an analogy of a bank. You choose one based on the features within their web platform, such as online banking, how long you must wait in line for the teller, and which ATMs are closest to you. You have an equally large array of characteristics to consider for the blockchain you choose:

- *Transaction speed.* The speed of transactions for a blockchain should be a significant consideration, as faster blockchains can reach a higher number of transactions per second than slower ones. This impacts the fees (i.e., gas) you'll pay and how long you must wait for transactions to occur.

- *Security.* Examine the blockchain's security record to determine if there is a pattern of breaches and other security issues. Specifically, a blockchain might be more vulnerable to man-in-the-middle attacks, while another might have vulnerabilities in its encryption algorithms. Do some research to ensure the blockchain you choose won't become a security nightmare for you.

- *Cost of transactions.* You probably wouldn't want to choose a bank with high transaction fees, right? The same concept applies to blockchains. Gas fees can be expensive, limiting what you can accomplish. A comparison of the fees of blockchains should also be part of your analysis.

- *Consensus.* Consensus mechanisms can significantly affect security, performance, or even climate change. A blockchain using the Proof-of-Work mechanism can be more insecure and use more energy than one using Proof-of-Staked-Authority. Take this into account when choosing a blockchain. Namely, if you are particularly concerned about the environment and climate change, then you'd want to avoid the Proof-of-Work mechanism because that requires extreme amounts of computing power.

Your choices for a blockchain include:

- Ethereum, which is currently the leading blockchain used for NFTs. It is one of the first that supports NFTs and includes support for smart contracts.
- Flow, which is a scalable and portable blockchain with many tools to aid in the development of NFTs.
- Solana, if you want a fast, scalable blockchain.
- Cardano, although it does not yet fully support smart contracts.

There are over 1,000 different blockchains with at least four types of blockchain networks for NFTs.

The following section examines tokens, which are essential components of NFTs and blockchain.

Tokens

A cryptocurrency, like bitcoin, is currency. Just as with any currency, you can place them in the bank (i.e., save them), invest them, give them away, buy with them, and receive them in return for selling goods and services.

It's important to understand that a token is *not* considered a currency. Instead, they are unique identifiers for something or someone. You've seen tokens in one form or another in the physical world: ISBN numbers for books, UPC codes for groceries, and serial numbers for equipment, for example. Each of these numbers uniquely identifies an object so it can be referenced.

For example, if you call the support line to get your television fixed under warranty, you will be asked for the serial number of your TV. Associated with this number are your television's characteristics, including the screen size, original cost, and several pixels (amongst many other things).

However, the token is *not* the object or person. It merely identifies the object or person.

The ERC-721 specification[3] defines the standard for NFTs. Each NFT has a uint256 variable. This number is a non-negative 256-bit long number that can store a number up to 1157920892373161954 2357098500868790785326998466564056403945758400791312 9639935 (or 2^{256}) in decimal. This number is the token or identifier for the NFT.

The ERC-721 specification goes on to define all the other characteristics of NFTs.

An additional native feature of NFTs is the ability to decentralize governance using decentralized autonomous organizations (DAOs).

Governance with DAOs

Currently, every form of government on Earth is centralized, meaning there is a central authority that makes and enforces the rules of society. In a dictatorship, a single person, a dictator, is in charge, while in democracies, this might be a parliament or Congress, a president, or some combination of people. But a single person or a group is in control.

Most organizations follow the same approach. In a corporation, the central authority is the CEO and the board of directors. In the US military, the head of the Joint Chiefs of Staff is in charge, although they report directly to the president. Every agency in government has a single person at the top of the organization. Beneath that person is a hierarchy of other ranks and titles that also make decisions, set goals, and enforce discipline on those at lower levels in the organization.

A decentralized autonomous organization (DAO) is a new type of organization made possible because it runs on a blockchain and bases decisions on rules within smart contracts. In this governance model, there is no need for centralized authority and hierarchy; once the

DAO has been defined along with its smart contracts, there is no need for human intervention in governance.

A DAO has the following characteristics:

- *Tokenization.* Blockchains may be used to represent voting rights. Only those who own tokens can participate in governing.

- *Self-enforcement.* Smart contracts enforce the rules.

- *Automation.* Many smart contracts combined, often in complex configurations, enable interactions between different people and groups. These interactions are automated and autonomous due to smart contracts.

- *Decentralization.* DAOs must be built upon decentralized infrastructure to prevent people with more computing resources from tilting decisions in their favor and corrupting the system.

- *Transparency.* Because DAOs are built on blockchain, the underlying data cannot be changed and is transparent.

- *Trust.* Smart contracts are the basis for trust. Because decision mechanisms are built into smart contracts, people can be assured that any decisions will follow the results.

Using DAOs, communities raise to a new level of fairness and freedom. Human bias and the potential for corruption are reduced, enabling a more fair and balanced approach to community governance.

Investing in NFTs

Disclaimer: This is just a brief overview of investing in NFTs. This is *not* investment advice.

Many investors are excited about the investment potential for NFTs. Headlines touting a $69 million dollar sale of a single NFT strengthens the idea that this new frontier offers many opportunities for significant returns on investment. Before jumping into the investment market, it's a good idea to understand more about your options.

To invest in an NFT, you must first establish your digital wallet and load it with cryptocurrency. You will use this money to fund your investments (i.e., to purchase one or more NFTs). Next, find a marketplace and set up an account. Make sure you choose a marketplace with a good reputation, good security, and a decent interface (as a poor interface can be very frustrating).

You can invest in any number of diverse types of assets, including:

- Art
- Collectibles
- Memes
- Music
- Domain names
- Virtual land

To sell an NFT, you can estimate its value using an online tool, such as DaapRadar. Simply enter a few parameters, including the NFT identifier, to determine the estimated value.

You can purchase an NFT or produce your own, depending on your investment strategy. You can also purchase NFTs and sell them to someone else or save them if you want.

Why invest in NFTs? Because of the following:

- Smart contracts enforce the rules.
- The popularity is increasing at a dramatic rate.
- NFTs are often increasing in value. As with any investment, though, some will grow, and some will decrease.

Yet, there are some downsides, including:

- Just as with any investment, prices can fluctuate.
- Buying and selling are not free. There is a fee for every transaction.
- Blockchains, especially those using the Proof-of-Work consensus method, harm the environment.

Once you've decided to use NFTs, whether for investment or some other purpose, you need to be concerned about security.

NFT Security

When you open an account with your bank, you naturally expect that your transactions are secure (meaning you won't lose your money) and private (meaning people can't find out how much money you have and how you spend it). Banks go to great lengths to pass security audits and rigidly enforce best practices, because their brand would suffer if a breach involves releasing information about people's transactions. In this case, they'd get visits from federal authorities, people might be fired, and the CEO and executives might find themselves under fire.

No single entity manages blockchain. The standards and protocols are designed with security in mind by incorporating strong encryption and secure authorizations. For the most part, you can depend on blockchain security, although different implementations might be more secure than others.

The data itself is stored elsewhere because of the overhead associated with placing data on the blockchain. For NFTs, the images, videos, or data are held outside the blockchain, generally on a central cloud server. The blockchain for the NFT may be perfectly secure, but the external data can be insecure, deleted, or moved. Because the NFT cannot be changed, there's no method for considering it. This data could also be hacked and altered to something else.

Marketplaces are just like any other technology company. Their security must follow best practices and must be of the highest level. Their safety is only as good as their security department. The NFTs and wallets they maintain could also be compromised if their platform is compromised.

Finally, blockchain, NFTs, smart contracts, and other mechanisms, as well as the underlying technologies, consist of code that is not perfect. There are always vulnerabilities in code because humans write it.

See the Security Fundamentals section of Chapter 3 for more information.

You must also understand how privacy works for NFTs and blockchains.

Privacy Concerns of NFTs and Blockchain

Blockchain is, by design, a public ledger of every transaction that has ever occurred regarding the chain. It's entirely possible (and it has happened) that law enforcement, the government, businesses, and even individuals can open the ledger on your blockchains and obtain the details on every transaction you've done.

In theory, blockchain is anonymous because you don't need to include your personal information (i.e., name, address, and so on) in your wallet. The transactions within the wallet are visible to everyone, but the wallet's owner is invisible... unless it's not.

Molly White, a software engineer, summed up the problem nicely in her blog:

> Imagine if, when you Venmo-ed your Tinder date for your half of the meal, they could now see every other transaction you'd ever made—and not just on Venmo, but the ones you made with your credit card, bank transfer, or other apps, and with no option to set the visibility of the transfer to 'private.' The split checks with all your previous Tinder dates? That monthly transfer to your therapist? The debts you're paying off (or not), the charities to which you're donating (or not), the amount you're putting in a retirement account (or not)? The location of that corner store right by your apartment where you so frequently go to grab a pint of ice cream at 10 pm? Not only would this be visible to that one-off Tinder date, but also your ex-partners, estranged family members, prospective employers.[4]

You can use obfuscation methods or employ a tumbler or mixer server to hide your transactions, or at least make them more difficult to trace, but these methods are not easy to use and do not work perfectly. They also add time and complexity to the process of doing a transaction.

NFTs add another layer on top of these concerns. You see, an NFT is a unique identifier. Let's say you fashion an NFT for your avatar and display it publicly. You bought the NFT using your digital wallet. All someone needs to do is follow the ID from the NFT to the wallet to find out every transaction you've ever done.

To make matters worse, none of the data in the blockchain can ever be deleted. That's by design. Therefore, all your data, once exposed, cannot be deleted or changed.

One of the oversights when the internet and web were designed, was the lack of security and privacy. Blockchain suffers from many of the same concerns. The transactions stored in blockchain and NFTs are not private. Keep this in mind when you use or invest in these new technologies.

Another problem is that NFTs don't natively support provenance and attribution data. To resolve this issue, there is an effort to add content authority to NFTs.

Content Authenticity for NFTs

If you've ever created a digital asset such as an image or video, then you know these technologies don't support an immutable way to preserve provenance and attribution data. The Coalition for Content Provenance and Authenticity (C2PA) is designed to record the context and history of digital media. Adobe, Arm, Intel, Microsoft, and Truepic formed this alliance to securely add a layer of trust to all types of digital content.

Digital provenance will effectively help resolve the problem of misinformation by including verifiable, tamper-evident signatures to prove that the metadata and the underlying data have not been altered. The design consists of options to maintain the privacy and security of content creators.

These attributes are added to a digital asset when they are constructed. The history of any alterations to the content and metadata is maintained. This attribution information is preserved throughout the publishing process and is viewable by anyone.

NFT Scams

Scamming investors is not new, as the practice goes far back into the past, even before civilization. Ponzi schemes are a well-known scam dating back to the 1920s when Charles Ponzi promised a 50 percent return on investment with little to no risk. Ponzi schemes accept money from new investors, take a little off the top, then disburse those funds to earlier investors. These scams depend on a constant influx of new investors. Eventually, they cannot find enough new people to scam, and everything collapses.

NFTs, like any other investment mechanism, suffer from many methods to scam money from people, including everything from artificially inflating prices to creating fake or duplicate NFT projects. The following are some of the scamming methods used:

- *Wash trading.* This is when a scammer artificially inflates the prices of their NFTs. They hope to make their NFTs appear more lucrative, and hence, get higher bids when they sell them. This effectively imposes a false or illusionary demand. Wash trading is frequently heavily promoted or publicized to bring in investors. Notwithstanding, there is some risk to the practice: gas fees can reduce their profits and even result in a loss.

- *Rug pulls.* It's legitimate to promote NFTs to sellers. Sometimes, promoters will heavily hype NFTs to get investors, but once the price has been driven up, they take the money and run.

- *Counterfeit scams.* It is possible to counterfeit an NFT. For example, you could take a screenshot of a graphic NFT, then make a new NFT that looks exactly like the real one. Because they are not the actual NFTs, the buyers bid on worthless NFTs.

- *Pump-and-Dump.* In this scam, an individual or group will buy NFTs to drive the price artificially. Sometimes, these prices can rise dramatically and even hit the news. Investors believe they need to get into the action while there is still time. But, when they feel the price is at its highest level, the unscrupulous traders will sell them off, making a considerable profit on worthless NFTs.

- *Airdrop scams.* Also called NFT giveaway scams, in this type of scam you'll receive an offer for a free NFT in return for some minor service, perhaps sharing a post or something equally trivial. You will also be required to link your metamask wallet credentials; they then record what you type to get those credentials from you. From there, they can steal NFTs from you.

How do you avoid getting scammed? First, remember the old rule that if something looks too good to be true, it probably is. Be suspicious if the return appears unreasonably high. Check the credentials of the people behind the investment and look at their track record. If they suddenly appeared out of nowhere and are offering a 50 percent return in a week, it's almost certainly a scam. You should follow these practices:

- Never share your private keys. Giving them out is, in effect, the same as handing out the keys to your home.
- Additionally, always use the services of reputable (i.e., official) sites.
- Avoid using bargain networks.
- Research before investing. Check the online reviews.
- Use caution when investing. If you invest wisely and use properly vetted sources, you'll have a much greater likelihood of success.

Scams aside, there are further challenges to the adoption of NFTs.

Challenges to Adoption

So far in this chapter, we've covered the advantages and disadvantages of NFTs, from the technology to investment strategies and risks. NFTs are a recent technology, although development and adoption are proceeding at a fast pace.

Yet, there are challenges to the broader adoption of NFTs for use by the masses or the metaverse. Let's look at a few of these:

Blockchain overhead. NFTs are based on blockchain technology with all the associated overhead in the use of computer resources. Because NFTs are decentralized and copies exist on every network node, they can take up massive amounts of disk space, and because they cannot be deleted, this space is used forever. The storage and bandwidth considerations must be addressed.

Proof-of-Work bottleneck. The Proof-of-Work Method is a consensus method that uses phenomenal amounts of energy to the point where it significantly contributes to climate change. Better and more efficient consensus algorithms exist, and new ones will be developed in the future. But until they become mainstream, the future of NFTs will be constrained.

Transaction fees. Transactions are not free—you can expect to be charged a hefty fee each time you implement an NFT or perform a transaction. These fees are based on the network activity at the current point in time; for mainstream adoption, these fees must come down by order of magnitude.

Regulation. Because NFTs are investments and can represent assets in the physical world, it won't be long before regulators step in. The developers must form rules to prevent the marketplace from being stifled.

Hazy legality. The law has not had enough time to catch up to the fast pace of NFT and blockchain development. For instance, smart contracts are a great idea, but they haven't yet been seriously tested in court.

Physical world implications. While NFTs are intended to provide proof of ownership (amongst other things), enforcing that ownership in the physical world is legally untested. If I associated an NFT with my home, does that mean I'm the owner? Will a court accept that as evidence or proof of ownership? These types of questions still remain open.

Lack of privacy. In my mind, the lack of privacy is the biggest impediment to the widespread adoption of NFTs. Because the transparency of ledgers is part of the blockchain and NFT design, this will be a challenging problem to resolve. After all, NFTs and blockchains must ensure complete privacy before the public will accept them in their everyday lives.

Remember, the early internet suffered from many of these same (or similar) problems early in its development, rollout, and adoption. Those problems were, to a greater or lesser degree, solved. Because NFTs and blockchain are new technologies, you can expect that any barriers to adoption will be addressed and resolved.

It's only time before regulators get involved with NFTs, especially as they become more prevalent in everyday life.

Regulation

As digital assets become more popular and have greater use, regulatory agencies will inevitably be formed to help prevent fraud, place money-laundering barriers, develop taxation mechanisms, require reporting, and protect consumer privacy. Requirements for security might also be regulated.

As with many modern technologies, existing regulatory standards and laws are not suited initially for digital assets of all forms, including NFTs. Because NFTs are often investments and cryptocurrencies are money, the government will likely step in sooner rather than later.

Executive Order on Ensuring Responsible Development of Digital Assets. In 2022, President Biden signed an executive order to set national digital asset policies. This order "requires the Attorney General, in consultation with the Secretary of the Treasury and Chairman of the Federal Reserve, to make a recommendation as to whether legislation is necessary for the development of a US CBDC within 180 days."[5] The order also directs and encourages existing financial regulators to expand their activities within existing mandates, requires a whole government response, and sets up the conditions for digital assets legislation.

Securities. Many NFTs are used to accomplish goals outside of the realm of securities. Meanwhile, regulators might soon classify some NFTs as securities. This would allow those NFTs to fall under securities law, subject them to taxation, and restrict their reselling.

Anti-Money Laundering (AML). To fight crime, the US government has established a whole suite of regulations and policies requiring banks and financial institutions to implement procedures to reduce or eliminate the practice. If NFTs become subject to AML regulations, suspicious transactions will need to be reported.

Copyright. Copyright for digital assets, including ebooks, blogs, music, and videos, is difficult and expensive to enforce if violations are detected. Copyright needs substantial change to address digital assets, and those changes will likely happen sooner rather than later.

International regulation and enforcement. Laws vary from nation to nation (and in some countries, from state to state). Governments will inevitably formulate their regulations, but they must coordinate their efforts to present a united front.

The effect on the environment is another area of consideration.

NFTs and the Environment

We've already discussed how NFTs and blockchain use substantial amounts of energy and consequently contribute to climate change. NFTs and blockchain are responsible for significant energy usage worldwide because of their centralized design and consensus mechanisms. Long term, these issues must be addressed through redesign, because they will interfere with the scalability of this technology.

Some ways to address these issues in the short term include using carbon offsets (such as planting trees to match the carbon emissions). Powering mining data centers using renewable energy is another solution. Neither is a long-term solution because you can only do so much with carbon offsets and renewable energy.

Using a different consensus algorithm, such as Proof-of-Stake, requires much less energy. Switching to these alternative consensus algorithms could significantly reduce the energy requirements (as well as reduce the gas fees for transactions). Additional viable solutions include batching multiple transactions together so that minting algorithms can mint many transactions simultaneously (i.e., batch minting) or delaying the minting until an NFT is sold (i.e., lazy minting).

Summary

NFTs provide new entrepreneurism for individuals, businesses, and investors. This technology enables more immersive, valuable, and pervasive experiences and offers various options for gaming, industry, retail, and other businesses. For example, in gaming, NFTs support in-game ownership of assets and land; supply chain management can take advantage of NFTs for better recordkeeping; and genealogical information can be recorded and shared.

Blockchain, NFTs, DAOs, DeFi, and dapps (as well as many additional technologies) form the foundation for the metaverse. NFTs give people a way to own the copyrights of digital assets and to execute smart contracts that give them personal control over royalties and compensation. The ownership concepts of NFTs reflect the broader promise of true ownership of assets, in effect merging the digital and physical worlds.

Businesses must consider NFTs, blockchain, and the metaverse when creating their overall digital transformation strategies. The emerging technology of NFTs provides greater customer utility, driving greater brand value creation.

Throughout this chapter, we've deliberated some of the many applications for the technologies of blockchain and NFTs. NFTs and the underlying technologies present the case for decentralization, and in a sense, break the traditional paradigm of a centralized approach to ownership and use of assets. In the new world of NFTs, it's about interoperability, which is also the true promise of the open metaverse. The metaverse has the potential to free human creativity and business innovation in ways we are only beginning to understand.

In the next chapter, we'll look at another use case for the metaverse—gaming. Gaming is arguably one of the first emergences of the metaverse. The immersive technology of the metaverse is the ideal environment for playing realistic games that provide captivating experiences.

Notes

1 M Quiroz-Gutierrez. Bored Apes and CryptoPunks Help Jolt NFT Market to Over 21,000% Growth and $17.6 Billion in Sales Last Year, 10 March 2022, fortune.com/2022/03/10/bored-apes-cryptopunks-jolt-nft-market-to-billions-in-sales/ (archived at https://perma.cc/S7WH-BUCL)

2 A Sundararajan. How Your Brand Should Use NFTs, 28 February 2022, hbr.org/2022/02/how-your-brand-should-use-nfts (archived at https://perma.cc/SV2D-JX4U)

3 ERC-721 Non-Fungible Token Standard, ethereum.org/en/developers/docs/standards/tokens/erc-721/ (archived at https://perma.cc/BAG9-SBR6)

4 M White. Abuse and Harassment on the Blockchain, 22 January 2022. blog.mollywhite.net/abuse-and-harassment-on-the-blockchain/ (archived at https://perma.cc/K5Z8-Q9UL)

5 New Layer to Crypto Policy Emerges with Digital Assets Executive Order, www2.deloitte.com/content/dam/Deloitte/us/Documents/risk/us-advisory-digital-asset-regulatory.pdf?nc=42 (archived at https://perma.cc/8BCD-SM5L)

05 >Gaming_

Gaming is possibly the closest representation of what the metaverse might look like. It's an ideal use case for the metaverse, because gaming involves already expansive, web- and cloud-based immersive experiences. In fact, many games take advantage of the computing power available on the client (i.e., a mobile device, desktop computer, or gaming console) they're on, having offloaded most of their complex functions to cloud-based infrastructures. The metaverse promises to knowledge transfer several best practices from the already-rich gaming world, thus creating a new level of immersion and features within the metaverse.

In fact, for many, gaming is their first entry point into a virtual world. Quite a few of the concepts of the metaverse are rooted directly in gaming. Individuals create avatars to digitally represent themselves or a character in the gaming world. These avatars allow them to interact with the game and other players and act as their point-of-view during gameplay. Many earlier games were heavily scripted; however, new versions allow players to engage in new and unscripted ways.

Gamers place substantial importance on their digital identity or persona within one or more games. They personalize how they present themselves to other gamers by customizing their avatars. These avatars reflect how each gamer feels about themselves and their personality, showing off their social standing, skills, and experiences to their fellow players. As people spend more time immersed in gaming worlds, they connect with other players, thus increasing the importance of their digital identity.

A Brief History of Computer Games

First, let's take a moment to look back at the history of computer and video gaming. By understanding the roots of computing games, we can better extrapolate its future and how technology will be used to create engaging, highly immersive multiplayer games and inspire the metaverse.

Since the early days of computing, people have used computers to play games. Long before the days of mobile phones, personal computers, and the internet, professors and students at universities and colleges designed and wrote computer games. In fact, in 1952, a British professor created OXO (a version of tic-tac-toe) for his doctorate program at Cambridge University. In 1958, William Higinbotham started a new game called Tennis for two that ran on an analog computer and used an oscilloscope screen for its display.

By 1962, computer technology had improved so much that Steve Russell at MIT created a game called Spacewar!, designed to run on the PDP-1. This game supported play on multiple computer systems and was the first game of this type.

Have you heard of Zork before? Zork was an interactive text game with no graphics or sound. The game was based on the earlier Colossal Cave text game (also known as Adventure or ADVENT) created in 1976 by a Stanford student named Will Crowther, and simulated Mammoth Cave in Kentucky. Don Woods, another Stanford student, added fantasy elements to the games structure. Colossal Cave's two-word command set was limited, so they created Zork, which had a much richer command set. They split Zork into three parts—Zork I, II, and III—and founded a company named Infocom. Eventually, Infocom created dozens of interactive fiction games for the primitive personal computers (by modern standards), including Hitchhiker's Guide to the Galaxy and the Leather Goddess of Phobos. Activision purchased Infocom in 1986.[1]

Eventually, the rise of personal computers with better processors, storage, and graphics led to the demise of test-based fiction games. In 1967, developers at Sanders Associates Inc (led by Ralph Baer) created a game called The Brown Box that was played on television. Known as the Odyssey, it became the first home video game console in 1972.

Advances evolved quickly in the video game world from 1970 to the early 1980s, including:

- Atari released the Video Computer System in 1977—a home gaming console with many new features, including joysticks, cartridges, and so on.
- In 1978, the Space Invaders arcade game was released.
- Activision launched in 1979.
- Pac-Man and Donkey Kong were released.
- Other games were released, such as Lunar Lander, Star Raiders, Pong, Galaxian, and Space Wars.
- Microsoft released a flight simulator game.

The early video games available to the public ran on specialized consoles typically sold to "quarter-grabbing" video arcades. Players paid for time (usually just a few minutes) with quarters and could extend their playing time by paying more in. Usually, these consoles consisted of a large, refrigerator-sized cabinet with joysticks (or other controls), coin slots, and a television vacuum tube. Sometimes, they would be very elaborate. In a racing game, for example, the player sat and operated their racecar with a gas pedal, brake, and steering wheel.

As personal computers became ubiquitous, many games were modified to work on the new home computers. At the same time, gaming consoles such as the Nintendo and Atari systems appeared on store shelves, and the video arcade games were ported to them. Of course, as the gaming industry matured through the 1980s and 1990s, new games were developed that never saw the inside of a video arcade. In 1983, the video game market crashed due to market saturation but soon recovered with the release of the Nintendo NES.

Each company designed and released new games and even developed movies that appeared in theaters based on the games. Ultimately, Nintendo sold more units than Sega, leading to Sega exiting the gaming console market.

The video game scene changed again in 1995 with the release of 32-bit consoles. Sony entered the video game market with its PlayStation console and quickly became the dominant company in the business. In 2000, Sony's PlayStation 2 became the number-one selling console. Microsoft also entered the market around this time with their Xbox console.

By 2005 and 2006, there were three dominant video gaming companies: Microsoft with their Xbox 360, Sony with their the PlayStation 3, and Nintendo with their Nintendo Wii. The PlayStation 3 became the first console to offer Blu-ray support, while the Nintendo Wii offered motion-sensitive remotes and the Xbox 360 sported a motion capture system. Specialized handheld consoles, such as the Game Boy, were also introduced and made playing video games easier and more accessible to younger audiences.

At this time, everyone began buying smartphones, and the gaming world quickly took notice. Games were developed so that people could play them anywhere they wanted from the convenience of their phones. At the same time, gaming appeared on social media platforms, requiring only a web browser on any device. These two environments allowed much larger audiences to play games, using the device or media of their choice.

In 2016, the release of a new Pokémon GO game that took advantage of augmented reality (AR) appeared. In this game, people used their phones to search for Pokémon characters in the real world. These colorful animated beings were overlayed on the video camera display of smartphones, and thus appeared to exist in the environment.

Modern video console games often consist of a client installed directly on the console and a cloud interface, which installs new modules, characters, and other things as needed. More recent games are entirely based in the cloud, with only a thin client required on the gamer's hardware.

Video games have evolved to use 3D graphics and sound to create strikingly real environments. Some can be played by individuals; others are enormous multiplayer universes constantly changing in real time. Advanced devices allow fully immersive experiences in virtual or augmented reality worlds.

The modern video gaming experience is, in many ways, the entry point to the metaverse. Many of the concepts, such as immersive and responsive environments, 3D graphics, high-quality sound, and a functioning economic system, are the basic building blocks for the leap to the next level—the metaverse.

Playing video games is a pastime that engages many people for many hours every day/week. What drives people to spend so much time in gameplay?

The Psychology of Gaming

As game equipment becomes more sophisticated, with better graphics, 3D, artificial intelligence (AI), augmented reality (AR)/virtual reality (VR), and other technologies, as well as more sophisticated storylines, game designers find they are reaching a much broader and more rapidly growing audience. These designers can use tools such as Experiential Sampling Methodology (ESM) to understand how the story, background, and non-player characters (NPCs) change players' engagement levels. The greater the engagement, the more it indicates that players enjoy and are fulfilled by their gaming experiences. These complex and deep storylines provide opportunities for players to interact with other players, NPCs, multiple storylines, barriers, goals, and rewards. Thus, people can step out of their daily lives to share new and different experiences with their gaming friends.

Game designers ensure their games give people opportunities to win and become more skilled. Players can immerse themselves in a game world, almost literally becoming a character, and achieve results that let them win on a gradient basis. Thus, games that are too difficult or too easy for most people (at least at the beginning) may not become as popular as those that find the right balance between effort and winning progressively larger goals.

The human brain is not designed to distinguish between reality and virtual reality (VR). To the brain, an attacking lion appears to be a real attacking lion, which triggers a dopamine response to react accordingly with all the reasonable fear and other emotional responses.

Complex multiplayer games go even further by addressing social needs as well. A player can make friends with other players, form groups, earn and spend money, and set and help achieve group goals. Players gain status, just as if they were in the real world, giving them even more reasons to continue playing.

In-game items and property serve an even greater purpose in fulfilling the needs of players. By purchasing virtual objects and property, they gain the sense that something tangible has been achieved—they own something for their efforts—even though these in-game possessions don't exist in the physical world. A person who buys a new set of virtual clothing for their in-game avatar can feel just as good as someone who does the same in the real world.[2]

Given that video games provide challenges, goals, results, and victories, it shouldn't be surprising that the popularity of video games continues to rise as games become more immersive and social; simply put, their popularity increases.

The Growth of Gaming

Video gaming has increased steadily since its beginning in 1972 with the introduction of *Pong*. At first, because consoles, mobile phones, and PCs didn't yet exist, this growth was the result of arcade games. By 1980, the arcade version of Pac-Man brought in over $1 billion in sales in one year, a significant percentage of the $39 billion in revenue from just arcade game sales.[3]

By this time, gaming consoles had already appeared. In 1980, sales of games in this area reached $20 billion a year. Growth continued for a few years, but the market dropped in the mid-1980s, only to resurge after 1985. PC games joined the mix around 1981, and hand-held games appeared on the market in the late 1980s. Finally, mobile games were born in 1997 when Nokia released their cell phone with a game called Snake.

All four types of video games continued growing in sales, except for arcade games, which dropped dramatically in the late 1990s. Games running on mobile devices, consoles, and PCs continued gaining popularity, and sales have grown consistently yearly.

Around 2017, cloud-based and virtual reality (VR) games appeared. These still account for a tiny but increasing percentage of gaming sales as of the writing of this book.

In 2020, the total gaming revenue was $165 billion (in 2021, this increased to $178 billion[4]), and was split as follows:

- Mobile: $85 billion
- PC: $40 billion
- Console: $33 billion
- Cloud and VR games: perhaps $7 billion

As can be seen from these sales numbers, video games are immensely popular, and the industry is proliferating.

Modern games are complex, immersive, interactive adventures with rich storylines. They can require millions or even hundreds of millions of dollars in funds to develop, and the investors naturally want a monetary return for the money they've invested into these artistic projects. Thus, developing, promoting, and maintaining these games requires a sound business strategy, good leadership, and management, just like any business.

As we've touched on previously, game designers and coders have been creating computer games for decades, and video games followed with the advent of more sophisticated hardware including graphics and faster CPUs. Nowadays, video games are even more popular due to revolutionary computer software and hardware improvements.

Their extreme popularity is evidenced by the fact that the gaming industry exceeds the total size (and revenue) of the total size (and revenue) of movies and music combined. This dominance means more people are purchasing (and presumably playing) video games by far than movies and music put together. Video games are the dominant attention media, and that dominance doesn't show any signs of slowing down.

The Evolution of Video Gaming

In the early twentieth century, everyone had a radio in their homes, and it was common to find families huddled around these receivers, listening to their favorite series, the news, or other entertainment. Later, television quickly superseded radio as the dominant medium for entertainment, first with black and white and later with color sets.

By the late 1950s and 1960s, virtually every family owned at least one television, and, as with radio, on many nights, you'd find them all sitting on the couch, watching their favorite shows.

With the advent of new technologies such as cable, the VCR (and later DVD players and Blu-ray), the entertainment potential of television continued to permeate society. Video games were a natural progression to this growth, because gaming consoles plugged directly into those TV sets. The development of the personal computer market also fed the evolution of video gaming.

Now that most homes are connected to high-speed internet and virtually everyone owns and operates an internet-connected mobile device, gaming has expanded into every venue and area of people's lives. In the past, to play a video game, an individual had to visit a specialized arcade or play them from their homes. Now with mobile computing, games can be played anywhere and at any time.

Combined with complex storylines, AI/ML, 3D, and AR/VR, these trends mean that gaming has unprecedented content leverage. It's not uncommon to overhear people talking excitedly about their favorite games, newest stories, and expansion modules. Games have spun off related content such as TikTok and YouTube Channels (for instance, Viva La Dirt League), movies, television series, and animated specials.

Remember when everyone seemed to talk about the most recent episode of *Game of Thrones* or *Breaking Bad*? That's the social aspect of media at work. People love to talk about their favorite shows, movies, or games. They become heavily engaged and want to share their experiences while socializing with friends. Video games have the same effect; because people become very immersed and devote much of their spare time enjoying these digital worlds, they naturally want to share them with others.

For business, gaming has the advantage of having a built-in feedback mechanism. Game designers create immersive worlds that people want to be part of because they are fun and enjoyable. Movies and series are scripted, much like novels, and the viewer follows those scripts. Video games are different because players are part of the action and can change the storyline based on their decisions. The games center around players and not authors, actors, or directors.

Because the medium is so flexible, video games have consistent growth. New devices, technologies, categories, and content continue to feed the desires and needs of players, enabling them to enjoy new worlds and new ways to expand their imagination. If you combine these trends with the social aspects of multiplayer games, it's easy to see how people can enjoy the immersive qualities of their favorite games and invest ever more time and money into these virtual realities.

For years, major companies have noticed the potential of these gaming trends and environments and have been busy inventing technical innovations such as streaming, the cloud, and decentralized processing. These companies share a goal of enabling the playing of video games without the need for a desktop computer or a console system. They are working towards making high-quality games available in the web browser, on whatever device the user happens to be using at the time. Video gaming is becoming an omnichannel media.

These growing video gaming trends introduce many merchandising possibilities. Players will (and already can) purchase products, services, and even property within a game. Of course, some games may support in-game advertising, say on a billboard in a racing game or via product placement. Furthermore, as we've already determined, there are countless possibilities for physical universe merchandising from movies to toys.

Additionally, the demographics of video games are evolving. Because of smartphones with their constant internet access and powerful computing capabilities, the audience for video games has expanded into virtually every niche, culture, and age. For example, many demographics have found short play sessions of games like Candy Crush to be a great stress reliever.

On top of these trends, the market for vintage video games is growing. People often scan auction sites to purchase a copy of their favorite console game they played when they were younger. Many older games are being released on Nintendo Switch and other platforms so that anyone can play an early version of Mario Brothers or Zelda. Original console versions of popular video games can demand prices of thousands of dollars or more for a single copy.

A vital component of video gaming is the effect of long-term intellectual property (IP). Many movies and their characters and scenarios are designed into these video games, and games, if popular, spawn successors. Thus, Spider-Man appears not just in movies and comic books but is also featured in video games to allow for a continuation of the experience in a more immersive and flexible format. New games are created based on older games. Examples include games like Resident Evil, Pokémon, Grand Theft Auto, and Call of Duty, which continue to spin off more complex and more advanced sequels.

The metaverse promises to boost gaming to an entirely new level. Video game technology is the walkway leading to the development of the metaverse.

Gaming Mechanics in the Metaverse

Modern online video games are an integral part of the metaverse, but to be fully integrated, a few concepts must be true. Games must be designed to operate with the following concepts or considerations in order to fully integrate with the metaverse and gain all the benefits it implies.

Real time. Games in the metaverse generally operate in real time, meaning there is a consistent clock running within the game. Action games are typically designed to run in real time because that's the best way to make the gaming world real for players. Racing games, Pac-Man, and any action game are examples of real-time games.

In contrast, turn-based gaming means there is a pause between each action to allow time for thinking. Chess is an example of a turn-based game.[5]

Persistence. It is vital that games persist, which means they must continue even when players are logged out. Games that support multiple players (i.e., hundreds or thousands of them) must persist because gameplay cannot stop for all the players just because one logs out.

Collaboration. Players, especially in multiplayer games, must be allowed to work together or collaborate with other players and with NPCs.

Social stickiness. When a player enters a game, they generally try to beat it. Furthermore, after they meet a few other players, form friendships, and join communities, they continue playing because that's where they find their community and friends. This solves the problem that most people become bored with games after a while. Once they form social bonds with others, they are no longer playing to win the game (for the most part); they are playing to be with their friends.[6]

3D immersion and immersive experiences. Immersive experiences are designed to grab the attention of a viewer or player and let them see a real or fantasy world. They can interact with the environment and manipulate objects. The concept of 3D immersion gives the viewer the perception (i.e., sight, sound, touch, and possibly even smell) using 3D glasses and virtual reality (VR) technologies.

Interoperability. This concept means players can purchase or gain possessions in one game and transport them (and use them) to another game (or other location in the metaverse). For instance, if players purchased a set of virtual clothes for their avatar, they could wear those same clothes in another game or even at a virtual sporting event or conference.

The Game Economy

Modern video games consist of complex worlds that provide exciting and challenging adventures for players. In-game economics gives players the additional goals and challenges of earning income within a game and using that to make purchases. These economic systems give players further incentive to continue playing and spend more, as items can be purchased with real money from the physical world, thus creating additional income streams for gaming businesses.[7]

When a game is designed, the designers must decide if they want to include an economic system and, if so, how it will work. Players need a way to know how much money they've earned and spent within their gameplay and how much various things cost. Then designers must define how players will earn income and whether they can use physical money in the gaming world. Following that, the game must allow players to make purchases, sell objects, keep those articles someplace safe, inventory them, and maintain a ledger of their income and what they've done with it. The game could even go as far as to include virtual banks, trading, and other mechanisms if that helps with the play.

To keep players engaged in the game, currency can be designed and objects assigned values. Substances for sale need to be promoted, perhaps in an in-game shop or by using carefully crafted clues, and mechanisms for making purchases and sales must be implemented. The game designers must balance the ability of players to earn money within a game with the ease they have to make purchases.

Additionally, game designers need to decide if they allow virtual money, which is earned in-game, to be converted to physical cash in the form of withdrawals. This can incentivize players to invest more time playing the game, making purchases, and solving puzzles because they can use that money in their everyday lives.

The Attention Economy

Many of the lessons learned by the gaming industry apply directly to the metaverse (and other businesses as well), especially concerning the attention economy. No business can remain functional if consumers are not engaged and active, which undoubtedly applies to games. For a game to become popular and generate revenue, it must hold the attention of its players. Players who become bored or feel that their needs are not fulfilled will look elsewhere for entertainment.

Alternative for "As we've mentioned", games in the past were owned by arcades and accepted quarters or tokens (coins issued by the arcades themselves) for a certain amount of playing time. Playing time was extended by inserting more coins into the game, which was an efficient way to increase profits. The games were challenging enough on a gradient, which kept players coming back for more.[8]

Modern games keep players engaged using a variety of means. Many games now charge on a pay-by-the-hour (or month) basis, while others are free to play but offer the option to purchase in-game objects, virtual skins, and even virtual currencies. Gaming's social aspect also increases the stickiness of games—people remain playing more because they've made friends within game worlds than due to gameplay.

Because the metaverse is an immersive experience, it shares many attributes with games, of which businesses can take advantage. These businesses can create opportunities to increase engagement by gaining and holding the attention of their customers, just as games do.

In the metaverse, web-based storefronts can improve consumer engagement by delivering good products and services using an enjoyable and valuable customer journey. These storefronts hold the attention of consumers because of these traits. To prosper in the metaverse, businesses must create the means whereby consumers remain engaged. Eventually, advanced 3D graphics and high-technology interfaces won't be enough because they will be familiar to every business. Consumers need a reason to place their attention on a business) and keep it focused, so they come back repeatedly. Both can be accomplished via good marketing and advertising.

Major businesses agree that gaming is the gateway to the metaverse and acknowledge its influence over future development and direction.

Games Influencing the Metaverse

The influence of gaming on the metaverse cannot be understated. Over 3 billion people actively game, and gaming is growing faster than any other form of entertainment. Microsoft chairman and CEO Satya Nadella agrees:

> Gaming is the most dynamic and exciting category in entertainment across all platforms today and will play a key role in the development of metaverse platforms. We're investing deeply in world-class content, community, and the cloud to usher in a new era of gaming that puts players and creators first and makes gaming safe, inclusive, and accessible to all.[9]

Roblox, Minecraft, Grand Theft Auto, and Fortnite are sports platforms that resemble the metaverse in many ways. They all provide immersive experiences, allow in-game purchases, and are invested in their communities, supporting them and driving their business. Each of these games provides its players a virtual world and an environment; players can freely socialize with other players and interact with the gaming world.

Epic Games, valued at $31.5 billion in 2022, created Fortnite, which currently engages over 350 million users. Tim Sweeny, CEO of Epic, highlighted the significance of the metaverse, saying: "The next three years are going to be critical for all the metaverse-aspiring companies like Epic, Roblox, Microsoft, Facebook [now Meta]. It's kind of a race to get to a billion users, whoever brings on a billion users first, would be the presumed leader in setting the standards."[10]

This gaming platform offers far more than just video games. They have created a fully featured immersive experience for their consumers based on the Unreal Engine, a set of tools to create experiences on the Fortnite platform. To further their expansion, they've acquired Twinmotion, Hyprsense, Cubic Motion, and other companies and added their capabilities to Unreal Engine.

Epic Games also offers a game store (Epic Game Store) where consumers can download and play various games. Their online services (Epic Online Services) provide the tools for developers to create games, and Epic Games Publishing helps developers build, publish, and monetize their games.

The platform has expanded into other forms of entertainment as well, as evidenced by the Travis Scott Concert, where the rapper and producer Travis Scott held a concert inside the Fortnite platform. In a tweet from April 27, 2020, he shared, "Over 27.7 million unique players in-game participated live 45.8 million times across the five events to create a truly Astronomical experience."[11]

In the future, games will continue to influence the metaverse by introducing new concepts, hardware support, and platforms. Gaming opens the door to the metaverse and proves that, conceptually, the idea is valid and can enhance the lives of billions of people.

Social Gaming

One of the first early indications of social gaming was Kim Kardashian: Hollywood, which has netted more than $157 million in sales since launching in 2014. The idea is for players to compete for notoriety by climbing up the ranks of the elite in Los Angeles. The business case for the game is based on the strategy of using famous personalities to create easy-to-play gaming experiences to virtually build up communities. Players can then purchase designer clothes and customize their makeup.

Zoe Henry quotes Niccolo de Masi in her Inc.com article titled "The Brilliant Business Model Behind Kim Kardashian's $150 Million App." Here's what's most notable from the exchange. Niccolo de Masi, CEO at Glu Mobile, said: "With the brand integration, we're adding more authenticity to the product than you would have if it were pretend clothing brands." He went on to say, "The world going mobile means you need to bring the whole world into your mobile product."[12]

This was an early precursor of the merging of social and gaming and will be a trend to watch throughout metaverse worlds. This introduces the question of how Freemium games and experiences can best generate revenue in the metaverse by allowing players to play at no cost while offering in-app purchases to supplement their experience.

Play to Earn

Businesses learned long ago that one way to motivate people is to offer them ways to earn income using their services. Games are no different, and gaming companies have taken advantage of the recent technologies of blockchain and NFTs to enable prizes, incentives, and other in-game assets.

Known as the play-to-earn business model, players are rewarded for achieving specific goals within the game. They can purchase objects in the game using "real" money or virtual currency, or they can perform activities that provide value to other players, the community, or the game and earn that way.

These players receive rewards in the form of cybercurrency or NFTS, representing in-game virtual pieces such as a sword, clothing, or even virtual land. Once a player has won a virtual object, they can sell or trade them in an NFT marketplace. They can even sell digital objects for real money that they can use outside the game.

Play to Own

In traditional games, assets are not owned by players. The play-to-own business model changes all that because they fully own the component they find or purchase within the game. These assets have an absolute value, and players can sell or trade them as desired inside or outside the game (in a marketplace).

As a result, these NFT-based "artifacts" create an entirely new economic system based on the ownership of virtual items. Because blockchain (i.e., the underlying technology of NFTs) is decentralized, the economy is under the control of the people and not a central authority. Players are free to remove their belongings from the game and use them in other games as desired.[13]

Both the play-to-own and play-to-earn business models are enabled by blockchain, which we've touched on previously and will describe in the next section.

What is Blockchain Gaming?

As we've said before, blockchain is the technology that enables NFTs and assets, which are owned by players instead of a central authority. Because blockchain and NFTs are usable anywhere in any game that enables the technology, said items can be transferred from game to game. Even more exciting, possessions can be sold or traded in marketplaces or the metaverse when it has been implemented.

This technology frees players from the tyranny of their hard-earned possessions becoming "stuck" in one gaming system (or, at best, in the games of a single company). As we highlighted in the last section, this enables the creation of a player-owned economic system that is not under the control of any entity.

Thus, gamers who spend countless hours building up their collection of belongings can rest assured that they can use them generally how they want. Nevertheless, there's another dimension to blockchain gaming: goods can be sold for "real" money, money that can be used to purchase groceries, pay debts, and rent, and even purchase new games.

Interoperability is critical, because the game mechanics must be based on blockchain and NFT technology. It is how assets can be owned by individuals and transferred from game to game to a marketplace or anywhere else.

The metaverse and its open design depend on the interoperability of NFT-based assets that can be used in any other open metaverse world. Although, the designers of closed worlds do not face interoperability concerns because assets cannot be moved elsewhere. Ownership is centralized to the world operators in these closed worlds (or games).

Games Built on Blockchain

As we spoke about earlier in this chapter, gaming is the largest and fastest-growing entertainment segment. Video games are superior in many ways to other forms of entertainment because they are interactive and interoperable in the case of blockchain-based games.

Blockchain games are gaining in popularity, although it is still not as popular or widespread as other closed gaming systems. Hundreds of games that take advantage of blockchain already exist, and the number continues to grow. Some are listed here:

- *Axie Infinity.* A digital world populated by NFT-based Axies (i.e., digital creatures). The game supports a vibrant economy; some in-game tokens trade for hundreds or thousands of dollars.

- *God's Unchained.* Inspired by Magic: The Gathering, this game allows players to create decks of cards and use them to fight opponents. Players own their cards that they can buy or sell at will.

NFTs in Gaming

An NFT certifies ownership of a virtual possessions. Each NFT describes one and only one thing. In gaming, NFTs can represent characters, skins, weapons, shields, bottles, land, or anything else that is considered unique. Any resource can be made unique by adding a serial number or via a similar method. When you are listed as the owner of an NFT for a digital article, you are the digital piece owner. The NFT proves that you are the owner.

Based on blockchain technology, NFTs may be traded, bought, and sold. Because blockchain is decentralized, any NFT and its associated resource can be transferred from anywhere to anywhere in the metaverse. To illustrate, your avatar and its NFT can move freely from game to game and even to social events or conferences.

Building Games

Gaming has evolved from simple, text-based computer games to today's complex, realistic, and immersive worlds. Hardware and software are advancing to the point where games can be truly immersive, real-time, persistent experiences for millions of people.

Modern Games

Modern gaming requires significant investments in the game's infrastructure. Immersive games require large disk farms containing hundreds of thousands or even millions of the newest and fastest drives (most likely solid-state drives because they are so fast), rooms full of memory and CPUs, and incredible amounts of bandwidth.

Adobe recently acquired Allegorithmic, maker of Substance 3D. Allegorithmic is a leader in 3D editing and authoring and has defined the standard for 3D material and texturing. The Substance 3D Collection consists of a set of tools to enable developers to create and manipulate 3D objects and images. It includes such tools as Stager, Designer, Painter, and Sampler.

Adobe Substance allows creators to design and apply skins and textures to enhance 3D gaming graphics, thus making those games even more realistic and immersive. The Allegorithmic set of tools was already used in games such as Call of Duty, Assassin's Creed, and Forza. Additionally, it was used to create special effects for movies such as *Blade Runner 2049*, *Pacific Rim Uprising*, and *Tomb Raider*.[14]

Cloud Gaming

Typical online video games run virtually everything locally on a console, PC, or mobile device. Thus, the game logic, rendering, video, audio, graphics, and everything else is done on the smartphone, tablet, or PC, which requires the game's installation and all its components to be downloaded and installed. A local machine does the work and only accesses the internet to collaborate with other gamers and the central gaming system.

Games are designed this way because the internet is not necessarily a reliable communication method. The connection slows down, gets interrupted, gets, recovers from errors, and consistently has other problems. Many of these issues occur in a fraction of seconds, but service interruptions can last for hours or even days.

The internet was designed in the 1980s when the typical communication method was a modem attached to a phone line. The original designers didn't even consider the possibility of persistent connectivity, which came much later with the advent of broadband, fiber, and digital subscriber line (DSL).

Finally, the internet was slow—much slower than today. In the 1990s, a 1-megabyte file could take minutes or hours to download; today, on a typical fiber-connected home, that same file could be downline in seconds or minutes at the most.

Games were first designed to run locally as much as possible and only transmit and receive when necessary. With today's fast internet connections, these constraints no longer exist for the most part, which has opened the door to a better approach to gaming.

The cloud consists of data centers located all over the planet. These data centers contain hundreds of thousands of CPUs, millions of disk drives, and high-speed communications. By leveraging these data centers, cloud gaming moves game processing from a console, PC, or mobile device to distributed computer systems.

Cloud-based games don't require consoles or other specialized hardware. They run directly from any supported web browser because most of the work is performed in the datacenters, not on the user's device. Thus, the browser-based game simply acts as a communication device to the player, sending commands to the data centers and receiving the results as commands, a video stream, and graphics.

Cloud gaming is not as easy as it sounds though. Just keeping everything in sync is a complex task. This complexity increases when latency, transmission errors, and other factors, combined with the high cost of running a game in a data center, are considered.

These are just a few issues that must be resolved before cloud gaming grows in its popularity. Cloud-based games offer advantages, including better graphics, larger maps, richer gameplay, and many more concurrent users, however.

How Gaming Influences Virtual Experiences in the Metaverse

It's not surprising that the popularity of the gaming culture influences our lives. The experience we gain from playing and socializing within games certainly carries into our daily lives and within enterprises, businesses, governments, and other areas. The gaming experience, indeed, is the closest yet to the up-and-coming metaverse. Additionally, gaming is only the beginning, and the lessons learned there will inevitably be applied to create immersive experiences for enterprises using and accessing the metaverse. Tim Draper, a Silicon Valley venture-capital investor, stated, "Every enterprise will want to reach people through the metaverse, whether to communicate, advertise, or do business with people who are making virtual reality their place of business."[15]

Slack, an office chat tool, premiered as a messaging service used by a video game. Slack became so popular that Salesforce Inc.

acquired the business for $27 billion. Stewart Butterfield, Slack CEO and Co-Founder, said of the acquisition in the announcement on Slack.com: "We have a once-in-a-generation opportunity to rethink and reshape how and where we work. Salesforce and Slack are uniquely positioned to lead this historic shift to a digital-first world. I could not be more excited for what's to come."[16]

Microsoft plans to acquire Activision Blizzard Inc., a major video game company, to use its technologies and other innovations from the gaming world in the enterprise. Jeremy Bailenson, a co-founder of VR-based training platform Strivr and founding director of Stanford University's Virtual Human Interaction Lab, went on the record for an article written about this by Angus Loten to say, "Microsoft has obviously been a leader in business-to-business technology in general, and also pioneers in virtual and augmented reality. Now, they instantly have access to one of the most elaborate and long-running metaverses of all time with World of Warcraft."[17]

Mesh for Microsoft Teams uses mixed reality applications to feel presence, enable collaboration on persistent 3D content, and to connect from anywhere. Mesh supports a variety of technologies, including Hololens 2, VR headsets, mobile devices, and PCs, enabling the sharing of digital experiences to create a collective understanding and allowing for more significant innovation.[18]

Gaming's influence on the metaverse will definitely change enterprises and businesses in many ways, enabling greater collaboration and innovation. Let's briefly examine a few of these changes here:

Sales and marketing. The immersive experiences the metaverse offers will allow customers to see and feel products, creating a more lifelike communication without needing to be physically present.

Advertising. Product placement within movies and other media has been and is a popular method to generate revenue from entertainment. The metaverse will give advertisers opportunities to advertise within digital worlds by placing products with users or players (in the case of games).

Events. Everything from comedy acts to major sporting events will see the size of their potential audience expand because people will be able to attend without a physical presence. These immersive experiences will look and feel natural without traveling to a crowded venue.

Engineering. Businesses will be able to create immersive simulations of their products. An engineer could create a simulation of a bridge and test it under various conditions to determine its strengths and weaknesses long before the bridge is actually built.

Workforce training. Businesses will be able to create immersive environments to allow employees to be trained. For example, a power company could set up an immersive simulation of a nuclear power plant to walk employees through various failure modes without any danger to help them learn what to do in those instances.[19]

Summary

As a reflection, the metaverse creates an immersive environment for shared experiences. Gaming provides a glimpse into the possibilities offered by the metaverse, indicating how the metaverse will act, what it will look like, and some of the business and consumer benefits. Much of the technology needed to create the metaverse is being actively developed and implemented for gaming, leading to a smoother, more robust, and more usable metaverse.

The development of previous gaming platforms, technologies, and experiences went in one linear direction: from a director, writer, or artist to the viewer. Gaming, even the early, primitive, interactive fiction games, allowed for two-way experiences, albeit in a limited fashion. Today's games allow for immersive storytelling in which players are enveloped by the game and become part of the story. They are no longer just idle viewers—they can see, hear, and even touch their environments, interact with other players, and create new forms of engagement and business in a virtual game world.

The result blurs the lines between gaming and other forms of entertainment (i.e., music, film, and media)—and even with real life. Games are becoming seemingly near real, and, in many ways, the virtual world can expand reality into new realms that, in the past, humans could only dream of.

As these gaming concepts and technologies are carried over to other forms of entertainment, there are virtually no limits on the artistic creativity available to humans.

In the next chapter, we'll evaluate how the metaverse is changing entertainment.

Notes

1 A Rosenberg. Microsoft Can Rescue a Historic Trove of Lost Games from Activision's Vault, 2022, mashable.com/article/microsoft-activision-acquisition-save-infocom (archived at https://perma.cc/7CA8-DV8V)

2 What Makes Games So Addictive: The Psychology Behind Gaming, 13 June 2019, f1pme.medium.com/what-makes-games-so-addictive-psychology-behind-gaming-e6ea6928586 (archived at https://perma.cc/F6EP-C3XL)

3 O Wallach. 50 Years of Gaming History, by Revenue Stream (1970–2020), 23 November 2020, www.visualcapitalist.com/50-years-gaming-history-revenue-stream/ (archived at https://perma.cc/M5E5-B4AV)

4 Video Game Industry Statistics, Trends and Data in 2022, 18 January 2022, www.wepc.com/news/video-game-statistics/ (archived at https://perma.cc/C856-33SZ)

5 D Norton. Real-Time vs. Turn-Based Mechanics in Learning Games, 20 April 2017, www.filamentgames.com/blog/real-time-vs-turn-based-mechanics-learning-games/ (archived at https://perma.cc/DL2W-V9MB)

6 S Pierce. "Stickiness" in Games, or: Why You Can't Beat WoW, 30 January 2010, www.gamedeveloper.com/design/-quot-stickiness-quot-in-games-or-why-you-can-t-beat-wow (archived at https://perma.cc/6WC3-YBNR)

7 Machinations. What Is Game Economy Design, 11 August 2021, machinations.io/articles/what-is-game-economy-design/ (archived at https://perma.cc/783B-QCSZ)

8 J Radoff. Game Economics, Part 1: The Attention Economy, 3 March 2021, medium.com/building-the-metaverse/game-economics-part-1-the-attention-economy-efb64312ad6b (archived at https://perma.cc/657V-U7CD)

9 Microsoft News Center. Microsoft to Acquire Activision Blizzard to Bring the Joy and Community of Gaming to Everyone, Across Every Device, 18 January 2022, news.microsoft.com/2022/01/18/microsoft-to-acquire-activision-blizzard-to-bring-the-joy-and-community-of-gaming-to-everyone-across-every-device/ (archived at https://perma.cc/X6KD-6NKN)

10 GlobalData Thematic Research. Epic Games Is Strengthening Its Metaverse Ambition, 28 April 2022. www.verdict.co.uk/epic-games-metaverse/ (archived at https://perma.cc/2CX4-PKKM)

11 W E K III. Fortnite's Travis Scott Concert Was Historic. But He's Not the only
    Artist Getting Creative, 30 April 2020, www.nbcnews.com/think/opinion/
    fortnite-s-travis-scott-concert-was-historic-he-s-not-ncna1195686 (archived at
    https://perma.cc/MW26-ST3P)

12 Z Henry. The Brilliant Business Model Behind Kim Kardashian's $150 Million
    App, 2 June 2016, www.inc.com/zoe-henry/kim-kardashian-hollywood-app-
    157-million-sales-strategy.html (archived at https://perma.cc/SC2A-2ADZ)

13 M Mulla. What's the Difference Between Play-To-Own and Play-To-Earn,
    1 March 2022, coinpedia.org/news/whats-the-difference-between-play-to-own-
    and-play-to-earn/ (archived at https://perma.cc/89J7-KRFT)

14 S Belsky. Adobe Acquires Allegorithmic, the Leader in 3D Editing and
    Authoring for Gaming and Entertainment, 23 January 2019, blog.adobe.com/
    en/publish/2019/01/23/adobe-acquires-allegorithmic-substance-3d-gaming
    (archived at https://perma.cc/EAY7-96PY)

15 Microsoft's Activision Deal May Bring "Metaverse" to Enterprise Tech,
    successwithsahil.com/microsofts-activision-deal-may-bring-metaverse-to-
    enterprise-tech/ (archived at https://perma.cc/JH4Q-3J4J)

16 Slack. Salesforce Completes Acquisition of Slack, 21 July 2021,
    slack.com/blog/news/salesforce-completes-acquisition-of-slack (archived at
    https://perma.cc/UQ5N-9TRH).

17 A Loten. Microsoft's Activision Deal May Bring "Metaverse" to Enterprise
    Tech, 18 January 2022, www.wsj.com/articles/microsofts-activision-deal-may-
    bring-metaverse-to-enterprise-tech-11642554025 (archived at https://perma.cc/
    3EA4-KDBF)

18 Microsoft Mesh, www.microsoft.com/en-us/mesh (archived at https://perma.cc/
    444Z-5SHV).

19 S Sharma. 7 Ways the Metaverse Will Change the Enterprise, 26 January 2022,
    venturebeat.com/2022/01/26/7-ways-the-metaverse-will-change-the-enterprise/
    (archived at https://perma.cc/6YMF-DPDG).

06 >Entertainment_

Entertainment has been a part of the human experience as far back as archeologists have been able to ascertain. One could certainly make a case for adding entertainment in addition to the three basic needs of humankind—food, clothing, and shelter. People not only enjoy being entertained but also need it to enrich their minds, relieve monotony, and, more importantly, expand their social circle.

Technology has infused even more depth to entertainment. Through the invention of the radio, people began telling their stories to thousands and millions. With the advent of movies and television, the entertainer's art could be displayed directly in homes throughout the world. In all these cases, advertisers and businesses gained in numerous ways from the ability to reach far more people with their messages and brands.

The metaverse promises to add an entirely new dimension to the use and value of entertainment. Entertainment in the metaverse will be a colossal growth driver for businesses to connect with consumers. Instead of just watching a pre-recorded movie on a screen, consumers can now participate in an immersive experience. Affectively, from the comfort of their own home, they can explore the far-off historic lands like the pyramids of ancient Egypt with their friends without even leaving their homes. They can experience the heat of the desert, the feel of the stones, and the sights and sounds of the ancient crowds of people.

But before we delve into the effects of the metaverse on entertainment, let's set the stage by reviewing the history of entertainment.

A Brief History of Entertainment

People need entertainment. Based on historical evidence, various forms of theater, dance, and music existed as far back as can be determined. In prehistoric times, it's easy to imagine members of a tribe dancing around a fire as part of a ceremony or an elder chanting the words of a story from long ago. Such entertainment was a part of the life of humans whenever and wherever they lived.

Archeologists have discovered evidence of musical instruments in ancient tombs dating back thousands of years. Evidence of stages for plays or oration exist in the ruins of ancient cities, and artwork depicting dancing has been found painted on cave walls and the homes of nobles.

Socialization is a common theme in these depictions of entertainment. Actors presented plays to audiences of all sizes and backgrounds, musicians played their instruments and sang songs to crowds of people, and dancers performed as part of ceremonies with their tribe members. On the surface, the reasons for entertainment can be attributed to religion, war, and sacrifice. Yet, its primary purpose was to gather people together to celebrate something important to the group.

All these forms of entertainment were performed locally, and the performances were never recorded because the technology didn't exist. Even the Romans, with their impressive coliseum, only gave performances and gladiatorial combats that had to be seen in person. Everyone could talk about the events, but to see them, they had to travel to lands near and far.

On December 28, 1895, history was made when Louis and Auguste Lumiere screened the first movie commercially for the first time, charging a small fee for people to view it. Their film showed clips of scenes from everyday life in France. This wasn't the first time people had viewed a motion picture—that occurred in the early 1830s with the development of the phenakistoscope.[1] This machine took advantage of a slotted spinning disc, creating the illusion of motion. Thomas Edison then invented the kinetoscope in 1891, a machine showing people a strip of film moving past a light source.

These and other analogous machines were useful, but they still required people to view them in a theater or room. Entertainment of this nature all changed with the invention of the radio. For the first time in human history, performances could be broadcast and heard by audiences outside of their local area. People all over a country and even the world could listen to the exploits of Flash Gordon, The Lone Ranger, and the Martian invasion of Earth as presented by Orson Welles. At first, these broadcasts could not be saved, but lacquer discs and magnetic tape inventions allowed the major radio networks of NBC, Mutual, and CBS to begin taping their recordings for posterity.

In the 1940s and 1950s, televisions appeared in homes throughout the United States and other countries. The first episode of I Love Lucy was broadcast in 1951; Bob Hope moved his comedy show from radio to television in 1952, and NBC launched The Tonight Show in 1954. By the end of 1952, televisions were in use in 20 million households throughout the United States, and advertisers spent $288 million on television spots. By 1963, television superseded newspapers as a news source for the population. By 1965, 96 percent of NBC's programming was broadcast in color.[2]

Innovation continued at a rapid pace. In 1964, The Beatles appeared on the Ed Sullivan Show to over 73 million viewers; in 1969, the world watched as Neil Armstrong walked on the moon; and in the late 1970s and early 1980s, ESPN, MTV, and CNN were founded and began broadcasting. Satellite dishes appeared on the market in 1996; digital video disks (DVDs) were introduced in 2000; and in 2005, flat screen TVs appeared.

Broadcast innovations occurred parallel to this timeline of accomplishments, enabling the rise of technologies. Radios took advantage of AM and FM frequencies, while television used its own series. Satellite television worked off direct links to communications satellites, and cable depended on a vast network of copper. Later, optical cables were laid under streets, hung on poles, and stretched across oceans. Currently, mobile technologies depend on their innovative uses for different bandwidths, enabling ever faster and more stable connections.

Over 150 years of innovations have led us to an intersection of stable and fast communications, advanced technologies such as artificial intelligence (AI)/machine learning (ML) and augmented reality (AR)/virtual reality (VR), cloud infrastructures, the internet and web, and development tools. All these (and other) components now lay the foundation of the revolution known as The metaverse. The stage is now set for the quintessential transformation in entertainment. From a paradigm of predetermined, predefined, and centrally owned content to a new one consisting of reciprocal immersive that happens in real time, the result will be unprecedented.

Connecting through Entertainment

At first, it might appear that people want to be entertained to escape reality. It's true that many watch movies, read books, or play video games to relax after a hard day's work or to distract themselves from everyday life. Nevertheless, this is only one motivation.

Consider that people often view movies with their friends or build relationships with other players inside video game worlds. Many watch movies and television series not so much to escape, but so they have something in common with their friends—something in common to talk about. Many religiously follow their favorite long-running series such as *House of Dragon* or *Westworld* because their friends are doing so. Many people gather in groups to watch these series together and enjoy what can be likened to sitting around a campfire and telling each other ghost stories. Entertainment is, in many ways, a communal experience.

There is no doubt that people, in general, enjoy escapist experiences. Life can be monotonous, with insurmountable barriers, and the lure of seeing the newest movie with a group of friends can be tough to resist. Modern entertainment helps people momentarily escape reality. It gives them time to immerse themselves in a different world—in a book, film, song, or whatever else—and helps them get through their days.

It's easy to see why people will be attracted to the next step in entertainment—immersive realities. Spending time in a virtual world can help them overcome many of life's adversities. For example, consider the possibilities for a person with quadriplegia "walking" in a virtual world?

The COVID pandemic pushed many to expand their horizons by engaging with virtual worlds in games, classrooms, and even digital shows and concerts. In virtual worlds, if only briefly, people can escape the unwelcome news of the day—inflation, war, high gas prices, and the news on the pandemic. Media companies have immense potential to help people by creating new virtual, immersive encounters.

The real aptitudes of the metaverse are the ability to share inter-connectedness—to experience a story in real time and participate in those stories. People can become a part of the entertainment. They can also visit those virtual worlds with their friends, make new friends while there, form permanent social bonds that span metaverse worlds, and even continue their socialization outside in the physical world.

The metaverse allows for infinite entertainment possibilities; the only theoretical limit is the designers' and participants' imagination and ingenuity. Anything from historical walkthroughs, to African safaris, to a trip to the moon can be presented as entertainment within the metaverse.

How we get from here to a fully functional metaverse is still being established. Many large businesses are investing billions into enabling new forms of entertainment via the metaverse. They will succeed in creating this new forum for entertainment to provide an escape and a new social reality for everyone.

The impact of the metaverse on entertainment and its resulting impact on new business prospects cannot be overestimated. The following section covers some of the outcomes in greater detail.

The Metaverse and Entertainment

Before the impact of the metaverse can be understood, it's essential to look at the current media landscape. Hundreds of billions, if not trillions, of consumer dollars are at stake, and the competition for the attention of those consumers is intense. The businesses that succeed stand to grab much of that attention and the ability to define the direction of the metaverse of the near future.

As of the writing of this book, the entertainment industry is very much in flux. The old technologies of DVDs, Blu-rays, cable and network TV, and desktop computers are giving way to streaming movie services and mobile computing. In the past, the big names were NBC, CBS, ABC, and to a lesser extent PBS. These gave way to VHS and Betamax (and, later, DVD and Blu-ray), cable TV, the internet, and the personal computer. Now, these technologies are fading and, with a push from the pandemic, are giving way to the new giants of Netflix, Disney, Apple, HBO, Comcast, Hulu, and Amazon.

The metaverse does more than merge the physical and virtual worlds; it also brings together media and commerce in new and powerful ways. In the following sections, we will explore this in more detail.

Evolution of the Media

In the past hundred years, media evolved from radio, to broadcast television, to cable television, and finally to digitally delivered TV. Personal computing began with large, clunky, desktop machines such as the TRS-80 and Atari. These evolved over the decades into much more powerful desktop machines and video game consoles, and are being superseded by mobile devices such as smartphones, tablets, laptops, and even digital watches. People can now receive entertainment in the form of movies, games, music, and books wherever they happen to be and whenever they want.

Technology tends to evolve towards the biggest and best prospects for market penetration. These evolutions, and in some cases revolutions, create shifts in the marketplace. Innovative, quick, and nimble businesses survive; those who are sluggish to adapt to technology shifts tend to do poorly.

A case in point is the current expansion of the streaming market—with a dozen or so major contenders and hundreds of niche services offering specialized content for a targeted subset of consumers. How many services will consumers adopt? Or, will they become fatigued with the vast entertainment platforms and limit themselves to just a few contenders?

It is a contest in many ways between media giants, but it won't end in winner takes all. People will subscribe to multiple services and channels because each service has unique offerings. People will not necessarily unsubscribe from Netflix just because they've found something they like on Disney+. In other words, people may not spend less time on Netflix merely because of their new subscription to another service.

Nonetheless, people generally allocate a more-or-less fixed amount of free time to their life. Of course, vacations and events like the pandemic sometimes provide more free time. Yet, the time spent watching movies and being entertained is relatively fixed.

Those companies that use their streaming services as a component of a much larger plan will thrive. Think of it as using media to funnel people to other products and services. Consider Disney: their media service offers premium content, and due to their intellectual properties, such as the Marvel Cinematic Universe (MCU) and Star Wars, they have attracted an enormous audience. However, each series and movie within them are part of a much bigger plan to encourage people to purchase merchandise and visit their theme parks. Apple and Amazon use a similar approach—they use media to funnel consumers to other parts of their business.

Roku was the market leader for a decade, starting when it was launched in 2008; The Apple TV hardware was released in 2007, and the Fire TV device went to market in 2014 and is now the most popular device of its kind. In 2012, Amazon had a market share of around 20 percent, and iTunes stood at 70 percent. Today, their shares of the market are still roughly the same.[3]

There's no question that streaming services are producing a large variety of content. Before considering how this will intersect with the metaverse, let's look at how they distribute this content.

Content Distribution

It's imperative to comprehend that these trends are coming to a head now, partially due to the long lead times for deals. One of the explanations as to why this is happening right now is that there are long lead times to each deal cycle.

Deals must be initiated and negotiated years in advance of the time movies are aired in theaters, released on Blu-ray or DVD, and agreement deals on which streaming platform the IP is shown. Contracts involving multiple releases, as with the Marvel or Star Wars universes, require even more coordination and lead time. This doesn't even consider the time needed to implement all the associated deals, including merchandising, theme park features, promotions, and a bounty of other things that produce even more revenue. All media-producing companies have some form of planning and implementation cycle and the associated lead times.

To top this off, companies must race against the clock to get their products to market. Taking too long to get these movies and other forms of entertainment to consumers can cause viewers to look elsewhere, say on other streaming services, to fulfill their needs. This race to get to market is fundamental to the creation of entertainment.

How Important is the Race to Market?

If someone has subscribed of a streaming channel like Hulu for many years, does this keep them from subscribing to other media like Disney+ or Amazon Prime? If a streaming channel launches content weeks or months before other channels release their own, does that give them a competitive advantage?

Let's look at the release a movie sequel. Blockbuster movies such as *Independence Day* or *The Matrix Trilogy* are often followed by sequels. So, the thinking goes, the original was a hit, so how could a sequel fail? After all, if the time between the original and its sequel is too great, producers may find the audience has moved on. To a certain extent, the producers of the sequel to *The Matrix Trilogy* discovered this with their release of the fourth movie in 2021. The film underperformed, partially because the audience had moved on.

No doubt taking too long gives the competition the time to enter and dominate the market. A new streaming service needs to motivate consumers to subscribe; they must somehow differentiate themselves from other available services. One excellent method is to be the first to market. Consumers like continuity and at least some of them will remain when the other services become operational.

An enormous number of media still have not transitioned to video. It's common, especially with less popular movies, to discover that they never made the jump from VHS to DVD, much less any other digital media. These older or less popular entertainments are a gold mine of content that streaming services can pick up to give their subscribers unique and interesting content.

As the competition for streaming services settles down, which likely will occur in 2024 or 2025, the market should stabilize surrounding those services that provide quality content designed by consumers. At this point, the ability for new competitors to enter the marketplace becomes more complex, costly, and time-consuming.

When you think about the large streaming companies, does their motivation for entering the market matter? Some businesses like Disney+ focus on their intellectual property, while others like Apple and Amazon are more aligned with selling hardware, products, or other services and use streaming as a funnel.

Pricing

Producing new content is expensive, especially when shows such as Amazon's The Expanse, HBO's Rome, and Disney's MCU series lineup are considered. To attract audiences, streaming companies are funding shows with substantial amounts of special effects, well-known names, and established intellectual property (IP). These and other factors combine to increase content costs to new levels.

Furthermore, the strategy of many streaming services is to use movies as funnels into other areas of their business. Disney, for instance, sells merchandise, cruises, and tickets to theme parks, and all of these help promote their movies, series, publications, and over-all brand. Apple also appears to attract consumers to their overall ecosystem of products and services, and we can assume that Amazon wants to entice movie watchers to sample the other services of Prime.

Consequently, streaming services tend to be priced to attract viewers and not necessarily to turn a profit. More significant numbers of viewers mean more people experience not just the streaming service but can be converted to other revenue streams.

Content Spend

The streaming companies know they are in fierce competition for consumer attention. To gain their attention (and revenue), each provider spends unprecedented amounts on new shows. All content providers are budgeted to spend over $50 billion in 2022, although that number could hike much higher.

Streaming platforms must use their content to generate revenue. Part of this revenue results from the monthly streaming fees charged to consumers. Indirect revenue results from merchandising benefits, including people purchasing a cruise after watching Disney's *Jungle Cruise* movie, toys, games, and premium services.

At the time of this writing, the following lists how much the streaming platforms spent on content:

- *Disney.* In 2021, Disney spent $25 billion on content, anticipating spending $33 billion in 2022. These numbers include Hulu and releases in theaters. Their quarterly report states, "The increase is driven by higher spend to support our DTC [direct-to-consumer] expansion and generally assumes no significant disruptions to production due to COVID-19."[4] Disney+ had 129.8 million subscribers as of the end of 2021.

- *Netflix.* In 2021, this company spent about $17 billion on streaming.[5]

- *WarnerMedia.* This streaming company, which includes HBO Max, HBO, CNN, CNN+, Warner Bros, and Discovery+, plans to spend over $18 billion in 2022. Before the merger, Discovery+ claimed 22 million streaming subscribers. HBO Max and HBO have a combined subscriber count of 73.8 million subscribers.

- *Amazon Prime Video.* In 2021, Amazon spent about $13 billion on video and music. They claimed to have 200 million subscribers at the end of 2021.

- *Apple TV+.* In 2021, Apple spent about $6 billion on original content.[6] As of July 21, 2021, Apple+ had fewer than 20 million subscribers.[7]

Gaming

We've already reviewed gaming in detail, but it will be helpful to examine it in the context of entertainment. Gaming is a principal entertainment sector because it enables audience interactions and creates immersive connectedness. Many find it far more fulfilling to play with friends in a video game than watch a movie or streaming series. The experience is vastly different—games interact with players in ways other media cannot.

The volume of technologic advances that can be applied to gaming is regularly increasing. These advances create the potential for gaming to become much more innovative about how they interact with audiences and about how media, in general, is monetized.

Case in point, newer phone technology such as the iPhone 10 enables face tracking. This technology, in turn, makes it possible to create unique and interesting interactive engagements that account for players' gestures and facial expressions. If a player frowns, the NPCs within the game could react as if the player is angry without any other input.

When radio and television first appeared, only a few channels or stations existed. You could listen to or watch your favorite series at home or your neighbor's house. Cable television added even more channels, but you still had to view the content from a fixed location. Today, with mobile computing and fast wireless internet, games and entertainment can be experienced anyplace, at any time.

As of 2021, half of US homes had a gaming console, with 3 in 10 planning to buy one in the next year. Three out of four Americans played video games in 2021, and the average play time equaled to 14.8 hours per week in 2020. Gaming is also spread across the generations, from the younger Gen Z to older Baby Boomers. These trends accelerated during the pandemic, because many were forced to remain sheltered in their homes for extended periods.[8]

As we've postulated, many engage in gaming more for the social experience, with gameplay being a secondary reason for investing time and money. For this reason, multiplayer games have become exceedingly popular because they provide safe places for people to get together and enjoy the company of their friends.

The ever-changing media landscape, increasing competition, and accelerating technological advancements have created an environment where games have become the go-to entertainment form. These same factors create new chances for media giants to expand their streaming services to gain viewers and funnel them to additional revenue streams and markets.

As the platforms evolve, a substantial focus has been placed on the metaverse because people demand more immersive and exciting interactions. Humans have finite attention spans, constantly forcing entertainment to evolve into more powerful forms. Immersive storytelling is becoming the new gold standard. People enjoy being part of the story and interacting with heroes, villains, and worlds. This pressures traditional media, such as television and movies, to improve and evolve the quality of their products to continue attracting viewers. Although the future cannot be predicted, the trends are becoming more apparent; a fully immersive metaverse will be the ultimate form of immersive entertainment.

With all these changes in gaming and entertainment, are they merging into a combination of the two?

Game-tainment

Games and gaming mechanics have been popular on television going back decades, if not to the beginning of the media. Games like *Wheel of Fortune* or *The Price is Right* have been popular with viewers; many have followed the game exploits of popular winners on *Jeopardy* as they won night after night.

For many years, games and movies have influenced one another, each building audiences and providing content for the other. This trend is accelerating, and the pandemic gave it a significant boost as people were locked down and hungry for entertainment. As a result, entertainment companies are creating gaming services, and gaming companies are producing their entertainment.

Streaming giant Netflix is building its gaming unit and adapting its movies and shows into games. They plan to release *Castlevania*, *League of Legends*, *The Witcher*, and other series into games.[9] When co-founder and co-CEO Reed Hastings explained his vison for Netflix's gaming platform to CNBC, he said, "When mobile gaming is world-leading, and we're some of the best producers, like where we are in film today, having two of the top ten, then you should ask what's next. Let's nail the thing and not just be in it for the sake of being in it."[10]

Gaming companies are also investing in this area. In January 2022, the global sports betting and gaming company Entain launched Ennovate, investing $133 million to use as funding for applications for NFTs, VR/AR, and other startups and applications. CEO Jette Nygaard-Andersen told CNBC that gaming companies are broadening their customer offerings. He said, "We want to lead the way with new, exciting products and experiences for customers and use our cutting-edge technology to pioneer innovations in sport, gaming, and interactive entertainment for the metaverse"[11]

In an investor presentation in early 2022, Sony proclaimed plans to acquire or invest in 10 gaming, communications, and other gaming-related companies. These include Discord, Housemarque, Nixxes, Firesprirt, Bluepoint, Devolver, Valkyrie Entertainment, Bungie, Haven, and Accelbyte. Sony CFO Hiroki Totoki noted after the news was publicized that they want to further expand its technology and media offering across Sony's electronics products, gaming, film, and music. TechCrunch quoted him saying:

> The strategic significance of this acquisition lies not only in obtaining the highly successful Destiny franchise, as well as major new IP Bungie is currently developing but also incorporating into the Sony group the expertise and technologies Bungie has developed in the live game services space.[12]

These investments and startups promise to widen the breadth of entertainment in the metaverse. Gaming, sports events, concerts, sports betting, and more will no longer be standalone worlds all to themselves. Instead, they will unify into a rich tapestry of entertainment options.

Think about the Las Vegas strip as an illustration of the entertainment possibilities of the metaverse. After donning a VR headset and other gaming gear, individuals will be able to walk through a virtual world, perhaps along a street, and be presented with options such as casinos, theaters, theme parks, shops, concerts, movie theaters, and about anything else that can be imagined.

Theme parks based in the metaverse will allow guests to visit anywhere in the world or a fantasy world and experience entertainment as extreme or as tame as they desire. A theme park could include complex, gravity-defying roller coasters, re-enactments of historical events, very frightening haunted mansions, and even hikes on the mountains of Mars or planets orbiting far-away stars.

The metaverse offers many prospects for sports betting, competitive entertainment, and casino-type familiarities. Imagine a virtual wrestling match allowing anyone (i.e., their avatars) to participate. Those who don't want to wrestle on a virtual stage can then bet on the outcomes. People can use their cryptocurrencies to bet on horse races, baseball games, casino games, and even private card games. The possibilities for betting and competition are virtually endless.

In 2012, a holographic rendition of Tupac Shakur performed at Coachella, even though he had died a decade before. This holographic concert took place in the physical world, as a 3D image of the performer was simply projected on a glass panel. Holographic performances have increased in popularity since that time.

Concerts held within the metaverse, also known as virtual concerts, are more like a live show in that audience members attend in mass and can interact with one another. For example, Scott Travis performed in Fortnite, interacting with audience members (via their avatars). He moved around various scenes, such as underwater and outer space, to keep the performance engaging.[13]

For metaverse travelers, the shopping experience will also be an inimitable and attention-grabbing experience. Imagine shopping in a store that changes frequently and is personalized to each shopper's needs. Simultaneously, someone who is interested in home-building supplies could be presented with an entirely different layout and product set than another person interested in clothing or books. Metaverse stores will become almost living things in that they react to shoppers, change based on their needs, and can present artistic or action points where needed. Sky Canaves, a senior analyst at Insider Intelligence, reinforces how the metaverse shopping experience will not have the constraints within the physical world, stating, "The concept of a virtual store that's just a replica of a real-world store is not terribly exciting because there's no need to be bound by four walls or a specific location in the digital world."[14]

Music, explicitly attending concerts and shows, is traditionally a shared experience. People typically go to these types of events with their friends so they can enjoy the experience together. The constraints in the physical universe no longer limit virtual concerts. Imagine any imaginative Cirque du Soleil shows being presented in the metaverse. Currently, these shows are determined by the physical strengths of the actors, the weight and bulk of the stage and props, and the audience's position in relation to the show. All these constraints would vanish if these shows were presented in the metaverse.

People can experience things like never before in a virtual show or concert. They could have imaginative adventures, such as boarding a rocket ship to the moon or a planet, hang gliding, seeing and hearing fantastic animals and plants that don't exist in real life, or even being a passenger on a virtual cruise ship.

In December 2021, Sawhorse Productions and Alo Yago collaborated to create a virtual sanctuary in Roblox. They wanted to create a virtual space that felt outside the real world but still resembled Alo Yago stores. In the virtual world, people enter using an avatar and enjoy a more fantastic yet grounded shopping experience.

Such mixing is not new. Roblox is putting the pieces together in a new and unique way. For instance, they combine a virtual concert with a video game and add to the social experience.

The mix of gaming and entertainment creates new and exciting ways for people to play and be entertained. They can engage in activities that only existed in the imagination. In the end, gaming will become immersive entertainment. Traditional types of entertainment will merge into gaming and the metaverse.

As such, the metaverse has a tremendous impact on the entertainment industry.

Impacts of the Metaverse on the Entertainment Industry

The metaverse promises to have as great an impact on the entertainment industry as the transition from silent films to sound had. If that seems like an exaggeration, think of the revolutionary change from watching a movie in a theater or a television screen to an immersive experience of a world. Consider that, instead of watching a super-hero movie, a person could be present in that world and even become one of their heroes in the virtual world.

If that sounds like a video game, the concepts are similar, only raised to a new level. Inside the virtual worlds of the metaverse, people can move their avatar from world to world, purchase items they can use elsewhere, visit a virtual bank, or even watch a virtual concept. And, unlike a movie, the viewer is inside the experience, with perceptions such as sight, sound, and touch. Video games might be the entranceway to the metaverse, but the metaverse is a whole new thing.

Your movie-watching experience will be heightened to entirely new levels. Instead of merely watching actors and computer generated imagery (CGI) on a theater or television screen, people will be able to immerse themselves in the movie world in full 360×360 vision. They could even stop the movie to get behind-the-scenes commentary or explanations of how things were done. Suppose that if a person were viewing a film about Alexander the Great, they could branch off to virtually visit the locations and cities as they existed back in ancient times. The possibilities are endless.

New forms of entertainment will result from the development of the metaverse. People will be able to create their games and worlds, then share them with others. Bands can create virtual tours that allow an infinite number of viewers and that can be replayed for years afterward. NFTs provide countless ways to merchandise the entertainment experience, and businesses will be able to advertise within virtual worlds in numerous new and interesting ways.

The metaverse presents a new and captivating potential for marketers and advertisers to offer their products and services to viewers. Advertisers will be able to create immersive moments centered around their products. Imagine a virtual clothing store that allows patrons to try on new clothes and makeup, or even see how they would look with a tattoo.

One result of the metaverse is raising the bar for content creators. Instead of just making and advertising a movie, content creators will need to create a wider variety of content to attract viewers and listeners. This creates new windows for creativity, but it will also increase the work required for any new release.

User Generated Content is another opportunity that is reinforced by the metaverse. Suppose that content creators like bands give their fans the ability to create music videos and sing along with the music. This could increase the fans' engagement, giving them additional incentives to follow the band.

Persistence is vital to the metaverse—meaning the world doesn't stop when someone is not inside the metaverse. On the contrary, everything continues in real time. Irrespectively, if a person leaves the metaverse to sleep or eat, time will keep flowing and things will continue happening.

It's also possible to associate an NFT with a real-world item. Suppose a person purchases an outfit in the physical universe with an associated NFT. They could then wear this same clothing in a virtual format within the metaverse. In the same way, content acquired in one world of the metaverse should work within any other world.

The Metaverse's Impact on Streaming

Streaming is and will continue to present significant evolution to the movie and entertainment industries. In the early days of television, the options were far more straightforward: you created a movie or show, advertised it in advance, then hoped viewers would show up at the scheduled time to see it.

Later, cable augmented the number of channels to hundreds of specialized outlets, and theaters continued to operate because there were not many options to reach audiences. The advent of VHS and Betamax, DVD, and Blu-ray changed everything, by allowing people to record and keep copies of their favorite entertainment at home. The rollout of fast internet to most households, and later to smartphones and other mobile devices, changed entertainment yet again.

The entertainment industry is again being disrupted by the proliferation of streaming services. This results in a surge of mergers and acquisitions, research and development (R&D) activities, and partnerships as technology companies and media giants try to position themselves for this new distribution method. Many of these services also position themselves towards the metaverse by ensuring their portfolio includes the necessary technology.[15]

Major companies that are involved in the proliferation of streaming and the build-out of the metaverse include the following:

- Adobe systems
- AdQuire Media
- Alphabet
- Aomen City
- Atom Universe
- Gamefam
- GameOn
- Hungama Digital Media
- Meta
- Microsoft
- Nvidia
- OverActive Media
- Qualcomm

- Roblox
- Scuti
- Snap
- Tetavi
- Zilliqa

Many of these companies are also investing deeply into the metaverse. Some examples with notes on what they envision accomplishing are listed next:

Hungama Digital Media. In 2022, this Indian entertainment company announced the creation of a new company called Hefty Entertainment, which is intended to be a metaverse platform powered by Polygon. This platform is focused on DAO and is designed to create what is expected to be the world's most extensive entertainment collective. The platform will onboard consumers, fans, and communities into Web3 using collectible NFTs and free virtual events to encourage them to use the service.[16]

Qualcomm. In early 2022, Qualcomm announced it was creating a $100 million fund to be used to provide financial support to metaverse-related foundational technologies and content rapport. They've named it the "SnapDragon Metaverse Fund" and intend to extend grants to creators of extended reality engagements, including gaming, health, media, entertainment, education, and enterprise. They also stated they would support AI and AR systems.[17]

OverActive Media. Also, in early 2022, global sports, media, and entertainment company, OverActive Media announced it was forming a partnership with Zilliqa, which provides eco-friendly, high-performance, secure blockchain solutions. With this partnership, OverActive Media's MAD Lions brand will be able to deliver brand activations that will be enhanced in the digital realm.[18]

GameOn Entertainment Technologies Inc. This leading NFT game technology company partnered with Tetavi in March 2022 to implement an NFT music discovery game that leverages GameOn's blockchain capabilities.[19]

Delivering Entertainment in the Metaverse

People now consume content very differently than they did in the past. The pandemic accelerated an evolving scene whereby people demanded streaming services that host their preferred content on any device they chose to use, especially mobile systems like smartphones.

Unity and Insomniac joined forces to deliver content and interchange to people as well as increasing access to content creators. They also desire to provide more choices for socialization so people have more ability to work and play together. One of the partnership goals is to deliver a persistent metaverse world, allowing people to attend virtual events anytime and anywhere. Peter Moore, Senior Vice President and General Manager, Sports & Live Entertainment at Unity, explained the partnership by saying, "The work with Insomniac is all about a mixture of AR, VR, mixed reality, and green screen motion capture. Having that all coming to play to create an in-home festival experience."[20]

Volumetric capture, a method that uses several cameras to allow movement in 3D, is a primary focus of Unity. Moore shared:

> That's really the next level; getting into the third dimension of entertainment and being able to look around on the six degrees of freedom. For a long time, we've just sat in the audience and watched as it washes over us. I think the future is being on the stage. That propels us into a sense of immersion that we've never had before.[20]

Moore also predicted there would be the same kind of development for eSports. He further elaborated:

> How do we get inside the game more? How do we start watching the game from the inside? Currently, it's just passive cameras on the teams. How do you get more immersed in what's going on? How do you listen in? How do you sit next to them? That's something you could do with a volumetric camera rig.[20]

Unity believes entertainment and eSports offer great options for enhancement and disruption. They believe the development of innovative engagements will attract people to events so they can experience things in ways that are undreamed of.

Not only is the metaverse changing these areas, but it is also strongly affecting the music industry as well.

The Metaverse is Disrupting the Music Industry

Music artists have seen the value of the metaverse and are leading the way in this new technology. They understand that NFTs and the metaverse give them new ways to create revenue and additional methods to reach their fans and promote their content. Elizabeth Moody, General Counsel at entertainment law firm Granderson Des Rochers, LLP, remarked on how the metaverse is opening new channels for musicians, stating, "What's exciting is watching the artists become excited about the space. I think that the creators and the performers in the music industry will lead the bigger companies into the space."[21]

These new options require more complex licensing agreements and more complicated music rights. Adding music to games, virtual concerts, and even shopping events is technically straightforward, but agreements must be made with the rights owners.

Moore went further:

> There's a little bit of a push-pull right now, in terms of who's going to share the dollars. There's only so much money that a fan is going to spend, and the artists should be getting most of that, especially if it's a live performance... But of course, all the gaming development work that's happening is expensive. And the gamers need to see a piece of that, as well as the record labels and music publishers, so there's a tension right now to work out new business models.[20]

Additionally, fans can contribute directly to the creative process—fans can appear in music videos and can help create music. Many content creators are purposely building in occasions for their fans to collaborate on their art creation.

Shara Senderoff, President/Partner of venture fund Raised In Space, said that many artists "see the level that other artists are pushing the envelope on utility and engagement and what that really means, I think those earlier artists who dipped their toe in with just minimal offerings will really step up their game."[21]

Virtual clubbing is another phenomenon that's becoming popular in the emerging metaverse. These are literally virtual representations of real-world clubs where people, or their avatars, can dance, socialize, and listen to music. Because they are based in a virtual world, these clubs can be very imaginative, with a Martian or fantasy world landscape, and are limited only by the imagination of the club's creators.[22]

The Metaverse is a Great Place to Promote Your Business

As quantified throughout this book, the metaverse is designed to be an immersive experience that can be explored and encourages interaction. The metaverse is growing exponentially as more companies and individuals create new and exciting technologies and creations. It is truly a new world begging to be explored. It is safe to say the metaverse will define the future of entertainment.

When we say the metaverse is immersive, we mean that people can interact with each other. They can view one another, talk to each other, and even feel the touch of others. They can sense the world around them in full wrap-around 3D with all the relevant sights and sounds. As the technology for the metaverse evolves, these instances will become increasingly lifelike.

Nonetheless, the metaverse is useful for far more than just entertainment. It is also the perfect avenue for education—offering the ability to hold a conversation with a virtual Julius Caesar or General Patton. Forensic experts use it to help recreate crime scenes and solve cold cases. Social betterment programs can create venues for virtual concerts or other attractions to raise awareness and funds. The possibilities are almost endless.

Because the metaverse is relatively new and still evolving, many employment and exploration capabilities exist. The metaverse encourages creativity in new and exciting ways because it is so malleable—it's virtual and not physical, it's easy to adjust and change.

Like video games, the metaverse encourages people to socialize and be with others. It's a great place to meet new people, form new relationships, and make friends. You can meet people from all over the world without leaving the comfort of your home.

The metaverse also offers many prospects for earning income. People can create content, build new worlds, open virtual clubs and shops, sell virtual items, and even run entire businesses.

To top that off, the metaverse can be used to promote a business— even one based in the physical world. This can be done with subtle product placements, prominent virtual billboards, or even substantial floating zeppelins that travel through the virtual world, advertising your brand.[23]

Brands in the Metaverse

People are already experiencing the metaverse, even though it is relatively young and is still being developed. Of course, brands follow people, so as more people use and play in the metaverse, more brands will find moments to reach out to this emerging consumer base. In other words, brands follow eyeballs (i.e., a term for people viewing content). Brands crave attention—its core purpose is to create awareness—and as people move to the metaverse, the brands will be close behind.

These brands will use virtual sporting events, concerts, movies, and other forms of entertainment to promote their products, services, and businesses. The metaverse is a new world; as people come together to socialize, the brands will become more and more interested.

Communal Storytelling vs. One-to-Many Approach

As much as we explain the changing media landscape, treating the metaverse the same as any other platform or media would be a mistake. Instead, the metaverse is new and unique, and the way for brands to succeed within it is by finding and creating new benefits and realities. They must experiment in meaningful ways, and because the metaverse is infinitely configurable, they can take chances and, occasionally, fail, and then learn from that failure.

The metaverse is unlike any existing traditional media platform we've seen before, because brands can now experiment quickly and meaningfully within its platforms. For instance, activating brands in the metaverse can leverage 3D multiplayer environments to co-create communal storytelling, instead of the traditional one-to-many approach. The metaverse will move us from a brand monolog to an immersive dialog.

Intellectual Property

The metaverse is being implemented by the world's largest media and technology companies. Names such as Microsoft, Adobe, and Meta, are investing billions and hundreds of billions of dollars. Many of these worlds in the metaverse will be operated and run by these large businesses. And, because people are spending more time in the metaverse (which will only increase), it will create a flywheel effect of attracting more content creators and brands, which inevitably will introduce new questions about how intellectual property is handled in the future.

It's important to understand that the metaverse is the new frontier for entertainment of all types, including music, live performances, movies, sporting events, and theater. It can be expected that the same kinds (and different) issues with privacy, security, and intellectual property theft will occur there.

Content creators, publishers, labels, and studios will be looking for ways to maximize their profits and the offerings from the metaverse. How will they enforce their content's rights within the metaverse and the real world? Will their content rights convert between the virtual and real worlds? How will they be implemented and who will do the enforcement? Other questions might also evolve around how royalties should be calculated and distributed.

Interoperability

A critical requirement for a functional metaverse is that everything works together. In particular, people can go to any website on the internet without worrying if it will display correctly or function as needed. Internet and web standards ensure that everything works together and is more-or-less the same, which is known as interoperability. The metaverse depends on content interoperability, including everything from avatars, to NFTs, to any other content. This means if a person buys clothing in one world in the metaverse, they can wear it to a virtual concert, a game, or anywhere else they desire.

Forecast for Entertainment in the Metaverse

According to TechNavio, the market share for entertainment within the metaverse is forecasted to increase to $26.92 billion by 2026, with the Compound Annual Growth Rate (CAGR) accelerating at 8.55 percent. It is estimated that in 2022, this saw a 7.41 percent year-over-year growth rate. Consumer spending continues to rise based on consumers' attraction to virtual concerts and events.[24]

In-Vehicle Experiences

It shouldn't be a surprise that automobile manufacturers are also looking for ways they can enhance the in-car experience for drivers and passengers via the metaverse. Currently, many companies are integrating augmented reality (AR) into automobile GPS systems, by displaying symbols on the viewscreen showing what's happening in the front of the car. Arrows may be displayed, offering directions to steer and off-ramp locations. Potential hazards like potholes, possible collisions, and bicycles may also be displayed as animated overlays on the viewscreen.

The metaverse offers many possibilities to keep passengers entertained while in vehicles. Gaming mechanisms may be installed in seats, to allow games to be played on screens in front of each passenger. Advertisers who show targeted ads during game or movie play might also subsidize some of these features.[25]

When united with self-driving cars, which many predict will be deployed within a few short years, the metaverse promises in-car experiences that can relieve the drudgery of trips, help with navigation, allow shopping, in addition to a wide variety of other possibilities. This will provide countless instances for brands to engage with consumers in a fun and entertaining way. Typifying this is metaverse Entertainment, a division of Netmarble, which recently partnered with Hyundai Motor Group to create and leverage virtual celebrities, known as *digital humans*. Netmarble virtual celebrity Lina contracted with Sublime Artist Agency in 2022 to promote entertainment.

Art in the Metaverse

As concluded earlier in this chapter, collaboration and co-creation are significant components of metaverse's entertainment. The metaverse will thrive because of the community spirit. People will want to socialize there because that's where they'll find new friends and connect with their old ones. By enabling shared social interactions, the metaverse enriches the lives of people all over the world.

The metaverse will become a bastion of art, bringing humanity, ethics, values, and perspectives to light so they can be contemplated and understood. Because these exchanges occur in a virtual universe, anything is possible; art will prosper like never before. Yet, in the metaverse, physical constraints will not limit art. Instead, art will be able to represent anything imaginable, regardless of if it obeys physical laws or is even physically possible.

Summary

Radical change can be seen emerging through several metaverse use cases, including NFTs, gaming, and entertainment, especially now that media, technology, and entertainment are converging and contributing to the metaverse. Because of this, businesses are moving beyond the theoretical to the practical—they are now collectively investing hundreds of billions of dollars to acquire or build platforms they need to prosper, creating new entertainment models in the process for the coming age of the metaverse. Streamline Media Group's CEO and co-founder Alexander Fernandez reinforced this by saying:

> The lines between media, entertainment, technology, and video games have converged into the metaverse. Now is the time to build a sustainable structure around it that progresses the evolution of business models and welcomes more people, voices, and talent to shape it.[26]

As we've seen, the metaverse offers an unlimited variety of possibilities for individual creators and businesses to leverage entertainment to connect with consumers, create new revenue streams, and supercharge marketing. Gaming technology has laid the groundwork by supporting multiple players, persistence, and real-time gaming worlds. These concepts will support and enhance the continuing advancement of the metaverse, providing new ways to deliver consumer and business value.

Streamline's founder, Fernandez, goes on to say it's clear that entertainment in the metaverse will be a prompt for consumer expectations and attention to continue to evolve:

> Digital transformation has arrived, and video game technology is the infrastructure that will bring immersive interactive interactions to every aspect of life. It will open new latitude for product discovery, commerce, virtual coworking, education, and social interactivity. Welcome to the metaverse.[26]

Ultimately, the metaverse will provide very human and entertaining exchanges that serve to make people lead happier, smarter, and better lives with a deep sense of purpose and fulfillment. Everything good about humanity will be amplified and enhanced by the metaverse. Similarly, companies will perform well, simply by doing well in the metaverse.

Case in point, let's take a look at how digital fashion is having a profound effect on digital identity in the next chapter.

Notes

1   History. First Commercial Movie Screened, www.history.com/this-day-in-history/first-commercial-movie-screened (archived at https://perma.cc/A6BU-H4QD)

2   Johnson Hur. History of the Television, bebusinessed.com/history/history-of-the-television/ (archived at https://perma.cc/B5WM-GVSN)

3   statista. n.d. *statista*, statista.com/statistics/1171132/global-connected-tv-devices-streaming-market-share-by-platform/ (archived at https://perma.cc/LVT2-CCTG)

4   Tony Maglio. From Disney to Peacock: Here's What the Top 7 Streamers Will Spend on Content in 2022, 8 May 2022, www.indiewire.com/2022/03/streaming-wars-content-spend-disney-netflix-hbo-paramount-1234703867/ (archived at https://perma.cc/8679-2C7V)

5   Paul Ausick. What's Up with Apple: Spending on Streaming Content, Trouble in Korea, and More." 30 December 2021, 247wallst.com/technology-3/2021/12/30/whats-up-with-apple-spending-on-streaming-content-trouble-in-korea-and-more/ (archived at https://perma.cc/44EN-4L5X)

6   Tony Maglio. Who Is Winning the Streaming Wars? Subscribers by the Numbers, 16 March 2022, www.indiewire.com/2022/03/how-many-subscribers-netflix-disney-plus-peacock-amazon-prime-video-1234705515/ (archived at https://perma.cc/UD92-2ZPR)

7   Time Spent Playing Video Games Continues to Rise, 26 October 2021, www.marketingcharts.com/cross-media-and-traditional/videogames-traditional-and-cross-channel-118663 (archived at https://perma.cc/3QSZ-X7TB)

8   Microsoft News Center. Microsoft to Acquire Activision Blizzard to Bring the Joy and Community of Gaming to Everyone, Across Every Device, 18 January 2022, news.microsoft.com/2022/01/18/microsoft-to-acquire-activision-blizzard-to-bring-the-joy-and-community-of-gaming-to-everyone-across-every-device/ (archived at https://perma.cc/X6KD-6NKN)

9   Shannon Liao. Amid losses, Netflix Bets on a Bold Strategy around Video Games, 22 April 2022, www.washingtonpost.com/video-games/2022/04/22/netflix-video-games/ (archived at https://perma.cc/UG7W-ABJU)

10 Alex Sherman. Netflix and Microsoft Show That Video Gaming Has Become Too Big for Tech Giants to Ignore." 21 January 2022, www.cnbc.com/2022/01/21/netflix-and-microsoft-show-video-gaming-has-become-too-big-to-ignore.html (archived at https://perma.cc/C7TR-NP8P)

11 Contessa Brewer. Global Gaming Company Entain Looks to Compete in Metaverse, immersive Entertainment, 30 January 2022, www.cnbc.com/2022/01/30/entain-looks-to-compete-in-gambling-in-metaverse-immersive-gambling.html (archived at https://perma.cc/2T6W-837A)

12 Taylor Hatmaker. After Buying Bungie, Sony Goes All in on Live Service Games, 26 May 2022 techcrunch.com/2022/05/26/sony-live-service-bungie-destiny/ (archived at https://perma.cc/WTZ5-4N6K)

13 Makena Rasmussen. Touring the Musical Metaverse: Virtual Concerts Are Here to Stay, 7 September 2021, www.virtualhumans.org/article/touring-the-musical-metaverse-virtual-concerts-are-here-to-stay (archived at https://perma.cc/45GZ-RB56)

14 Queenie Wong. Shopping in the Metaverse Could Be More Fun Than You Think, 23 March 2022, www.cnet.com/tech/computing/features/shopping-in-the-metaverse-could-be-more-fun-than-you-think/ (archived at https://perma.cc/FA49-YZSM)

15 Kevin Westcott and Jana Arbanas. Can Streaming Video Survive the Metaverse? 29 March 2022, fortune.com/2022/03/29/streaming-tv-movies-metaverse-entertainment-industry/ (archived at https://perma.cc/LNU4-LSEW)

16 e-DAO Spearheads Media & Entertainment Web3 Revolution: Hungama Entertainment and Hindustan Talkies become anchor partners, 23 February 2022, www.globenewswire.com/en/news-release/2022/02/23/2390726/0/en/e-DAO-Spearheads-Media-Entertainment-Web3-Revolution-Hungama-Entertainment-and-Hindustan-Talkies-become-anchor-partners.html (archived at https://perma.cc/WD6M-GKLX)

17 Catherine Sbeglia Nin. Qualcomm Announces $100 Million Metaverse Fund, 22 March 2022, rcrwireless.com/20220322/business/qualcomm-announces-100-million-metaverse-fund%EF%BF%BCQualcomm announces $100 million metaverse fund (archived at https://perma.cc/5ZJ2-45FW)

18 Overactive Media Enters the Metaverse with a Multi-Year Zilliqa Partnership, 2 March 2022, overactive-media-group.prezly.com/overactive-media-enters-the-metaverse-with-a-multi-year-zilliqa-partnership (archived at https://perma.cc/6TWX-DLUS)

19 GameOn Partners with Tetavi to Launch Innovative NFT Music Discovery Game, 24 March 2022, www.globenewswire.com/news-release/2022/03/24/2409250/0/en/GameOn-Partners-With-Tetavi-to-Launch-Innovative-NFT-Music-Discovery-Game.html (archived at https://perma.cc/VMA8-PSZL)

20 Tyrone Stewart. Delivering Entertainment in the Metaverse, newdigitalage.co/technology/unity-metaverse-virtual-augmented-reality-insomniac-events/ (archived at https://perma.cc/6DWU-P9A7)

21 Victoria Copans. 3 Ways the Metaverse Is Disrupting the Music Industry, 24 November 2021, www.xliveglobal.com/fan-experience/3-ways-metaverse-disrupting-music-industry (archived at https://perma.cc/YDL7-JKN5)

22 Clara McMichael. I Went Clubbing in the Metaverse, and It Wasn't What I Expected, 2 May 2022, www.digitaltrends.com/news/clubbing-festivals-in-metaverse/ (archived at https://perma.cc/G87E-7KFY)

23 Mujahid Ali. 10 Reasons to Get into the Metaverse Entertainment Industry, 8 April 2022, www.scoopearth.com/10-reasons-to-get-into-the-metaverse-entertainment-industry/#The_Metaverse_Provides_a_more_Immersive_and_Social_Experience_than_Traditional_Media_Platforms (archived at https://perma.cc/4US9-X2H2)

24 Metaverse in Entertainment Market by End-User and Geography—Forecast and Analysis 2022–2026, May 2022, www.technavio.com/report/metaverse-in-entertainment-market-industry-analysis (archived at https://perma.cc/LB4S-ETRV)

25 Emilio Campa. How the Metaverse Could Disrupt the In-Car Experience, 9 April 2022, venturebeat.com/2022/04/09/how-the-metaverse-could-disrupt-the-in-car-experience/ (archived at https://perma.cc/S738-7ZWX)

26 Rebecca Oi. Will the Metaverse Encapsulate the Future of Digital Entertainment? 20 September 2021, techwireasia.com/2021/09/the-dawn-of-the-future-of-interaction-the-metaverse/ (archived at https://perma.cc/C75N-M2SR)

07 >Digital Fashion_

Digital clothing, as the name implies, doesn't exist in the physical universe. Instead, it's fashion that exists within metaverse, games, and digital social events. These clothes are not made of cloth, don't take up space in your home's closet, and don't require a tailor to fix a missing button. Instead, these clothes are made up of pixels and data. Technologies like 3D graphics, artificial intelligence (AI), augmented reality (AR)/virtual reality (VR), amongst others are these garments' components.

In digital worlds, clothing shops can be discovered as people browse for clothing. In some shops, people can generate clothing that they add to a picture of themselves. They can even consult with 3D designers (i.e., human or AI bots) who perfectly fit the clothing onto their image. Inside a game, they can buy clothing for their avatar in a theme suitable for that gaming world. An increasing number of games allow these articles of clothing to move between games operated by or outside the same company.

In this chapter, we'll elaborate about six use cases for digital fashion. These are abridged here.

Digital fashion for avatars. People can purchase digital fashion for their avatars in games and digital malls. Currently, these fashions are not easily movable to other worlds and games. Notwithstanding, as the metaverse evolves, there will be more interoperability, meaning that digital clothing will be usable between games and other worlds.

Fashion show events. The fashion industry is increasingly moving into the virtual world. Companies like Decentraland host digital catwalk shows, after parties, and other immersive experiences to celebrate their fashion. People will be able to show off their digital clothing in these digital showcases.

Digital fashion for persistent e-commerce. Further out as the metaverse is implemented on a broad level, the digital fashion that people purchase will be transferable to other worlds. For instance, the clothing purchased in a digital fashion shop will be usable in video games, fashion events, and even reproduced for general day-to-day use in the physical world.

Immersive shopping experience. Digital fashion creates opportunities for implementing immersive shopping experiences. Hence, instead of simply navigating through pages on a website, a consumer can walk through aisles in a simulated store to choose the clothing and items they want to purchase.

AR and VR usage for trying on clothing in the real world. An emerging use case is the ability for people to use smart mirrors and other technologies to "try on" clothing and makeup, namely, before a purchase. Consequently, people can see themselves wearing glasses, makeup, shoes, and other clothing in their digital mirror before they spend any money.

Augmented reality (AR)/extended reality (XR) fashion in the real world. Remember the Pokémon game, where people could use their smartphones to "see" Pokémons in the real world? Carry that forward a few years, and technology advances, glasses, and contact lenses will include the ability to overlay images against what people see. Accordingly, people could digitally change their hair color, and anyone with those special glasses or lenses would see the new color. The same can be done with any type of fashion and accessories.

Reviewing What We Know So Far

We are now halfway through the book; before we proceed and to better understand digital fashion in the metaverse, let's do a quick recap of what we have covered. Currently, there are many different game and entertainment platforms. Many of these platforms in their current state are a walled garden, meaning what happens in one world does not necessarily translate into others. Over the coming years, the barriers between these worlds will relax as the metaverse is implemented. Some obstacles might still exist, however, because differences will exist between the worlds. Yet items, avatars, and fashion items will be transferrable. In other words, these worlds are precursors to what's yet to come in the future of the metaverse.

Additional platforms such as Decentraland are growing in popularity, increasing their market share and value. As all these cyber worlds mature, many will build in new technologies and features that allow people to do the same things they did in the physical world and now in the metaverse. For example, it will become increasingly common for individuals to visit clubs or shows in computer-generated worlds like the physical world.

The ideal end-state for the metaverse is to become an immersive experience that takes on a reality of its own. People will enter the metaverse to play, do business, engage in commerce, and socialize. Additionally, emerging technologies and business models will interlink these environments so they are interoperable and can be delivered on a large variety of different devices.

It should be critically noted that implementing the metaverse is not entirely dependent on Web3, blockchain, or crypto economic systems to operate. Yet, Web3 is critical to realizing the metaverse's full potential. Many vendors are developing other technologies, including Microsoft Mesh, Meta Presence, and NVIDIA Omniverse, that use complimentary technologies to enable the metaverse.

Ownership is a central feature of Web 3.0 and the metaverse because it gives users control of the digital properties they create and purchase. These include metaverse-based clothing, shoes, avatars, art, skins, and a wide variety of other content. Because the content created by users is based on blockchain and NFTs, it is not stored on a central server. These features are destined to become decentralized, persistent, and live in real time.

A whole new generation of customer experiences will be realized by implementing the metaverse. Many of these possibilities were considered only science fiction and even fantasy just a few years ago, but now they can be achieved within the metaverse. Anything that can be imagined can be accomplished directly, in a game or social world or another yet-to-be-created magical world as the metaverse continues to mature.

Many video gamers and visitors to social worlds are already spending real money on assets purchased within game worlds. They use these items to decorate their avatars, furniture, property, and so forth or to be used as tools or weapons. This trend will increase as visitors to these and other worlds will want to enhance their explorations and fantasies. Additionally, once such items become easily transferable between worlds, this trend will accelerate even more.

Due to significant investments in the technologies needed for immersive experiences, social experiences and social media platforms are poised to become dominant players in the metaverse as it evolves. Some social media companies are investing billions, or even tens of billions, of dollars per year in these technologies.

How We Got Here

Digital fashion began to emerge in the early 2000s with games and social platforms like Final Fantasy, The Sims, and Second Life, among others.[1] Before that, players applied skins to their characters, which was a straightforward way to change their avatar's texture color. As video games grew to be more complex and competitive, game manufacturers added the ability to change clothing, makeup, hairstyles, and accessories. It wasn't until around 2015 that game companies began selling accessories to players using microtransactions.

Scarlett Yang, a digital fashion designer, stated, "There's more creative freedom in the digital [realm], there are no constraints, no gravity."[2]

People want to look their best, especially in a social situation, and gamers are no exception. Gamers want their avatars to reflect their identity, whether that means being outfitted in a way to fit a particular role or in some fanciful costume that defies the laws of physics. The same standards hold for people who "walk" around a web-based shopping mall or socialize in a simulated club.

Jo-Ashley Robert, an associate producer for Dead by Daylight who oversees the creation of characters and cosmetics, offered, "It's a new trend, but it's not a trend that's going to die; it's only getting more popular. For players, it's a type of expression and immersion. By dressing your character how you want, it pushes the imagination a little further."[3]

Digital fashion includes everything from head to toe of a character, comprising of the following:

Footwear. These can include custom socks, sneakers, high-heel shoes, and any other type of imaginable footwear. Gamers can outfit their character with armor for their assorted footwear.

Clothing. Any clothing type that can be imagined can be designed and sold within virtual games and social platforms. The choices range from plain t-shirts and jeans to fantastic science fiction and fantasy outfits.

Hairstyles. Computational characters can receive different hairstyles, from standard haircuts to elaborate styling.

Makeup. Of course, no outfit would be complete without makeup and accessories, including jewelry and watches.

Avatar. An avatar can be designed to take on any form, from a hulking monster, to an intellectual librarian, to a space traveler.

Digital fashion is improving rapidly, with higher quality and more available choices. One aspect of this improvement can be seen with microtransactions—small transactions performed within a game or computerized world, further enabling digital fashion as it continues to accelerate.

The digital fashion trend is progressively attracting the fashion and beauty industry. Several fashion companies such as The Fabricant, DressX, and the Dematerialised are fully involved in digitalized clothing. These companies don't sell physical fashion—their wares are confined to the experiential world. They've even created simulated fashion shows and catwalks to show off their creations.

Because protection from the elements (i.e., storms, heat, and the like) is not needed in the virtual world, you might be asking yourself, why do people purchase digital clothing? Communicating, "signaling," and as some might call it "flexing," are what many industry experts believe is a significant motivation behind digital fashion. People use clothing, accessories, and makeup to show off their social status, and this trend carries over into interactive environments. They also use style to communicate power, desirability, happiness, and a wide variety of other emotions.

Many times, cyber clothing is represented as NFTs, which, when the technology matures, will enable fashion to move from world to world freely. In other words, players can purchase virtual clothing in a shop in the metaverse and wear it in all their video games and social platforms.

Lest you think digital clothing is just a fad, in 2019, the world's first digital blockchain dress sold for $9,500 at the Ethereal Summit in New York. This dress, called "Iridescence," was created by Dapper Labs and Johanna Jaskowska and was unveiled by Dutch startup The Fabricant.[4]

While it is true that investors are attracted to the opportunities of digital fashion, going forward, self-expression may be the primary motivation behind most purchases of replicated clothing.

Self-Expression

Self-expression can be defined as the way that people share themselves with others.[5] The ways that we represent ourselves with others—through speech, movements, writings, and art—are a foundation for our personalities. What we express and how we express ourselves are essential to being human.

Self-expression is so important that in the United States, the US Constitution's first amendment (and in many other countries around the world) protects the freedom of every individual to express themselves. But what does that mean? It is the expression of your beliefs, thoughts, and emotions. You can express them in words (i.e., spoken or written), symbols, dance choreography, music, computer programs, and digital media.

Self-expression is your freedom to communicate about anything you want in any way you want. There are limits, of course, such as, "You can't yell fire in a crowded theater." Your freedom stops when it puts the lives of others in immediate and grave danger.

You need to express yourself for many reasons. Many creative people share their creations with others to communicate something.

For instance, an art installation might initially appear to be a pile of trash, but on a deeper level it could symbolize the damage humanity has done to the planet. Many people express themselves in the things they collect, or through their hobbies, the games they play, or the words they write (and many other ways).

Self-expression is vital because it improves communication between individuals and groups. Viewing a painting, reading a novel, watching a dance, or listening to poetry provides us the opportunities to know more about an individual and to understand their viewpoint better.

An individual's clothing also communicates a bit about their personality. An extrovert may wear a loud, multicolored outfit because they want to be unmistakably seen and recognized by others. An introvert, on the other hand, may choose to wear more traditional, reserved clothes and makeup, communicating that they are in a serious mood.

Fashion often goes through fads (i.e., short-term activities or styles) and trends (i.e., long-term developments). Remember growing up when some new fashion style was released, and everyone had to dress that way? This hunger for that latest style only lasted a few weeks—it was a fad. On the other hand, many young adults started wearing purposely torn jeans, and that tendency continues to this day. It's a trend—a long-term behavioral change.

In other words, people consciously or unconsciously identify themselves by the way they dress and by their appearance, and this carries through to virtual worlds and the metaverse. Some people won't (or don't) care about their augmentative appearance, just like they may not put significant importance or focus on their looks in the physical world. Others may want to wear the most colorful, fabulous fashions and makeup they can find or design because they want to be seen, which is their way of expressing themselves.

Fashion is a not to be overlooked aspect of worlds in the metaverse. It is a significant aspect of digital identity—how people dress and look in the digital world identifies people and their personalities.

Digital Identity

The metaverse provides people with a new way to explore distinct aspects of their identity. Because the metaverse consists (or will consist) of virtual worlds that don't follow "normal" physical laws, just about anything is possible. Suppose a person feels more comfortable in the digital universe as a two-headed person wearing an elaborate, gravity-defying dress and incredible makeup. In that case, they can feel free to embed those characteristics into their digital identity. This malleability allows people to continuously explore their identity in a new way, without the physical constraints of the real world.

Visitors to the metaverse can pick their wardrobe, purchasing clothing and fashion accessories from computerized shopping malls. They can also create custom fashion by hiring digital designers or making their own creations. This action flips luxury on its head, as high fashion is no longer as exclusive as it is in the physical universe. Everyone can participate in metaverse fashion; people from all walks of life, from the extreme introverts to blazon extroverts, from the wealthy to those living paycheck to paycheck—everyone can join the metaverse and create their own unique identity.

Due to this accessibility to everyone, the metaverse has democratized fashion. Anyone can create their own clothing, makeup, and accessories. Of course, high-end users can still purchase expensive fashions, but even so, clothing of all types can be made or purchased for little-to-no cost. In fact, there will be wear-to-earn and advertising options to make digital clothing free of any charges.

The rise of digital fashion also enables designers of all social classes to create their fashion masterpieces for little-to-no cost. New tools and techniques will allow designers to create incredible fashions of all types. Once this digital clothing has been designed, it can then be displayed on social media sites like Instagram.

Nowadays, fashion companies are releasing brands that exist only in the digital world. These fashions can only be seen in virtual worlds because they do not exist in the physical universe. There are two camps of fashion in the metaverse: traditional clothing and those that live only in pixel form.

Another area of fashion that's becoming more prevalent is with the use of augmented reality (AR). In this case, people wear special glasses or use their smartphones to overlay images on top of the view. The Pokémon game is one well-known application of this technology, where Pokémon creatures can be viewed in the real-life environment using a smartphone.

In 2020, Ralph Lauren introduced technology allowing consumers to scan the Ralph Lauren logo to create an AR image, sent through Snapchat, of their gift boxes with red ribbons. Before that, Snapchat and Ralph Lauren collaborated to create Bitmoji—asynchronous avatars that can be used on Snapchat and elsewhere.

Digital Fashion Overview

Anything is conceivable in the digital universe (i.e., games, social platforms, and the metaverse). As we've touched on previously, the limits of physical laws, practicality, weight, materials, and gravity don't apply. It will become commonplace for designers to create fashion that appears to be alive or defies gravity. Anyone will be able to create digital fashions, and high-profile (and priced) fashion experts will be able to design digital clothing that is one-of-a-kind or available for mass sales.

Digital fashion can mirror physical counterparts or be completely independent of the real world. People can replicate the contents of their real-life closets in their "home" in the metaverse if they desire, they can start fresh with all new virtual clothing, or they can mix the virtual with the real stuff. It's entirely up to them how much they want to invest in their digital identity.

Daniella Loftus, founder of This Outfit Does Not Exist, concluded, "You can be anyone or anything. This will bring in a whole new group of people who historically never used fashion as a medium because of the physical element."[6]

Digital fashion helps to create a quality immersive experience. The younger generations, especially Gen Z, find these new fashions appealing and are boosting the appeal of these new additions to virtual experiences.

There are several areas for digital fashion:

Trying on products. AR technologies, such as smart mirrors, allow people to see how fashion products appear before purchase.

Avatars. Digital fashion lets people dress their digital avatars in new and exciting ways. This includes everything from applying makeup to wearing shoes to complete outfits.

Fashion shows. People can view and show their digital clothing in live venues, such as fashion shows and catwalks.

Morgan Stanley recently estimated that the value of digital fashion may exceed $50 billion by 2030. Conversely, a senior advisor for the PTD Group, a marketing research company, is more cautious, stating, "I don't see a direct commercial opportunity here. There are business reasons why you want to be [in that space]. And I have a feeling we will see several brands jump into the space simply because everyone is talking about it, maybe not even understanding the consequences of it."[7]

Caroline Rush, the CEO of the British Fashion Council, believes that digital fashion could comprise 10 percent and 15 percent of people's wardrobes. That number might be high, but given that people want to look their best and show off their digital identity, it's likely that many people will invest in digital clothing.[8]

Digital Avatars/Digital Twins

> All truths pass through three stages. First, it is ridiculed. Second, it is violently opposed. Third, it is accepted as being self-evident.
>
> ARTHUR SCHOPENHAUER

Digital fashion will similarly pass through these three stages.

Several companies, including Arteec, Sketchfab, and 3D Celebrities, are creating full-body 3D digital scans of celebrities and characters from movies and television. These scans then are converted into avatars and digital twins—a virtual model that mirrors a physical object.[9] This capability unlocks many new opportunities for brands to use the metaverse for marketing and revenue. Metaverse tools allow people to map the interplay between physical and digital in various virtual environments and worlds.

A foundational concept of Web3 is that platforms do not control underlying data; rather, people own the content they create or purchase. In the metaverse, people can move their virtual objects to any world they desire, because their data (and virtual objects) are stored on the decentralized blockchain rather than on a platform's services. Along these lines, digital avatars and twins can move about the metaverse freely as designed by their owners.

Wear to Earn

The fashion industry is already creating brands of clothing and accessories to be worn in the metaverse, games, and social platforms. Each fashion item is an NFT, minted and owned by people. Some fashion companies are giving away their digital articles of clothing, while others are selling them and/or using them as incentives in marketing campaigns.

To help spread the word about these digital fashion lines, articles of clothing, and accessories, consumers can take advantage of the wear-to-own model. Meaning they are granted ownership of the fashion item as compensation for wearing it.

Megan Kaspar, managing director at Magnetic Capital and member of Red DAO, explained this model, stating, "Brands will compensate customers for wearing pieces by giving them access to exclusive items or airdropping fashion pieces to their virtual wallets, or by paying them in the form of a fungible token."[10]

Fashion Houses That Don't Sell Physical Clothes

Some fashion houses use digital clothing to incentivize people to purchase physical clothing. Other fashion brands don't sell physical clothing at all. Alternatively, their entire business model is to create, sell, and distribute digital lines of apparel and accessories. These include Fabricant, DressX, and The Dematerialised.

Luxury Labels Teaming Up with Game Developers to Outfit Players

As we've seen previously in this book, gaming is more than just solving puzzles, shooting zombies, and flying airplane simulations. A more critical aspect of multiplayer games is that it provides a place for players to socialize with their friends and family.

When people socialize, they often want to signal various aspects of their identity, such as their social status, appearance, interests, and feelings about themselves. They do this by selecting an avatar who represents their identity, then they add clothing and accessories to add more context.

Luxury labels, such as Balenciaga × Fortnite, Ralph Lauren × Roblox, and Lacoste × Minecraft are taking advantage of the social aspects of games to create fashions for various games. Gucci jumped into this arena in 2022, collaborating with Roblox to create Gucci Town, a virtual store where players can purchase Gucci accessories for their avatars.[11]

Digital Native Brands

People collect clothing, and sneakers are no exception. It's common for limited edition shoes to sell for hundreds or even thousands of dollars. Some high-end brands can even achieve prices in the hundred-thousand-dollar range. It should not be surprising that these collecting tendencies follow people into virtual worlds in the form of NFTs.

Digital native brands are bringing digital gaming aesthetics to virtual fashion. Nike purchased RTFKT (pronounced "artifact") in December 2021. The two companies collaborated to launch the Genesis Cryptokicks collection, which consisted of 20,000 NFTS. Ninety-eight of the 20,000 sneaker collections were designed with a specific design, which meant it would become a sought-after collector's item.

In addition, Adidas partnered with the Bored Ape Yacht Club to create and release their collection of 30,000 NFTs, while Gucci placed their clothing designed on various avatars.[12]

These creative endeavors marry fashion and art to create new and exciting opportunities for the brands to reach and engage with consumers.

Virtual Fashion Shows

Fashion brands have been showing off their clothing lines in fashion shows, catwalks, and other venues for over a hundred years. It's not surprising that the same concepts are being carried over into the digital fashion world.

Runways, a form of a fashion show, is already making an appearance in the virtual world. Digital designer Jeremy Scott created a line of doll-size clothes and showed them off on a digital catwalk in the summer of 2021. Prada put on a virtual fashion show in 2021 as part of Milan Fashion Week. Oliver Rousteing showed off his designs for 2021 using giant TV screens mounted on the runways of a physical fashion show. Dozens more major and many up-and-coming virtual fashion shows and catwalks occurred in 2021 and 2022, with more to follow.

These fashion shows are popular ways for people to be entertained by viewing fashion from anywhere in the world. As the metaverse is implemented, more advanced immersive, 3D technology will enable this trend to reach new heights.

Metaverse Stylists

Fashion plays a big part in how people view themselves and defines how others view them. People can shop in virtual clothing, shoe, and accessory stores to find the right look. Now, they can even engage with metaverse stylists, who are artistic designers skilled with the tools needed to create the graphics for digital clothing.

Michael Felice, an associate partner at consulting firm Kearney observed, "While it might seem the height of virtual vanity for individuals to professionally style their avatars as they prepare for entry into metaverse high society, it's actually quite logical."[13]

VR Headsets and AR Eyewear

VR headsets and AR eyewear are noteworthy entry points into the metaverse, although experiencing the metaverse doesn't necessarily require this kind of hardware. The early metaverse and its predecessors (such as games) will use smartphones, mobile devices, PCs, and other existing hardware, but newer technology will replace these earlier forms.

Once the technology becomes available and less expensive, AR glasses (and later contact lenses) will enable fashion overlays on real life. In this way, while wearing your AR glasses, you could see someone wearing a dress made of snakes; without the glasses, the physical dress is just a typical piece of clothing. These AR overlays do not need to conform to physical laws or any other objective reality because they are virtual images projected on physical forms or backgrounds, as was the case with Pokémon Go, introduced a few years ago.

NFTs are associated with a unique virtual object, but that object, such as the snake dress, can also carry over into the physical world through AR glasses. Just like that, it gives the appearance that the same clothes and accessories purchased and worn in the virtual world carry over into the physical universe.

These technologies unlock opportunities for individuals to be part of the creator economy (outlined later in this chapter) and for brands to explore new and exciting ways to engage people in their products and services.

Niantic bought 8th wall, a startup that sold AR development tools for the web (instead of mobile devices). This startup plans to enable AR experiences that access their mapping technology. Their goal is to understand and track real-world environments without using mobile applications such as ARKit.

These advances will provide prospects for brands to enhance the customer experience by creating an emotional connection with consumers using AR. For instance, using a standard webcam, a web application like an e-commerce storefront, could let customers "try on" clothing and makeup before purchasing by blending their image in the camera with the image of the product. This will increase conversion rates, reduce returns, and open new business models related to digital fashion.

3D Fashion

People view objects and the environment in three dimensions in the physical world. Enabling 3D in the virtual world makes digital fashion (and everything else) appear more authentic and dimensional. It also allows people to zoom in or out, swirl, or twist objects and, to a certain extent, the electronic environment.

For brands, this improves the customer experience by giving consumers a better understanding of how a product looks and operates, creating a more immersive shopping experience. Affectively, 3D sits at the intersection of the physical and metaphorical worlds.

Different Entry Points

There are several ways a brand can enter digital fashion in the metaverse:

- They can directly create clothing to sell in digital marketplaces so people can purchase them for their avatars.
- They can create promotional events that use NFT fashions in some manner.
- They can create a more persistent presence by setting up their virtual world so people can visit anytime. Alternately, they can create a 3D space that is part of a larger world—conceptionally the same as owning a store within a shopping mall.

Components of an Overall Brand Presence

A *brand* is how others perceive a business, product, or individual. We must also observe that a brand is the sum of all its interactions, not just siloed experiences. The more a brand is in-sync with its customer expectations, the better it will attract and retain consumers, which translates into sales and return visits.

The mechanisms for a brand follow:

- Identify the purpose of the brand. What is the brand attempting to accomplish?
- Define the value proposition.
- Create the visual representation (i.e., identity) of the brand.
- Get the brand out in front of people.
- Use public relations to get your brand known.
- Use social media and other means to promote your brand.
- Create content that consumers want to read, see, or experience.

World Building for Fashion

Digital fashion is not just about creating 3D clothing or accessories; it's also about building worlds. These worlds will become immersive, multisensory experiences that excite people by entertaining or educating them. For starters, a computer-generated shopping mall could be set up with a particular look and feel, like a botanical garden or medieval marketplace. This style will make the goods and services sold more accessible to people and generates a strong interest in visiting and returning.

Digital Platforms

A *digital platform* creates an ecosystem that allows communities of users to engage with the platform and each other. Social media, knowledge platforms (such as Reddit), service platforms (like Uber), and e-commerce are the four main types of platforms for the web.

Metaverse digital platforms will be defacto stages that support a creative environment, giving developers everything needed to create for the metaverse. The investments of major companies like Microsoft, Roblox, Fortnite, and Epic Games (among many others) contribute to the growth of these platforms. Subsequently, they provide a platform for digital fashion to continue to thrive.

What's the Point of Digital Fashion?

Why is digital fashion important? More simply, why would anyone want to spend money on virtual clothing and accessories that doesn't exist in the real world? From the individual's viewpoint, digital clothing enables them to show their digital identity. They can wear futuristic, magical clothes or simple, conservative outfits depending on their mood or the activities in which they are participating. It's a way for people to express themselves fully.

Businesses gravitate toward viable markets, and accordingly they will follow individuals into the metaverse. Advertisers will create billboards and signs, use product placements, and sponsor virtual events. Marketers will design entire campaigns around using the metaverse to improve brand recognition. Businesses will set up shops in the metaverse to sell their products and fashion brands will create stores that allow people to choose and purchase clothing.

Investors can (and already are) attempting to find ways to invest in the metaverse or in metaverse-type products like NFTs to make money.

Think of the metaverse as a newly opened world, full of wonder and interesting things, waiting to be explored, used, and augmented for good. As the metaverse and digital fashion are implemented, people and businesses will find new ways to expand their lives and happiness.

Creator Economy

As has been mentioned, there are two distinctly different models/schools of thought for implementing the metaverse: decentralized and centralized. The decentralized model doesn't depend on (or even allow) control by a central authority, while the centralized model envisions the metaverse being controlled by one or more centralized entities. It's likely that the eventual implementation of the metaverse will be a combination of both models, much like the internet today is comprised of centralized platforms, such as social media or e-commerce sites, that can be accessed using decentralized services.

An open metaverse encourages and supports the creator economy, defined as the millions of independent content creators, bloggers, videographers, and writers working to create quality content. DAZ3D is a business that moved from providing a platform for 3D artists, to selling their 3D models, to a modern service supporting 3D NFTs. They encourage creativity, and on their platform, creators thrive because they have access to all the tools needed to design NFTs and market and sell them.

Metaverse-as-a-Service

As the metaverse becomes more fully realized, enterprises will use metaverse-as-a-Service (MaaS) to enable them to unlock the creativity inherent within, such as digital fashion. MaaS will support a range of functions and services needed, including cryptocurrency, workflows, collaboration, and many other functions a business needs to take advantage of the metaverse. The advantage of MaaS is that companies will not need to invest in the large infrastructures required to support their entry into the metaverse. Extensible platforms enable greater collaboration, scalability, simulation, and 3D creation through MaaS.[14]

MaaS will lower the barriers and costs for businesses to enter the metaverse, and therefore, allow the creator economy to thrive like never before.

Challenge of Interoperability

Without the metaverse, moving clothing, accessories, and other items from world to world isn't possible in most instances. The standardized formats of NFTs and blockchain enable this kind of movement. As the metaverse is implemented, digital clothing will be worn in video games, graphical clubs, simulated fashion shows, and even traded or sold in online stores.

Because digital items, including fashion, are based on blockchain, interoperability will be an embedded possibility. Any world that supports NFTs and blockchain should be designed to allow items to move in and out without issue. This requirement will enable the metaverse to function at its total capacity.

Additionally, ownership of digital fashions and other items will remain with the creator or purchaser. The design of NFTs and blockchain enforces it.

Summary

The offerings of the metaverse are multifaceted and are changing the creation dynamic. In the past, a sizable portion of creative energy occurred in or for the physical universe, which meant physical laws constrained creations. Over the past decade, businesses have been increasingly focused on the need for digital transformation for growth and, more recently, embracing 3D worlds in gaming and the metaverse. With its forced isolation, the pandemic has accelerated digitization even more so, intending to support and address people's need to use the internet and virtual worlds to be entertained, educated, informed, and socialized.

These trends and the immense change in our world today, such as deglobalization and supply chain constraints, require businesses and brands to take more risks to remain competitive. Those businesses will acquire first mover advantage in the arena, in addition to having the opportunity and responsibility to help define the standards and gain more significant market share.

Core to the metaverse is its underlying technical complexity hidden from users through an interface of frictionless, personalized, expressive immersive experiences. The design of the metaverse as an open, decentralized arena gives users control over their digital identity, enforces their digital property rights, and ensures there are incentives for creativity. This way, data, interactions, relationships, and behaviors will fully be realized in the metaverse.

The revolutionary design and implementation of the metaverse and the associated hyper-realistic 3D renderings will cause concepts like digital twinning to be embraced, as we've seen early indications with the digital fashion use case. Organizations can monitor historical and real-time metrics and use data to forecast, inform, and simulate future events and concepts. The metaverse will be an ideal place to go beyond digital fashion and create simulated environments for autonomous vehicles and other trends. Using real-time, physical-world sensor data as inputs to simulations, designers and engineers can work together to develop innovative products and entire production lines. Doing so will improve quality and result in a faster time-to-market turnaround.

Businesses must equalize their purpose with the promise of these new technologies and trends by planning for future opportunities. Because competition is and will remain high, big or small and established or emerging companies must be willing to take calculated risks. Digital fashion is just one area where there are great opportunities for market leadership.

Many people will find negative things to say about every technological advancement. It's now difficult to believe that there were people who didn't see the value of the World Wide Web in the late 1990s. Nonetheless, astronomer Clifford Stoll wrote in *Newsweek*, "How come my local mall does more business in an afternoon than the entire Internet handles in a month?" Similarly, businesses and brands must work hard to overcome this kind of resistance to expand into new markets successfully.

The internet fundamentally altered how people interact with one another, and the metaverse promises to extend these tendencies by several orders of magnitude. Many use cases will only become available and visible after the metaverse is implemented; those use cases might even result in changes to human interaction beyond our current understanding.

The key to succeeding as a business in the metaverse can be seen in digital fashion and its focus on human centricity. Businesses must create compelling user experiences to attract and retain consumers. Ideally, the metaverse will be fully inclusive, foster creativity, and be beneficial emotionally and economically to people. If this is kept in mind as the metaverse is developed, it could help people come together and learn to live in greater harmony.

Notes

1   D. F. I. T. Metaverse, dissrup.com/editorial/digital-fashion-in-the-metaverse (archived at https://perma.cc/XCX2-4RDK)

2   R Jana. The Metaverse Could Radically Reshape Fashion, 11 April 2022, www.wired.com/story/extreme-fashion-metaverse/ (archived at https://perma.cc/2QWG-UP7U)

3   C Allaire. Video Games Are Becoming a High-Fashion Playground, 12 October 2021, www.vogue.com/article/video-game-fashion-designer-collaborations (archived at https://perma.cc/KBM7-FG72)

4   R Mowatt. The World's First-Ever Digital Dress Is Sold for $9,500 USD, 28 May 2019, hypebae.com/2019/5/first-digital-blockchain-dress-sold-9500-usd-fabricant-dapper-labs-johanna-jaskowska (archived at https://perma.cc/Q6WH-TLCA)

5   M Courtney and E Ackerman. What Is Self-Expression and How to Foster It? (20 Activities + Examples), 6 August 2018, positivepsychology.com/self-expression/ (archived at https://perma.cc/5EGP-NYQD)

6   B Girmay. The Metaverse Has Arrived—Here's How It's Changing the Way We Dress IRL, 7 Mar 2022, www.whowhatwear.com/digital-fashion/slide2 (archived at https://perma.cc/3QC3-8TEE)

7   D Masoni. Metaverse: A $50 Bln Revenue Opportunity For Luxury—MS, 16 November 2021, www.reuters.com/technology/metaverse-50-bln-revenue-opportunity-luxury-ms-2021-11-16/ (archived at https://perma.cc/97KM-86MX)

8   C Erdly. Fashion Embraces the Metaverse: Will 15% of Our Wardrobe Become Digital?, 6 March 2022, www.forbes.com/sites/catherineerdly/2022/03/06/fashion-embraces-the-metaversewill-15-of-our-wardrobe-become-digital/ (archived at https://perma.cc/BQQ8-MWEH)

9   T Lewis. Gallery: 3D Scans in Hollywood and Hospitals, 21 August 2014, www.livescience.com/47452-gallery-3d-scans-hollywood.html (archived at https://perma.cc/4QVP-RLDL)

10 R Wolfson. Wear-to-Earn NFTs Target the Billion-Dollar Fashion Industry, 1 December 2021, cointelegraph.com/news/wear-to-earn-nfts-target-the-billion-dollar-fashion-industry (archived at https://perma.cc/48PZ-G9J6)

11 A Webster. Gucci Built a Persistent Town Inside of Roblox, 27 May 2022, www.theverge.com/2022/5/27/23143404/gucci-town-roblox (archived at https://perma.cc/2U43-NBX5)

12 D V Boom. These Nike NFT "Cryptokicks" Sneakers Sold for $130K, 28 April 2022, www.cnet.com/personal-finance/crypto/these-nike-nft-cryptokicks-sneakers-sold-for-130k/ (archived at https://perma.cc/W8GG-4TBL)

13 N Sayej. Metaverse Stylists See a Booming Business in Virtual Clothes, 13 March 2022, www.businessofbusiness.com/articles/metaverse-stylists-virtual-clothes/ (archived at https://perma.cc/59PU-2K95)

14 Arti. Metaverse as a Service Will Take Web3 Motive to Next Level, 16 May 2022, www.analyticsinsight.net/metaverse-as-a-service-will-take-web3-motive-to-next-level/ (archived at https://perma.cc/S4QS-WJPU)

08 >Tokenomics_

Beginning in 2020, the COVID pandemic placed the lives of most of the world on hold. Two years later, in 2022, millions of people were ready to get out of their homes and rejoin life. Unfortunately, the world was not finished with the challenges: that year brought COVID variants, deglobalization, bear markets, snarled supply chains, and rapid inflation. All these trends will (and are) resulting in an erosion of customer sentiment.

Technology has not been immune from the fallout. Chip shortages are reducing the number of cars that can be manufactured; war and the resultant supply chain complications are reducing the raw materials required for solar panels, batteries, and electrical components; and inflation is raising transportation and manufacturing prices.

One survey found that 51 percent of consumer households in the United States stated they wouldn't purchase new technology soon because of inflation, and 68 percent believe that technology products will be more expensive in 2022. Out of 83 products, the survey found an average 1-point drop in consumers' purchasing plans from 2021–2022.

In contrast, the same survey found that more people (8 percent) were first-time purchasers than repeat purchasers. This jump in first-time purchasers results from people returning to their "normal" lives after the pandemic.

Additionally, college students are heading back to school after schooling from home for two years, and they want to purchase the devices they need to remain entertained and connected. Also, rental property vacancies are historically low, suggesting that people are moving around the country at an increased rate. This is another factor fueling the technology demand as these new tenants need to equip their new residences—and naturally, they want to get the latest equipment they can afford.

Several studies and analysts show that the nation is in flux. Consumers are looking for technology because they feel the world is opening up after the pandemic. Further, they are wary of the effects of a looming recession, inflation, and worldwide instability, hereby pursuing their shopping with a more conservative agenda, especially regarding their budget. All signs, in any event, indicate that consumer technology will continue to be relevant even with the disruptions occurring.

Given these disruptions and market factors, the metaverse, with its immersive experiences, might provide alternative customer solutions and business economic drivers.

In Chapter 3, we parsed blockchain, the underlying technology enabling cryptocurrency. *Tokenomics*, which is an interconnected economic system based on cryptocurrency, sits at the core of the metaverse. As we indicated earlier, the metaverse doesn't necessarily require Web3 and cryptocurrency technologies. However, they both provide functionality that can be leveraged to enable greater economic activities in the metaverse.

The media tends to focus on investment opportunities of non-fungible tokens (NFTs) and cryptocurrency. Clearly, video games paved the way, using blockchain and NFTs to power microtransactions (i.e., small purchases of in-game items and services). The most popular games, such as *Fortnite*, are free but use in-game currencies that may be converted to fiat (i.e., real-life) currencies like the dollar. *Fortnite* earned $2.4 billion in revenue in 2018 and $1.8 billion in 2019.[1]

These in-game currencies may be converted to fiat currencies at a fixed price. Exemplified, as this is written, in *Fortnite*, 1,000 V-Bucks cost $7.99, and in Roblox, 800 Robux cost $9.99. Inside these games, the currencies purchased using fiat currencies may be used to acquire items and services.

Let's assess tokenomics in more detail.

What is Tokenomics?

Tokenomics defines the underlying economy of cryptocurrency, including the mechanics of the creation (i.e., minting) of tokens, how the tokens are issued, where they can be used, who accepts them as payment, and how they are converted to fiat currencies. Currencies, crypto or not, will not be accepted and used unless they have value and can be exchanged for valuable goods and services.

These are some of the essential components of tokenomics:

Mining. It's the creation of new tokens using an algorithm. Bitcoin and Ethereum are examples of cryptocurrencies that use mining. (This is probed in detail in Chapter 3.)

Staking. Instead of mining, Ethereum 2.0 and Tezos use smart contracts to lock away coins. When someone stakes tokens, they set them aside to support the blockchain network and for transaction confirmation. People use staking to create a passive income, because many cryptocurrencies offer generous interest rates to those who stake their tokens. In other words, staking is the pledging of coins, which are then used in the Proof-of-Stake minting algorithm.

Yields. Offering higher yields is the method that cryptocurrencies use to attract investors to purchase and stake tokens. Yields are paid out in tokens.

Token burns. By permanently removing tokens from circulation (i.e., burning them), some blockchains, including Ethereum, purposely reduce their token supply to support their price.

Supplies. Some tokens, such as bitcoin, limit the maximum number of tokens that can be in existence. The design of bitcoin imposes a strict limit of 21 million coins. Others, such as Ethereum, are not limited by their design but impose limits to keep their price stable (countries' currencies are controlled similarly). NFTs set a limit of one because each token applies to a unique item.

Many of these rules and procedures are defined by the design of the technology underlying the token. Designers often detail the limits and uses of their token systems in a whitepaper.[2]

What is the Role of Tokenomics in the Metaverse?

Because the metaverse is, in many ways, intended to provide an immersive experience that simulates and enhances the physical universe, it is understandable that an economic model is essential. Without an economy, people couldn't make purchases, trade, or perform other similar things. Without an economy and the under-lying currencies (tokens), very few people would visit the metaverse, much less remain in it.

Transactions within the metaverse are done using cryptocurren-cies; although many games currently accept regular fiat currencies such as the dollar as payment, crypto adoption is still low among the overall population. Irrespective, within games (and eventually the metaverse), people can convert their fiat currency into the equivalent value of cryptocurrency.

Ideally, and in all likelihood, metaverse tokens will be used within it instead of either fiat or cryptocurrencies. These virtual tokens make it easy for people to engage in digital transactions. They can be used to buy and sell items, to provide voting rights, and, if the token is unique, to function as NFTs. In many cases, metaverse tokens can be exchanged for fiat currencies (i.e., cashed out into the physical world). Tokens can also prove ownership of real-world items if an NFT is linked to a physical object.

Some examples of the tokens used by video games and platforms include the following:

The Sandbox. This popular NFT game uses a specialized token called *SAND*. The Sandbox is extremely popular, has a billion-dollar market cap, and has the highest growth potential for an NFT game in 2022.

Decentraland. This platform allows people to purchase land and then monetize those plots. Decentraland uses a token called Mana.

Star Atlas. This space exploration game uses a currency called Atlas. Players form alliances (i.e., factions) and build intergalactic econo-mies in this game. Players use the Altas currency to purchase in-game items.

Meta. This platform, formerly known as Facebook, developed a token known as Libra, which was intended for cross-border payments. The currency was not approved by regulators but is an indication of potential uses for these currencies in the future.

Now that we've evaluated the role of tokenomics, let's unpack the basics of the subject.

Tokenomics 101

Tokenomics is a newly coined term to describe token-based economies such as video games, virtual shopping malls, platforms, and, when implemented, the metaverse. These token-based economies don't use fiat currencies like the dollar or euro. Instead, they use cryptocurrencies for trade. Many current video games and virtual platforms use various cryptocurrencies, although the trend is for them to create their version for simplicity.

Crypto assets have real value in the virtual world, although many of these cannot be transferred directly from world to world. In other words, the currency used by Alpha cannot be used within the Star Atlas game.

All cryptocurrencies are based on blockchain technology. Many of them use ERC20 (Ethereum) tokens, which support smart contracts on the Ethereum blockchain. The Mana and SAND tokens follow the ERC20 standard.

When investing in cryptocurrency, people are investing in the digital world, which means they are using blockchain.

How Blockchain Helps the Metaverse

As proposed earlier in this book, blockchain is a data structure that permanently records transactions. Blocks cannot be changed, and they are never deleted. Cryptocurrencies are based on blockchain.

Blockchain is very secure, although like all technology, it can theoretically be compromised by hackers. The technology confirms transactions and supports protected transactions, which, in turn, helps the metaverse.

Crypto Payments happen On-Demand

People who make purchases at physical stores or online using their credit/debit cards expect the payments to be processed promptly. The use of physical form cash is becoming less common, and people depend even more on how well these digital payment systems operate.

A significant benefit of cryptocurrency is that it can be used as a payment method in much the same way as credit/debit cards. Some e-commerce sites and stores are beginning to accept bitcoin and other cryptocurrencies as payment, and this trend is expected to continue. The major card processors, including Visa, Mastercard, and PayPal, have already implemented cryptocurrency.

People who shop in the metaverse will naturally want to purchase virtual and physical items in the virtual shops. The things they buy will be a form of an NFT, such as in a clothing store, an art gallery, or a weapons shop for their favorite game. Transactions of this nature within the metaverse must occur quickly, securely, and without errors. For the metaverse to gain traction with the population, people must have confidence that they can acquire and spend money and that their transactions will be quickly completed.

As time passes, more businesses and platforms will support payments via cryptocurrencies, even with the current price fluctuations. Central banks are even supporting cryptocurrencies, which in the short term may introduce instability in the market. Understandably, with their support, the long-term prospects for cryptocurrencies look good. In any event, cryptocurrencies are and will continue to be a standard payment method in the metaverse.

Where Can Metaverse Tokens Be Purchased?

Cryptocurrency is at the base of the digital economy of the metaverse. As these currencies stabilize and become more ubiquitous, people will feel safe using them for payment with the metaverse and in the physical world.

As with any crypto transaction, you must begin by setting up a crypto wallet, such as Metamask, Gemini, or Coinbase. Your crypto wallet acts the same as a physical wallet or purse. Instead of debit/credit cards, it holds all a person's cryptocurrency. Each of these wallets includes tools to convert fiat currency into metaverse tokens and to convert one cryptocurrency into another.

Metaverse tokens can be purchased using an application such as Binance, which accepts deposits in dollars or other currencies, or SWIFT. Other cryptocurrency exchanges include Transak and Wyre. Note, all these services charge a small fee.

Types of Tokens in the Metaverse

The metaverse alters how computers and the internet are used and viewed. People can enter the metaverse using standard computers or mobile devices, or they can use more advanced virtual reality (VR) and augmented reality (AR) technology to give them a more immersive experience.

Cryptocurrencies are a new form of capital, and as a result, they are capturing the attention of investors, traders, and even average people with money to invest. Gaming takes advantage of the properties and convenience of cryptocurrencies to support purchasing in-game items, governance, and various other features. Most games define cryptocurrencies using blockchain (usually Ethereum) and support in-game purchases through NFTs.

Modern games are putting smart contracts, governance (decentralized autonomous organizations [DAOs]), and NFTs to use, so that players have a wide variety of options and capabilities without the limitations and burden of a centralized authority. In many games, players and developers purchase real estate in virtual worlds, upon which they then use to "build" games and other attractions. This mimics the real world, in which a parcel of land would need to be purchased to host a theme park, theater, or other attraction.

Let's review several major virtual worlds to demonstrate how their new monetary systems work.

Decentraland (Mana)

Decentraland is owned by users and is based on Ethereum. People enter this virtual world to play, be entertained, interact with others, participate in activities, and explore. While they are engaged in these activities, they earn Mana tokens. This world was designed to be an outlet for people to create, experience, and earn from the applications and content they develop.

Mana is the official, native currency for Decentraland. It consists of ERC-20 tokens that are usable throughout Decentraland to purchase and lease virtual property; said properties can be improved (applicably with applications) and monetized. Mana can also be used to buy anything else in Decentraland, including avatars, digital fashion, names, and any other items.

Players purchase land from the fixed supply of the 90,000 parcels available using Mana tokens. By design, there is a maximum of 2.2 trillion Mana and a circulating supply of 1.3 trillion in Decentraland. Some of the use cases for Mana are described as follows:

· Mana can be used to purchase land and in-game items.
· Using Decentraland and DAO, people may use their Mana tokens to engage in governance decisions.

As of January 2021, there were 2.19 billion Mana tokens, of which 1.49 billion (68 percent) were in circulation. Initially, there were 2.8 billion Mana in the supply, but over 600 million were burned due to land sales.

Decentraland has a fixed supply of 90,000 land parcels that users/developers may purchase to develop games and other attractions. Land is purchased by burning Decentraland's native token Mana, making it deflationary (and indirectly redistributing value to token holders). Mana has a maximum supply of 2.2 trillion and a circulating supply of 1.3 trillion. At a market capitalization (MCAP) of about $800 million, the Mana token has two use cases. As of June 20, 2022, Decentraland traded at $0.828 and had a market cap of $1,536,194,523.[3]

The Sandbox (SAND)

The Sandbox metaverse was launched in 2011. Based on blockchain, this platform is community-driven and lets creators monetize voxel assets and gaming experiences. Players can create voxel art using VoxEdit, buy and sell assets in the Marketplace, and make and play games using Game Maker. The Sandbox is where creators, artists, and players can be creative without physical constraints.

In 2012, The Sandbox was implemented as a Web 2.0 platform. Between 2012 and 2018, there were over 40 million downloads and a large user base, which gave The Sandbox the credibility it needed to get ahead of the competition.

The Sandbox whitepaper sums it up nicely:

> SAND holders will also be able to participate in the governance of the platform via a Decentralized Autonomous Organization (DAO), where they can exercise voting rights on key decisions of The Sandbox ecosystem. As a player, you can create digital assets (Non-Fungible Tokens, aka NFTs), upload them to the marketplace, and drag-and-drop them to create game experiences with The Sandbox Game Maker. The Sandbox has secured over 50 partnerships, including Atari, Crypto Kitties, and Shaun, the Sheep, to build a fun, creative 'play-to-earn' gaming platform owned and made by players. The Sandbox aims to bring blockchain into mainstream gaming, attracting crypto and non-crypto game enthusiasts by offering the advantages of true-ownership, digital scarcity, monetization capabilities, and interoperability.[4]

In addition to introducing blockchain to mainstream gaming, The Sandbox encourages people to be players and creators simultaneously with their play-to-earn model. It is designed to be a decentralized platform for gaming.

The Sandbox uses its token known as SAND (a standard ERC-20 token) and limits the amount of land that may be purchased using SAND. Alternatively, unlike Decentraland, The Sandbox doesn't require participants to burn SAND tokens to make purchases. Instead, tokens used for the purchase are split between the seller and The Sandbox Treasury.

The SAND token has the following use cases:

- SAND may be used for purchases, trading, and sales.
- Owners of SAND tokens can participate in governance.
- SAND users can stake SAND tokens, which entitle them to shares of advertising and transaction fee amounts.

Most of the 123,000 available land parcels were purchased by 2020 in roughly 1,000 unique sales. An additional 900 sales have occurred since that time in the secondary market. Approximately 23 percent of potential SAND tokens are in circulation (as of this writing). Most of the remainder is held in reserve in the Foundation and Company, which reduces the chances of a token dump.

The SAND token lets people purchase and trade lands and assets within The Sandbox. Some of the things that it can be used for include the following:

- Trading digital assets in The Sandbox.
- Buying digital land.
- Interacting with user-created content.
- Purchasing services, play, and governance.

As of June 20, 2022, The Sandbox traded at $0.8631 and had a market cap of $1,086,266,218. There is a maximum supply of 3 billion tokens.[5]

Gala Games (Gala)

The foundational concept for Gala Games is that players own their winnings in their games. Any item earned or won belongs to the winner or earner. Game items are stored in the blockchain as NFTs, which allows their ownership to be verified, sold, purchased, or transferred.

The Gala Game ecosystem is powered by 16,000 player computers (i.e., nodes), making it fully decentralized. Players use voting mechanisms to contribute to decisions about the development of Gala Games, including what games should be added and what should be funded.

The token used within Gala Games is called Gala. It is an ERC-20 token, cryptographically secure and native to the platform. These tokens provide a safe and effective means of payment within Gala Games.

As of June 20, 2022, Gala traded at $0.0571 and had a market cap of $391,500,00. As of June 2022, there are 6.98 billion Gala tokens in use, with 35.24 billion in circulation.[6]

DeFi Kingdoms (Jewel)

DeFi Kingdoms is a new play-to-earn gaming protocol that launched in 2021. They use their cryptocurrency known as Jewel, which allows players to make in-game purchases using NFTs. Their goal was to create a yield farm within the game. They are based on the Harmony blockchain network, use Uniswap's V2 protocol, and support smart contracts and NFTs.[7]

DeFi Kingdoms is a gamified decentralized exchange. Players take part in yield farming and earn Jewel tokens. This token has two main functions:

- Deposits in the DeFi Kingdom Bank
- Delegating Jewel tokens into a liquidity pool in the Gardens

Once Jewel tokens have been deposited, customers may exchange them for xJewel governance tokens. These include a yield, giving participants an incentive to participate in governance. Another option is to exchange their tokens for a liquidity pool, theoretically generating higher returns.

When DeFi Kingdoms was launched, 10 million tokens were pre-created (i.e., pre-mined) and distributed as follows:

- Game development: 5 million
- Marketing: 2 million
- Original liquidity pool: 2 million
- Founding time: 1 million

Jewel's supply of Jewel tokens is limited to 500 million (note that the maximum supply of tokens can be changed). Yield-farming mechanisms will be used to introduce new tokens into the collection.

CRITICISMS OF DEFI KINGDOMS

The tokenomics of Jewel are well-designed and functional. In any case, there has been criticism of DeFi Kingdoms because it lacks an authentic gaming experience (however, the developers acknowledge this). The platform's focus has been on a decentralized exchange and gaming has become secondary, although planned. Part of their roadmap includes the creation of new realms, including a new token called Crystal using the Avalanche network.

INTEGRATING AVALANCHE AND THE CRYSTAL TOKEN

Avalanche was launched in 2020 as an alternative to Ethereum. It supports blockchain, smart contracts, a governance model, NFTs, dapps, and a cryptocurrency called AVAX. Avalanche prioritizes scalability and transaction processing speed (reportedly 4,500 transactions/second), and the rate of coin creation and the associated fees are set using a governance model. Transaction fees are paid with AVAX tokens, which are burned (i.e., no longer circulated), potentially making them scarcer over time.

In late 2021, DeFi Kingdoms (DFK) announced it would begin using Avalanche and become a new realm with its token named Crystal. With this integration, DFK would become more flexible with faster transaction times. The new realm, called DeFi Kingdoms, would bridge to the primary realm of DFK, effectively expanding the use case.[8]

Both tokens (Jewel and Crystal) are linked, so either can be used for a variety of purposes:

- Minting new NFTs (Heroes)
- Using as liquidity
- Being used as currency in the realm

The main DFK blockchain uses Jewel for gas fees for the DFK blockchain. This is where Crystal transactions are settled, which implies that Jewel is the power source for Crystal. This increases the reasons for using Jewel, because people who hold them also receive the benefits of Crystal.

Merging DeFi Kingdoms with Avalanche grants people more reasons to use DFK and provides additional incentives to use the Jewel and Crystal tokens. As a result, DeFi Kingdoms is growing fast, and that growth is expected to continue.

Non-Crypto Tokens

Games based on blockchain and NFTs require players to undergo a learning curve to participate. Several new games have been developed that use their Tokenomics model and currencies instead of the standard cryptocurrencies.

Bezorge, a play-to-earn crypto-game, defines an environment where players pillage the SHIBs and DOGEs of their enemies to rid the virtual world of FUD (i.e., Fear, Uncertainty, and Doubt). This game operates on a play-to-earn model where players earn blocks and gain rewards. Those who own two or more Bezogi NFTs can get more by summoning or renting them.

The game is different from others because it does not charge collateral or gas fees, which allows any gamer, regardless of their understanding of crypto, to participate in the game without charge.[9]

Token Economy/NFT Economists

According to Dell and the Institute for the Future, 85 percent of the jobs that today's learners will be doing in 2030 don't yet exist.[10] The field of NFT/Token Economists, fueled by the demands of the token economy, is one such job.

JTTM is an example of a company that will need people with skills and experience in this area. They are building a mobile game that combines their tokens with gaming functions. In a recent job offering, they stated they want to find an experienced Tokenomics Lead. Their ideal candidate would be an enthusiast of NFTs and cryptocurrencies, with the skills to deconstruct and design token economics, understand data, and be able to handle the evolution of complex systems in time.[11]

The new role will be responsible for the following:

- Token creation
- Token design
- Token development
- Token compliance
- Go-to-market
- Operations
- How the token will operate in gaming and staking functions
- Analyzing existing NFT projects and tokens
- Analyzing game theory and how it impacts the Tokenomics model
- Developing macroeconomic agent-based models for testing tokenomics

Token Gating

A new, emerging technology known as *token* gating is designed to control access to content by requiring consumers to buy a particular NFT and several tokens. The particular NFT is an access key verified through a digital wallet.

Using token gating, creators and businesses can tap into new opportunities to monetize content and allows visitors VIP access, which converts services and products into assets that can be used just like any other assets by providing utility. This is an evolution of paywalls and loyalty clubs by providing value incentives.

It opens an opportunity for businesses to create no-code tools to simplify the implementation of token gating their content. By taking advantage of token gating, content and access can be converted from something consumable to a commodity.[12]

Creating Delightful Experiences with Tokenomics

Crafting a metaverse experience that engages the general population must be immersive, good-looking, easy to access, and fully featured. Additionally, accessing and using the metaverse must be more than just profitable—it must be fun, entertaining, and offer rewards beyond what is available in real life. In other words, the metaverse must entice people to enter, remain, and return, by providing more than they can get from their own lives and environments.

Currently, most worlds in the metaverse offer a one-dimensional economic experience. Players can do the following:

- Buy and sell virtual land
- Buy and sell NFTs
- Stake their tokens
- Gamble
- Play to earn

The worlds also charge taxes on transactions, gas fees for minting, and entrance fees (sometimes requiring the purchase of NFTs or in-game items).

The above actions can be accomplished without spending much time in the metaverse. Many can be performed outside the metaverse entirely. Specifically, a person doesn't need to put on 3D goggles to buy and sell NFTs. They can do it straight from a website.

How can the metaverse be implemented so that most people don't just visit occasionally but make it part of their daily lives? People spend much time in games, but how can that experience be replicated in the metaverse, which requires (to be successful) that people be engaged, immersed, and it becomes as common as going to the local supermarket?

The metaverse will not be helpful without content that entices people to repeatedly visit and return. Games are popular, but people don't play them all the time, and many don't play them at all. The key to creating a long-lasting metaverse is to provide Persistent Utility by making it interesting, entertaining, fun, and valuable—so much so that people feel they must use it regularly.

The answer lies in creating a metaverse economy that gives individuals the right rewards at the right time to motivate them to return. The worlds of the metaverse must be engaging and provide an economic incentive. At first, people will be attracted because it's new and exciting, but that newness factor might quickly wear off as other interests vie for consumer attention.

People must be given reasons to visit and remain in the metaverse on a daily, or even more than daily, basis. The result must be that they not only react to the economics of the metaverse, but that they want to come to the metaverse because they can't get what they want anywhere else, at least not as quickly anyway.

There is more to the picture than simply creating a play-to-earn model to get players to come back. Unfortunately, that model can become monotonous—rote—quickly, and players (i.e., users) will find something else that they feel deserves their attention. This is one of the reasons why lottery games occasionally change and why there are so many variations on a simple gambling theme. By increasing the scratch card design's variability, even by simply printing assorted designs, increases the odds that people will participate more often even though the new card is the same as the old one.

The metaverse must be designed to give rewards in return for accomplishments. These rewards often mean gaining experience points, increasing power, and receiving NFTs or cryptocurrency in game worlds. Players face barriers—monsters, puzzles, and challenges—and then earn their rewards. This creates a feedback loop, making them want to return to gain ever-higher rewards. Games also expand by creating new, add-on worlds, allowing players to explore new areas and rewards.

There are eight core drives of human motivation, according to Octalysis:[13]

1 Epic meaning: Doing something greater than yourself
2 Accomplishment: Making progress
3 Empowerment: Engaging in a creative process

4 Ownership: Owning things

5 Social influence: Having friends, groups, companionship, and social responses

6 Scarcity: Having a drive to want something that another cannot have

7 Unpredictability: Wanting to know what will happen next

8 Avoidance: Avoiding something negative

It's easy to see how these eight core motivations drive people through their lives. A lawyer, for one, may get into the field because they believe they are defending the innocent. They win cases more quickly as they become more experienced. Moreover, they accomplish something. Winning complex cases can be highly creative and they gain the rewards of high income, which lets them own things.

A goal is to design the metaverse or a virtual world so that it gives stockholders as many of these core motivators as possible. The more people are motivated by these factors, the more they will engage and be fulfilled.[14]

Traditional economics also play a role additionally to engagement motivators. The Quantity Theory of Money[15] explains how the money supply and the price level are related:

$$MV = PT$$

where:

M is the total money supply.

V is how often money changes hands during a specific time.

P is the price level.

T is the total output.

Blockchain projects tend to use the Buterin Model, named after Vitalik Buterin, the inventor of Ethereum:

$$MC = TH$$

where:

> M is the total number of tokens
> C is the price of each token
> T is the volume of transactions
> H is how long the user holds the transaction

These theories can be baked into the design of the metaverse or separate worlds to create a real working economy, such that, as more tokens enter the system with a constant volume of transactions, it will cause the token price to decrease. Furthermore, costs can be increased by burning tokens, which reduces the supply and makes each token more valuable. Minting more tokens decreases the value and can even result in inflation. Tokens can even be given away to attract new practitioners. By manipulating these variables, a vibrant economy can be created and maintained.

Combining these concepts together will result in a vibrant, engaging, and enriching experiences for people in the metaverse and mimic real life. By creating an environment that appears real, motivates people, and gives them economic incentives, designers will be well on the way to creating a metaverse that is used and provides daily value.

The foundation of the metaverse is Web3, which creates new and additional opportunities to build out the metaverse economy. By its design, Web3 is decentralized and built on blockchain, so it naturally supports DAOs, NFTs, and cryptocurrency. It's easy to see why blockchain, Web3, and the metaverse are linked.

The flexibility of Web3 and its associated technologies are the basis for creating virtual environments where users and players can create their content, including everything from artwork, to businesses, to entire theme parks. All these are within reach of user capabilities, depending on the capabilities of the metaverse world.

Tokenomics provides the fuel to enable the entire metaverse because, without economic drivers, consumers have little to no incentive for return visits. The ability to earn, buy, sell, and trade is the energy needed to keep the whole metaverse operating and expanding.

Tokens, by themselves, provide the incentives for contributors to create new content. Additionally, tokenomics lets games and worlds create a taxation system, collect gas and other fees, and even invest in various parts of the economy, just as in real life.

Without an engaging user (or player) journey, the expansion and proliferation of the metaverse will be constrained. Users must have consistent reasons to return. An immersive story, engaging services, and the entire economy gives clients the multiple incentives they need to incorporate the metaverse into their lives.

Artificial intelligence (AI) and machine learning (ML) will enhance personalized user experiences and give the metaverse, games, and other worlds a more immersive, interactive feel. By leveraging these technologies, designers and implementers can improve consumer engagement and increase profit margins.

Software as a service (SaaS) platforms like Wappier aim to accelerate the go-to-market speed with many features baked into their platform and inasmuch don't need to be reinvented or reimplemented. Wappier's Web3 acceleration technologies allow global brands to build their on-chain presence and give customers cross-reality interactions. This technology is helpful for the following reasons:[16]

- Game Publishers can use Wappier's AI-powered optimization suite to increase prices, improve customer retention, and increase consumer loyalty. The product also includes NFT tools to help designers use blockchain and NFT economies.

- NFT-first publishers will find Wappier helpful in improving their infrastructure using multiple chain solutions, keeping people returning and improve the economy.

- Brands will use Wappier to find new ways to interact with customers by using blockchain technology to create new marketplaces, mint NFT collections, and design cross-reality interactions.

Summary

This chapter examined how tokenomics are essential to the metaverse, gaming systems, and virtual worlds. Tokenomics gives consumers and players significant reasons to try new experiences and frequently builds loyalty and retention. Without the economic foundation set in place by tokenomics, people who visit virtual worlds could lose interest and move on to a different world or game that does include these concepts.

Decentralized gaming is an ideal use case for tokenomics because people are already engaged by the game mechanics. Virtual worlds that don't depend on gameplay are rising in popularity because people can purchase land (i.e., virtual real estate) and then build on top of their plots. Both use cases put tokenomics to work to give customers and players a reason to visit and return often. This analogous use case resolves the complex and often overlooked problem of retention and keeping people engaged over the long term.

In the next chapter, we will survey virtual worlds, which are moving to the forefront of metaverse development and implementation. Our discourse will center around the methods and strategies businesses, patrons, and developers can use to build and trade their virtual assets in virtual worlds. Many are rushing to establish in this space, as these virtual worlds may become worth billions.

Notes

1 R Nambiampurath. Blockchain Games: NFTs as an Integral Part of In-Game Tokenomics, 4 April 2021, beincrypto.com/blockchain-games-nfts-as-an-integral-part-of-in-game-tokenomics/ (archived at https://perma.cc/7U2T-8QT9)

2 R Stevens. What Is Tokenomics and Why Is It Important?, www.coindesk.com/learn/what-is-tokenomics-and-why-is-it-important/ (archived at https://perma.cc/KDA7-4QQT)

3 CoinMarketCap. coinmarketcap.com/currencies/decentraland/markets/ (archived at https://perma.cc/5Q9R-ZDNS)

4 The Sandbox. installers.sandbox.game/The_Sandbox_Whitepaper_2020.pdf (archived at https://perma.cc/XZP7-9NWX)

5 CoinbaseMarketcap The SandBox. coinmarketcap.com/currencies/the-sandbox/ (archived at https://perma.cc/V879-VE3G)

6 CoinBase Gala. www.coinbase.com/price/gala (archived at https://perma.cc/7SFR-VXD2)

7 DeFi Kingdoms. game.defikingdoms.com/ (archived at https://perma.cc/ EE78-269B)

8 Z Lorance. Metaverse Weekly: The Expanding Tokenomics of GameFi Protocol DeFi Kingdoms, 8 April 2022 www.gmw3.com/2022/04/metaverse-weekly-the-expanding-tokenomics-of-gamefi-protocol-defi-kingdoms/ (archived at https://perma.cc/9HU8-XP4N)

9 S Jansen. The First Metaverse Designed for Non-Crypto Gamers Releases Theatrical Trailer Ahead of Launch, 22 April 2022, cointelegraph.com/news/ the-first-metaverse-designed-for-non-crypto-gamers-releases-theatrical-trailer-ahead-of-launch (archived at https://perma.cc/9V9V-X225)

10 IFIT, Dell. The Next Era of Human|Machine Partnerships, 2017, www.delltechnologies.com/content/dam/delltechnologies/assets/ perspectives/2030/pdf/SR1940_IFTFforDellTechnologies_Human-Machine_070517_readerhigh-res.pdf (archived at https://perma.cc/ EQS9-ZJV6)

11 Tokenomics Lead / NFT Economist, cryptocurrencyjobs.co/engineering/ journey-to-the-metaverse-tokenomics-lead-nft-economist/ (archived at https://perma.cc/8LDW-5UDX)

12 C Heidorn. Token Gating: Everything You Need to Know in 2022, tokenizedhq.com/token-gating/ (archived at https://perma.cc/QM7Z-TVX5)

13 The Octalysis Framework for Gamification & Behavioral Design, yukaichou. com/gamification-examples/octalysis-complete-gamification-framework/ (archived at https://perma.cc/FZM9-Q6CR)

14 J Beerda. Designing the Metaverse: Making the Economy Work, octalysisgroup.com/designing-the-metaverse-making-the-economy-work/ (archived at https://perma.cc/F4J4-3Z46)

15 Quantity Theory of Money, www.toppr.com/guides/fundamentals-of-economics-and-management/money/quantity-theory-of-money/ (archived at https://perma.cc/V8JL-4B8Y)

16 Wappier, wappier.com/ (archived at https://perma.cc/UGM5-A724)

09 >3D Worlds_

The metaverse is our new frontier. Now is the time to create new worlds, venture into them, and explore what is there.

3D Virtual Worlds

"Meta" derives from the Greek word *meta*, which has many meanings, including *after* and *a higher order*. Both definitions apply to the metaverse, the successor to the internet and a consolidation of all (or most) web technologies that preceded it. The metaverse will enable communication and social interaction on a scale hitherto undreamed except by the most forward-thinking science-fiction authors. Because the metaverse is a conglomeration of virtual worlds, it will be the most powerful system (or systems) humans have ever created, and it will inevitably become part of everyday life for most humans.

Every metaverse user contributes in the experience. Because the metaverse is designed to be persistent and immersive, everyone participating will feel a sense of presence and belonging, more so than felt with earlier technologies. When users leave the metaverse, time there simply continues onward, just as in real life. There will be no pause button, which will provide a greater sense of reality.

Users will be able to partake in a viable and thriving economic system, complete with currency (i.e., cryptocurrency) that they can spend or use to purchase virtual or real items as non-fungible tokens (NFTs). This financial system will include banking, exchanges, and even gambling houses. The economy's completeness of the metaverse will give users a significant reason to visit and return.

Generally, the metaverse is created and supported by contributors who give their time and efforts to keep it growing and expanding. Individuals, standards organizations, and businesses will continue to invest heavily into the promise and actuality of the metaverse.

Building 3D Worlds

Virtual worlds are built on blockchain technology, meaning that the metaverse will be owned and created by users. A spectrum of companies will be involved; some will create their own "islands" or worlds, while others will focus on interoperability, being that the metaverse in itself and many of its worlds will be free and decentralized.

These worlds will be (and already are) real with the same needs and concerns as the physical world. The people who enter them form communities and cultures that need order and laws (or rules) on top of the "merely" technical aspects of the metaverse.

The possibilities are indeed endless, and the potential of the metaverse is vast. Everyone can contribute to the greater whole, whether as a visitor, a creator, or a game player. They can purchase assets in the form of NFTs, buy and develop land, play games, view works of art, or just stroll in a virtual garden. Not only can they observe these things, but they can also create them. The metaverse does not consist of hard rock, glass, and asphalt; instead, it is made of infinitely malleable digital impulses.

In this chapter, we'll be investigating the metaverse with an eye toward attracting and accumulating consumers in a way that makes sense and has meaning.

Digital Twins/User Avatars

In 2002, Challenge Advisory hosted a presentation for Michael Grieves. During this presentation about product lifecycle management, the concept of digital twins was introduced to the mainstream. Originating at NASA in the 1960s, this term involved the idea for space programming. NASA created duplicate systems that they used to match the systems in spacecraft.[1] Apollo 13 is a notable example of how this was done and what it was used for.

In virtual worlds, the term *digital twins* means to create a digital version of physical objects. These twins are used to help manage product lifecycles. Dale Tutt, the Vice President of Aerospace Defense at Siemens Digital Industries Software, highlighted, "... the digital twin is the precise virtual representation of a physical product or process. In aviation, the digital twin is used to help design new products or make changes to existing products faster because engineering teams have a rich, robust understanding of the product and how it performs."[2]

In the metaverse, a digital twin often refers to a hyper-lifelike avatar. There is some discourse, however, about whether an avatar should be very realistic or if it is better to practice taking advantage of the malleability of virtual worlds to make them more pliable, fanciful, and unreal. Presumably, some factors can restrict the acceptance of digital twins and lifelike avatars, especially the uncanny valley effect.

The *uncanny valley effect* is the perception caused when a robotic or on-screen character image causes individuals to feel like there is something off or wrong. Often, the viewers will not consciously notice it, but they may come away from the movie or video games thinking it was somehow wrong. Illustrations and other artwork also walk a similar tightrope—they can be too abstract, ideal, or realistic. Digital twins and avatars must walk this line carefully to ensure that the images do not alienate consumers due to this type of effect.[3]

Several platforms and enterprises provision a range of approaches to digital twins and avatars:

ObEN. This artificial intelligence (AI) company is creating Personal AI (PAI) to improve digital interactions in virtual worlds. They created an app featuring a 2D PAI avatar, which they named Satoshi. This app acts as a news presenter on subjects including blockchain and cryptocurrency.[4]

Soul Machines. This technology is an example of using AI and high-definition 3D graphics to create an interactive experience. The business sector can use this technology to create digital twins, avatars, and on-air personalities who can act as entertainers, teachers, customer service representatives, and so on. Using this technology, digital citizens can provide a more lifelike experience for customers than current chatbots, thus reinforcing brands.[5]

Ready Player Me. This platform enables designers to create 3D characters and avatars, which brands then use to fulfill their metaverse, gaming, and other platform strategies. They provide the tools for designers to change skin tones, body types, and shapes and to add clothing and other accessories. One of the goals of Ready Player Me is to create cross-game avatars that can be used in any game and the metaverse.

Off-White. Virtual clothing is a requirement for avatars. Virtual fashion, as indicated in the previous chapter, adds a layer to the digital identity desired by consumers in the online world. Virgil Abloh, Founder and CEO of Off-White, and one of the most prolific designers of our time, reaffirmed, "I want to make virtual clothes to paint pictures physical clothes cannot, and let buyers access a new dimension of their style—no matter who they are, where they live, and the virtual worlds they love."[6]

Meta. Mark Zuckerberg, the CEO of Meta (previously Facebook), announced on June 17, 2022, that the public would be able to purchase clothing and fashion from a virtual avatar store. He noted that people could enhance their avatar with high virtual fashion items, including a Balenciaga sweater or Prada purse. He underscored, "Digital goods will be an important way to express yourself in the metaverse and a big driver of the creative economy. I'm excited to add more brands and bring this to VR soon too."[7]

Horizon World. This world is a social virtual reality (VR) app from Meta. Using the app, users can customize their avatars, including making them look like themselves. Meanwhile, these avatars can be missing legs and only have a head, arms, and feet. Andrew Bosworth, Meta's VP of Reality Labs and incoming CTO, explained, "Tracking your legs accurately is super hard and not workable just from a physics standpoint with existing headsets."[8]

Shapify. This device, by Artec3D, allows for the accurate scanning of a person's entire body, which is scanned from all angles and acquires everything, including the smallest details, from posture to creases in clothing. An entire body can be scanned in just a few seconds.[9]

Veeso VR Headset. This headset scans a person's face in real time, sends that information to a smartphone or mobile device, and then transfers the data to avatars. Subsequently, the avatars will gain the person's facial expressions and emotions.

Designing Immersive 3D Spaces

In the past, creating 3D objects necessitated many hours of tedious work by artists who used tools, such as Poser and Daz3D's Daz Studio, to hand-generate the mapping, textures, and characters of each object. While that process can and still is performed by 3D artists, it's now possible to use scanners to create 3D maps and textures automatically.

Using these scanners, users can transfer actual physical objects directly to the metaverse. They scan them using object capture technology, then optionally add other details using 3D modeling tools if desired. To contextualize, someone could scan a 3D image of a book, then edit that 3D image to change the title and cover art, which they then edit to modify the textures and colors.

The industry uses more advanced technologies, including Lidar cameras and satellite shots. A tool such as Quixel can create photo-realistic 3D images using Unreal Engine and Megascans. Adobe Substance is an expressive tool for texturizing 3D models.

Why is it necessary to create virtual worlds that look like the physical world? By adding realism to the metaverse and games, it makes users feel more comfortable, and gives them a familiar experience with similar reference points to the real world. Specifically, a light switch in the virtual metaverse looks the same and does the same thing as a light switch in the metaverse. The term used to describe objects that mimic real-life objects is skeuomorphism. As the visual design language of the metaverse evolves, so will the visual vocabulary.

Conceptually, by making the virtual world look and feel more like the physical world, it provides a more immersive experience. With some exceptions, such as games, virtual worlds will initially be designed around specific physical laws. In particular, some may enforce gravity, while others may have unique rules depending on their purpose. Of course, this functionality requires a significant amount of computational power. The processing load must be appropriately balanced between the cloud (i.e., server-side) and the user device (i.e., client-side) to improve performance. Nonetheless, the metaverse requires decentralized computing to enable splitting the loads as needed.

Software can solve the complexity of 3D simulations by using advanced algorithms to optimize performance, reduce the amount of data transferred, and distribute the load to different computers and resources as appropriate.

Creating Engaging Experiences

All these efforts are needed to create an engaging experience because if visitors are not engaged, they will not have much incentive to return. Users must be entertained, educated, enlightened, and delighted at every turn to have reasons for entering and continuing to use the metaverse. To achieve this, powerful storytelling is required, in addition to game mechanics like those used by Fortnite, Roblox, and Minecraft.

Moreover, metaverse's virtual worlds must be designed with a creator economy at its core, based on content, services, and asset creation for economic opportunities. A fully functional economic system is also needed so that users can buy, sell, trade, and own virtual items, which provides a method of rewards that will motivate the masses to participate.

A vital feature of the metaverse is providing users with a sense of ownership. Blockchain and NFTs, by design, grant this sense to users because they form the basis for ownership. An important reason for using the metaverse in day-to-day life disappears without ownership.

Accordingly, other strategies encourage long-term participation, including:

- Play to earn
- Rewarding users for their contributions
- Achieving goals in much the same way as games

The metaverse is decentralized and will never have a single owner. Of course, there will be vast worlds owned and operated by corporations, such as Meta, Fortnite, Roblox, and games. Moreover, the metaverse will depend on interoperability and decentralized autonomous organizations (DAOs) for its success. This is similar to the internet, which is not owned by any government or corporation, although specific websites and platforms on it are.

Enterprises are already using the metaverse's virtual worlds in some ways. Accenture announced that 150,000 new hires would be onboarded using VR and the metaverse. They will use this technology to educate their clients and train them on strategies and operations.

Metaverse's potential is enormous, as evidenced by a new report from McKinsey. This report predicts that annual metaverse-related spending could top $5 trillion by 2030, and e-commerce could make up between $2 trillion and $2.6 trillion. McKinsey compared this to AI spending, which they emphasized totaled $93 billion in 2021.[10]

One of the primary aptitudes of virtual worlds might be the connection between the physical and virtual. As the metaverse matures, the boundaries between virtual and reality will blend, primarily due to immersive technologies such as augmented reality (AR) and virtual reality (VR). This will increase the importance of virtual worlds and create opportunities for personalization so that inhabitants will see their world through their lens.

Personalized Experiences in Virtual Worlds

Adobe provides several tools to enable virtual ad buyers to track how their metaverse campaigns are performing. Adobe Analytics explained in an interview that the virtual world must generate revenue to succeed. Companies must be able to gain insights for their customers as they use the metaverse, in the same way, that Web Analytics lets website owners personalize experiences for their visitors based on their affinities and preferences.[11]

Accessibility, Privacy, and Security

According to the US Census Bureau, there were 41.1 million people in the United States with a disability in 2019. It is compounded by the fact that hundreds (if not thousands) of languages and cultures worldwide exist. The metaverse must be accessible to everyone globally, limited only by the availability of technology.

With its immersive experience, 3D graphics, and changeability, companies will find virtual worlds ideal for onboarding clients and employees. Functionally, Framework for Log Anonymization and Information Management (FLAIM) Systems offers immersive VR solutions to train communities for hazardous situations and emergencies. Firefighters are already using this system to learn firefighting techniques safely, so they don't need to be exposed to dangerous situations.[12]

The metaverse will be available to billions of users on devices of their choice, making it a true omnichannel experience. Thereby, audiences can access it on their PC, smartphone, tablet, personal assistant, and so forth. Devices such as VR and AR headsets and visors may also be used. Predictably, metaverse input devices must support smooth and robust voice interactions and gestures, which must be standardized.

Privacy, security, and safety are paramount concerns. The populace will come to depend on the metaverse, blockchain, and NFTs in their daily lives, and they will expect their personal information to be kept private and their environments to be secure. For example, protecting children from nefarious individuals will be paramount, and this might require some level of moderation of the virtual space, including some level of parental control.

Connecting to the Metaverse

Many influencers begin by developing their audience on a specific platform, such as YouTube or TikTok. Understandably, they might grow frustrated with the limitations of the platform they initially choose but find it difficult, if not impossible, to transfer their content and community to something else. For instance, many content creators on YouTube felt they would be better served with a different platform model, so they created a new platform called Nebula to host their videos.

For creators to be enticed to transfer to the metaverse, it needs to provide a way to monetize their content easily. Doing so will provide them with the incentives they need to tackle the significant task of moving their content and audience to the newer platform. Expectedly, the metaverse must earn the trust of brands, so people use it by default.

Scott Belsky, Chief Product Officer at Adobe, explained in an interview that many startups focus on existing users instead of creating new ones. He explained:

> in ultimate irony, that first mile of the user's experience tends to be the last mile of the team's experience when building the product. It's really toward the end where people ask, "What should the tour be, and what copy should we slap in there? Let's just use the form fields that we think are logical." It doesn't make any sense. It's all about the first mile.[13]

Arvind Krishna, the Chairman and CEO of IBM underscored, "It's a question of verticals versus horizontals. We believe that we are best positioned to take these technologies. We will always have an industry lens through our consulting team. We want to work on technologies that are horizontals across all industries."[14]

Summary

The metaverse is emerging from various technologies, gaming systems, social platforms, and designs that will interoperate to create a virtual, engaging, real-time, persistent environment that people will find useful to improve their lives. Because there are so many players (including companies and individuals) and the task is immense and not yet fully defined, there won't be a single growth period. Instead, expect growth in spurts and waves as recent technologies, designs, processes, and ideas occur.

A vital part of the design of virtual worlds in the metaverse is decentralization. Hence, there will not be a single place for individuals to visit in the metaverse. Instead, think of the metaverse as the glue (or strings) that connects many different virtual worlds and enables them to interoperate for the benefit of users and organizations. These virtual worlds—games, banks, entertainment venues, and social platforms—will empower societies and brands to find new ways to communicate, interact, earn money, and live their lives.

Humanity will become fully immersed in the metaverse, especially as the costs of the hardware and software fall, growing the digital economy.

Virtual worlds in the metaverse must provide the following:

- Companies and people must be able to sell, buy, trade, service, and market goods within the metaverse using their current enterprise technical stack.

- The commercial sector must be able to integrate products into their existing architecture stack.

- Full 360-degree views of customer relationship management (CRM) are required to evaluate marketing and advertising performance.

Now that we've explored virtual worlds, let's go into detail about the infrastructure that supports the metaverse, including endpoints, central systems, networks, software, and AI.

Notes

1 C Miskinis. The History and Creation of the Digital Twin Concept, March 2019, www.challenge.org/insights/digital-twin-history/ (archived at https://perma.cc/Z58K-MLJ2)

2 J Careless. Digital Twinning: The Latest on Virtual Models, 29 August 2021, www.aerospacetechreview.com/digital-twinning-the-latest-on-virtual-models/ (archived at https://perma.cc/D22T-NUEC)

3 Not Too Abstract, Not Too Realistic, Just Right, www.ferdio.com/notebook/not-too-abstract-not-too-realistic-just-right (archived at https://perma.cc/XYW3-ASYV)

4 ObEN. ObEN Launches AI Newscaster with 3D "Satoshi" Avatar to Deliver Content via PAI News App, 14 May 2019, www.globenewswire.com/news-release/2019/05/14/1823951/0/en/ObEN-Launches-AI-Newscaster-With-3D-Satoshi-Avatar-to-Deliver-Content-via-PAI-News-App.html (archived at https://perma.cc/KYY7-XAXL)

5 Soul Machines, www.soulmachines.com/ (archived at https://perma.cc/7V2Q-AX98)

6 D R. Virgil Abloh's Off-White Entering the Metaverse, 13 August 2021, www.conten.tech/post/virgil-abloh-s-off-white-entering-the-metaverse (archived at https://perma.cc/Y7AE-F5FJ)

7 V Bondarenko. Mark Zuckerberg Wants to Sell You (Meta) Fashion, 18 June 2022, www.thestreet.com/lifestyle/mark-zuckerberg-wants-to-sell-you-meta-fashion (archived at https://perma.cc/EH47-SA9W)

8 R Metz. Why You Can't Have Legs in Virtual Reality (Yet), 15 February 2022, www.cnn.com/2022/02/15/tech/vr-no-legs-explainer/index.html (archived at https://perma.cc/ZXR6-5XEM)

9 3D Full Body Scanning with Shapify Booth, www.artec3d.com/portable-3d-scanners/shapifybooth (archived at https://perma.cc/49DA-8V4X)

10 A-M Alcántara and P Coffee. Metaverse Spending to Total $5 Trillion in 2030, McKinsey Predicts, 14 June 2022, www.wsj.com/articles/metaverse-spending-to-total-5-trillion-in-2030-mckinsey-predicts-11655254794 (archived at https://perma.cc/HM7F-C3ZN)

11 E J Savitz. Adobe Moves to Track Ads in the Metaverse, 14 June 2022, www.barrons.com/articles/adobe-stock-metaverse-51655218195 (archived at https://perma.cc/PVR7-RZYQ)

12 Fully Immersive VR learning Solutions for Training in Hazardous and Emergency Situations, flaimsystems.com/ (archived at https://perma.cc/9ENR-6ZUV)

13 D O'Dwyer. From Conversion to Retention: Industry Experts on Improving Your Onboarding, 7 March 2019, www.intercom.com/blog/podcasts/expert-advice-improving-user-onboarding/ (archived at https://perma.cc/QB76-A7ZL)

14 International Business Machines Corporation's (IBM) CEO Arvind Krishna Presents at Bernstein 38th Annual Strategic Decisions Conference (Transcript), 2 June 2022, seekingalpha.com/article/4516142-international-business-machines-corporations-ibm-ceo-arvind-krishna-presents-bernstein-38th (archived at https://perma.cc/3AK5-YWW8)

10 >Infrastructure_

Endpoints, Central Systems, Network, Software, and Artificial Intelligence

In World War II, the allies and the axis countries used analog computer systems to code and decode secret messages. At the time, these technologies were considered highly advanced. After the war, larger, more sophisticated computers were built. These behemoths took up large rooms filled with equipment that needed to be air-conditioned and kept free from contamination. Nobody had even dreamed of the supercomputers that followed, much less smartphones, the internet, web, and artificial intelligence (AI). Science-fiction writers did not even touch on these concepts except in the broadest strokes.

Since that time, technology has evolved and gone through many transformations. Before each change, people, even those "in-the-know", made inaccurate or completely wrong conclusions about the future of technology. Highlighted by Ken Olsen, the former president of Digital Equipment Corporation, who famously argued in 1977, "There is no reason for any individual to have a computer in their home."

Fast-forward to today. It's striking that just a couple of generations ago, people watched four channels of pre-programmed material on heavy television sets using vacuum tubes. Today, virtually everyone carries what would have been referred to as a supercomputer, from which they can watch millions of different videos on demand.

Underneath it all, invisible to most people, is the vast amount of technology to support business and individual use of computers, the internet, web, and their associated applications. For most people, the extent of their knowledge stops at getting their smartphone configured or calling their internet provider to install a cable modem. The details behind the scenes are invisible, which is how they should be.

For this chapter, *infrastructure* is defined as the technology that underpins the computing-related needs of end-users and businesses. This includes endpoints (i.e., mobile devices, PCs, smartphones), central systems (i.e., servers both cloud- and non-cloud-based), network (i.e., digital subscriber line [DSL], broadband, and other technologies), and software (i.e. operating systems, firmware). We're also grouping artificial intelligence (AI) and machine learning (ML) into the mix, because these technologies are essential for our discussion of the metaverse.

Overview

We begin our investigation with *endpoints*, which are defined as devices that provide input/output services to users, whether they be consumers or business processes. Endpoints include smartphones, laptops, desktop computers, and Internet of Things (IoT). We're also including augmented reality (AR), virtual reality (VR), mixed reality (MR), and extended reality (XR) into this set because these technologies are required for the metaverse to operate. For businesses, endpoints include robots; industrial IoT devices; medical IoT; and other smart, business-oriented devices.

Consumers and businesses use endpoints to put computing and, down the line, the metaverse to work. It's what they see and how they experience computers, virtual worlds, games, and the metaverse. All these devices are connected, in one way or another, to central systems that store data and house applications.

We join servers and their associated databases (whether cloud-based or not) into central systems. These devices and databases on the back end are wholly unseen and usually unknown to users. Despite the name, central systems may be decentralized (as in the case of blockchain and NFTs). We're simply differentiating the back end from the endpoints for clarity. Central systems perform much of the work, store vast amounts of data, and usually host applications.

A vast web of networks connects everything. In consumers' homes or businesses, routers and wireless routers enable endpoints to connect to the greater internet. These routers understand and hide how a user (or application) request sends and receives information to other systems in the cloud, in server rooms, or, in the case of decentralized systems and applications, to all the places where the data and resources may be found.

Endpoints, central systems, databases, and everything else on the internet and within the metaverse, games, and other virtual worlds require software and applications. Looking more closely, your smartphone runs applications that connect over a network to get to central systems that run applications which perform calculations and manipulate data in databases. Applications run on the endpoints (i.e., smartphones, smart glasses, factory manufacturing robots), on routers (to route your requests to the right places), and on the central systems (to manipulate data and return it to you in some form).

Finally, AI and ML are essential components to adding intelligence (or the appearance of intelligence) to endpoints, central systems, and applications. AI/ML enables non-player characters to appear more lifelike and act like real people. This is also essential for AR and VR to become lifelike and interact with people and objects. Without AI/ML, there simply is no metaverse.

With that brief overview in place, let's begin by discussing endpoints and how they apply to the metaverse.

Endpoints

In the earliest days of computing, computers took up entire rooms, filled with refrigerator- and washing-machine-sized machines that vibrated voraciously. These machines, which had memory measured in kilobytes (not megabytes), needed copious amounts of air conditioning because they generated lots of heat.

"Today, it's so much easier," explained the director of computer operations of a major retailer. "In the early 1980s, I worked with a machine by Digital Equipment Corporation known as a PDP-11/34. Each morning we had to boot the machine by typing in 20 machine-level instructions on the front toggle board. This caused it to boot from paper tape, which is exactly what it sounds like, to get the boot code for the disk drive. We accessed the PDP-11/34 from teletypes, which operated at a few dozen characters per second, and huge television screens. However, this machine, which only sported 128 kilobytes of memory and 10 megabytes of disk space, ran over 100 jobs simultaneously for an accounting firm."

Those early machines' input and output didn't have any intelligence. They were connected to a computer system with thick cables, and data only traveled in one direction: either from an input device such as a teletype or keyboard or to an output device such as a printer or television screen.

There were no smartphones; mobile phones of any type didn't yet exist. The internet and the World Wide Web didn't yet exist either, and cyber currencies didn't even appear in science-fiction novels. Graphics, much less 3D graphics, were still a dream. Even personal computers and gaming consoles had not yet been invented. As far as technology was concerned, it was a different world.

Technology has undergone many iterations, and the evolution of endpoints is the most profound as far as users are concerned. Before personal computers and video game consoles came on the scene in the 1980s, the users of computers were people in businesses, universities, government, and other organizations. Home users didn't yet exist (and were not even imagined by anyone).

That all changed with the advent of personal computers, such as the TRS-80 and, later, Windows 95, along with the rising popularity of video game consoles. People wanted their computer and video systems, along with the associated applications and games. Even though the internet and web didn't yet exist, these early users connected to new online services, known as bulletin boards like AOL, CompuServe, and Prodigy using rotary phones. These connections were painfully slow, but it was better than nothing.

Progress continued onward. The internet and web became widespread and replaced all those tedious dial-up connections. At this point, personal computers and video game consoles began to take advantage of the always-on potential of the internet to send messages, receive updates, and download graphics.

After the year 2000, cell phones began their explosion into the pockets of virtually everyone. The invention of the iPhone, Android, and other phones brought instant communication across the planet. Add to that DSL, broadband, fiber, and satellite networks (covered in the network section of this chapter), speed of connection, and even the possibility of connection, became a non-issue for most people.

At the time of the writing of this book, telecom giants are in the process of spending billions of dollars to roll out the infrastructure needed to support 5G cell phone technology. This standard will enable 20 gigabits per second peak and 100+ megabits per connect average data rates. In less than a decade, 6G is slated to begin its rollout, promising delivery speeds of 800 gigabits per second.

These breakneck communication speeds of the various networks (i.e., fiber, DSL, broadband, satellite, 5G, 6G, and others) enable and support the development and use of smarter and better endpoints. Without a fast network (which we'll address in more detail later in this chapter), endpoints have limited value for users, businesses, and industry.

What is an Endpoint?

Endpoints are any device that is physically located at the end of a network. Examples include smartphones, tablets, laptops, personal computers, gaming consoles, personal assistants such as Alexa and Google Home, IoT devices, medical IoT devices, and manufacturing IoT devices (among many others). Speakers, VR helmets, haptic devices, AR glasses/contact lenses, and XR devices also count as endpoints. For this chapter, we examine servers in the Central Systems section, even though they also qualify as types of endpoints.

An endpoint, or computing device, communicates over a network (wired or wireless). For instance, when someone plays a video game on an Xbox 360, the endpoint is the Xbox 360 console. When two people talk to one another on smartphones, each phone is considered an endpoint.

Consumer endpoint hardware becomes more advanced and more capable every year. Newer models are built with enhanced batteries capable of longer life and can hold more considerable charge for extended times. Sensors are becoming more capable, smaller, and less power-hungry; camera quality is increasing to the point where some smartphones take better pictures than professional gear; and with the arrival of 5G (and by the end of this decade, 6G), bandwidth is quickly becoming a non-concern.

These advances all progress the quality of our devices and allow people to communicate in more ways than ever, and they also are becoming so advanced as to where they can support the metaverse with all its functionality.

Examples of Endpoints

Let's look at the following standard endpoints and inspect how they might be helpful in the metaverse.

Personal computers (PC). These were among the first devices made available to home users, and they grew in popularity until smartphones and mobile devices superseded them because they simply aren't as mobile. Many homes no longer even own a PC, instead doing everything they need on a tablet or smartphone. PCs are often used as gaming consoles, primarily custom-built with high-capability hardware. More powerful graphics cards will make these excellent platforms for the metaverse.

Video game consoles. These consoles have been around as long as personal computers. Their built-in graphics support internet connectivity, making these platforms ideal for the metaverse, especially as newer and more powerful models are released in the coming years.

Smartphones. These pocket computers now support everything from making phone calls and sending text messages to playing complex video games and keeping the family finances. Smartphones are equipped with an array of sensory devices, including cameras (at least two in most cases), speakers, and microphones. They also connect to the internet over high-speed communications like 4G and 5G, can use wireless, and are small enough to carry in a pocket. To support the metaverse, they will need to become even more powerful and offer support for VR, AR, and XR devices. Luckily, the technology is well on the way to becoming an ideal metaverse endpoint, especially because nearly everyone owns one. Although, at the very least, 5G speeds will be required to support the metaverse fully.

Tablets and other mobile devices. Tablets are mobile devices, like smartphones, only larger. Some tablets are specialized for specific roles, such as Kindle for reading books, while others are for general use. They tend to use Wi-Fi and not cellular networks (with exceptions) and typically do not sport the array of sensors present in smartphones. Depending on the purpose and model, and with hardware upgrades, these might support the metaverse.

Personal assistants. Amazon Alexa and Google Home are examples of personal assistants. These virtual assistance devices use voice commands and speakers, although newer models include small video screens. These devices will be able to connect to the metaverse, but in their current form, they cannot support the 3D graphics, fast communications, and applications needed to do so.

IoT devices. Smart light bulbs, alarms, and plugs are consumer-grade IoT devices. Irrespective, many smart devices, including sensors and motion detection, are not visible to consumers. All these devices access the cloud to receive and transmit information and commands. Devices such as smart light bulbs can be accessed from the metaverse, while smart sensors can deliver data to the metaverse.

Medical IoT devices. The metaverse provides many possibilities for medical technology. Virtual worlds can be used to train surgeons and other medical professionals. In the future, virtual doctors in the metaverse will be able to diagnose medical problems without physically contacting patients by taking advantage of wearable IoT devices.

Manufacturing IoT devices. Manufacturing no longer consists of highly specialized people standing over a moving belt, screwing on bolts on wheels. Today, these tasks are performed by autonomous and semi-autonomous robots; manufacturing plants are becoming fully automated, which introduces opportunities for the metaverse to test designs, try new types of robots and other equipment, and even control live manufacturing plants.

Each of these endpoints serves a valuable purpose in improving people's day-to-day lives in gaming and virtual worlds and, of course, in the metaverse. In addition, other technologies are needed to enable genuinely immersive experiences and extended reality. Let's explore a few more critical technologies (i.e., endpoints) in the following sections.

VR, AR, MR, XR, and Haptic Devices

One of the prime attractions of the metaverse is the option to take part in partially or fully immersive experiences. Technologies such as augmented reality (AR), virtual reality (VR), mixed reality (MR), extended reality (XR), and haptic devices (i.e., those which support other senses such as touch) are endpoints (or components of endpoints) that support partially or fully immersive experiences. These capabilities bring virtual worlds and the metaverse to life as truly immersive experiences. In this section, we'll describe the technologies in more detail.

To put these technologies into perspective, begin with a straight line. At one end is the physical reality, and the other is fully immersive virtual reality. This is known as the virtuality spectrum—a scale beginning with the entirely physical and ending at the completely virtual. The area between these two extremes is called mixed reality. It is also known as the reality-virtuality continuum.[1]

AR mixes virtual objects or information into the real world; on the other hand, mixing physical objects into a virtual world is known as augmented virtuality (AV). Typically, you might encounter AV while watching a virtual screen in the metaverse, which includes physical objects.[2]

Check out this diagram:[3]

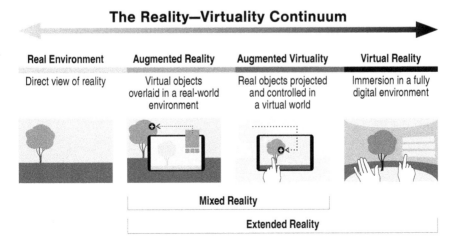

The Reality—Virtuality Continuum

Real Environment	Augmented Reality	Augmented Virtuality	Virtual Reality
Direct view of reality	Virtual objects overlaid in a real-world environment	Real objects projected and controlled in a virtual world	Immersion in a fully digital environment

Mixed Reality

Extended Reality

Mixed reality (MR) is the fusion of AR and AV, while XR consists of AR, AV, and VR. We'll talk about all these concepts later on.

Augmented Reality

Augmented reality, also known as AR, enhances objects in the real world by overlaying them with computer-generated information. AR occurs in real time, is three dimensional, and interactive. AR is more than just images—it can also include sound and haptic sensations (i.e., touch).

AR debuted in 1968 with the invention of a head-mounted display by Ivan Sutherland. Later, the US Air Force and NASA used AR to enhance navigation. Tom Caudell came up with the term augmented reality in 1990, and the technology came into use on the internet in the early 2000s. The furniture store Ikea created a smartphone app to allow consumers to overlay their furniture in their homes through the smartphone display.[4] Of course, AR became a common household term with the introduction of Pokémon Go in 2016.

Some examples of AR include:

Snapchat filters. These filters let users add images to their pictures. They can add everything from navigation aids to costumes to funny photos. All that's needed is a smartphone and the Snapchat app.

Pokémon Go. This app went live in 2016, made $207 million in its first month, and was the top download in the world.[5] It lets users search their local environment for Pokémon, which can be found by looking through a smartphone display.

Heads-up display (HUD). These are displays mounted in automobiles, planes, and so forth that display information on windows to aid in navigation, play games, and perform other functions.

AR is based on a device equipped with a camera. These include smartphones, specially equipped contact lenses, smart glasses, and other mobile devices. When a consumer view objects through the screen or lens, complex software uses computer vision to analyze the video stream and superimpose computer-generated images as appropriate.[6]

Technically, AR software is loaded onto the devices including smartphones, glasses, or contact lenses. Users see the physical world through these devices. When a user looks at something, the cloud-connected AR software analyzes the video stream and inserts the appropriate image information into the user's view. A user then sees a combination of natural and virtual images.

Pokémon Go overlayed images onto the display view without considering depth, distance, and other complexities. Snapchat filters and other use cases add cartoon or animated images to a video stream by recognizing facial contours and basing their algorithms on that. A similar example, more complex AR applications, such as adding an animated bird flying through the woods, must understand the concepts of foreground/background, depth of field, the angles of vision, and movement of many objects. The solutions to these more complex AR scenarios require artificial intelligence and machine learning.

Understanding images might seem to be simple because the human brain is exceptionally good at it. Also, to note, images are not something that computers are inherently programmed to do. For a computer, an image is just a stream of ones and zeroes—understanding the patterns is the problem. This is addressed by breaking the image down into semantics, understanding the parts of the image, and 3D geometry, which further breaks down the image into components. Let's say, in a picture of a person standing in front of a building holding a flashlight, 3D geometry breaks out the person, the building, and the flashlight (and anything else in the image). Semantics then interprets each of the parts to understand their meaning.

Of course, the geometry of a flashlight is vastly different from that of a building, and even that is different from a face or body. To make it even more complicated, objects break down into subobjects. The image of a person is composed of a face, arms, and legs, and that person could be wearing clothes and jewelry and even have tattoos. The human brain excels at breaking down complex composite images into their parts. However, computers have a more challenging time than our brains, so much so that an entire branch of computer science known as computer vision is devoted to this subject.

To add another layer of complexity, the image is viewed in two dimensions, and from that, the third dimension must be extrapolated. Again, the human brain does this quickly—but the human brain has evolved over hundreds of millions of years.

Adding the third dimension is critical because AR must insert objects into the image before it reaches the human eye. Consider the complexity of this operation. A person wears AR glasses or contact lenses to view the world. Two images are received of a moment in time from these viewing devices—one from the left and one from the right just as occurs without AR. Each of these images must be interpreted and understood, then a new image of those two original images must be inserted in places that make sense in under a second. The new images, which include the inserted elements, are then sent to the human eye.

This process requires some specialized technology:

Depth-sensing camera. AR requires a camera (or, in the case of glasses and contact lenses, two cameras) that records the view's visual information and then determines the distance and angle to the focal point (i.e., the place where the human eye focuses), typically an object. It also needs to do the same for other things in the view.

Registration tools. Hardware-based sensors and accelerometers help AR understand the geometry of the space so that images can be placed in the right places.

Computer vision. As we've maintained, complex ML and AI algorithms are necessary to break down the images within the view and understand their meaning.

Output. Naturally, the composite image must be displayed for it to be seen. On AR glasses and contact lenses, this occurs on the glass of the lenses; on a smartphone, it occurs on the device's screen; on a personal computer, it occurs on the computer screen.

There are distinct types of artificial reality, each with its specific purpose:

Marker-based AR. This form of AR uses markers, such as QR codes, logos, or artwork, to understand where to insert AR objects.

Markerless AR. Another form of AR is to insert images into the view. A fitting example is the Home Depot app that allows consumers to insert their merchandise into their view of a room in their home. The merchandise is simply overlayed onto the display. Pokémon Go is another example of markerless AR.

There are also several types of markerless AR:

Location-based AR. The travel and tourism industries use location-based AR, which uses the GOS system to overlay items onto the view depending on physical locations. This AR type is useful in mapping applications to place appropriate images in a map context. For example, a Grand Canyon National Park tourist app could insert arrows indicating hiking paths or signs describing sightseeing topics.

Projection-based AR. This AR type is commonly used in training applications. It allows people to move around objects freely to see them from all sides.

Superimposition-based AR. This AR form performs full or partial replacement of one or more objects in the view with other entities. This is used by social media filters such as Facebook and Instagram.

Outlining AR. Also known as contour-based AR, this AR type is commonly used in car navigation systems to outline view areas to make them easier to see after dark, giving a better view to the observer.

In addition to the displays on smartphones, tablets, and other mobile devices, these are a few of the devices that support augmented reality:

Smart contacts. Miniaturized LCD displays and electronics have enabled the implementation of AR contact lenses. These lenses add images, navigation information, and other data to the view only seen by those who wear them. Mojo Lens has developed contact lens technology.[7]

Glasses. Smart glasses add images, videos, and information to the lens view. They send and receive their information via connected personal computers or smartphones.

Hoods. These hoods cover the entire head. AR technology is used to display images, video, and information on the window of the hood. These hoods have many uses in manufacturing and business.

There are many applications for AR, both in and outside of the metaverse. Equally important, for a truly immersive experience, we need to evaluate virtual reality (VR).

Virtual Reality

Whereas AR superimposes images and information on physical reality, virtual reality (VR) immerses a person into a virtual world. VR creates simulated environments where a user's senses are engaged within the virtual world. If you've seen the movie *Ready Player One* or *Free Guy*, you've seen an example of VR. Most video games use VR to create worlds where players wander around solving puzzles, hunting monsters, and purchasing in-game items.

The concept of VR began in 1935 with a story written by Stanley Weinbaum called *Pygmalion's Spectacles*. In this science-fiction story, a character uses a pair of goggles to enter a fictional world. These glasses gave the wearer a fully immersive experience.

The first "real" VR device was patented in 1962. It was created by Morton Heilig and was called Sensorama; this device consisted of a large booth that could fit up to four people and simulated several senses, including 3D sight, audio, vibrations, smell, and even wind.

The first flight simulator was created by a military engineer named Thomas Furness in 1966. In 1969, Myron Krueger began creating AR experiences using computers connected to video systems. Later, in 1975, he created an interactive VR platform called Videoplace that used a dark room and large video screens surrounding the viewer.

In 1980, a company called StereoGraphics created stereo vision glasses. In 1985, Jaron Lanier and Thomas Zimmerman founded VPL Research, Inc to sell VR goggles and gloves. In 1989, Crystal River Engineering, founded by Scott Foster, developed VR training for astronauts, which, in addition to images, included 3D audio. In another application for space exploration, a NASA scientist named Antonio Medina created Computer Simulated Teleoperation, a VR application intended to help drive Mars rovers from Earth.

Fast-forward to 2010 with the development of a prototype (the first) for the Oculus Rift headset. It was created by Palmer Luckey and featured a new feature allowing a 90-degree field of vision. He later raised $2.4 million through a Kickstarter campaign to implement the technology. In 2014, Facebook bought the resulting company, Oculus VR, for $2 billion.

By 2016, the field of companies developing VR products became crowded, with well over a hundred developing products, including Google, Apple, Amazon, Microsoft, and many others.

In 2019, the number of VR headsets connected to Steam was reported to have exceeded 1 million for the first time. Finally, in 2020, the Oculus Quest 2 was released—and has sold millions of units since then.[8]

VR has appeared in many movies, including *Ready Player One* and *Free Guy*. These two films are notable examples of how immersive experiences and virtual reality will work in the future.

There are three types of virtual reality:[9]

Non-immersive. Most VR today is non-immersive in that the virtual environment is displayed on a screen. The user is not immersed in the scene. Instead, it's like they are watching a movie.

Semi-immersive. Flight simulators and disaster training programs often use semi-immersive technologies. Projectors and viewing screens might surround the user. Physical devices might simulate movement, such as devices that lift one side of the simulator to make it seem a plane is banking or a theme park ride that raises the ride's front end into the air to give the appearance of climbing.

Fully immersive. This type of VR is often portrayed in movies such as *The Matrix*, *Free Guy*, and *Ready Player One*. The user is fully immersed, and it feels to them like they are within the virtual world. Haptic gloves and full-body suits simulate touch, and goggles and headphones simulate sight and sound. Future advances might even allow other senses such as taste, smell, and motion to be simulated to a certain extent.

HOW DOES VR WORK?

So, how does VR work? How does it place a person into an imaginary, virtual world that appears real to a greater or lesser extent? VR headsets (i.e., goggles), headphones, hand-trackers, treadmills, and other devices can make the brain think the imaginary world is real. The more senses can be mimicked, the more the illusion appears real.

To embrace fully immersive experiences and truly feel like the real world to its users, VR needs to be believable, interactive, and immersive.

Users must also be able to explore and experience virtual worlds. This is all done by using real-time computer-generated 3D graphics, high-quality sound, and simulating as many other senses as possible.

Some of the components of a good VR experience include the following:[10]

Sound. Without high-quality sound, VR simply doesn't work. Mono and even stereo sound are not good enough. Instead, spatial audio is required—this is sound that syncs in real time with the visual images in the virtual world, thus creating a sensation of immersive audio.

Head and eye tracking. VR would be nothing if it were static. In many ways tracking the movement of a user's head and eyes is critical to creating an immersive experience. Users move around a VR world, and it changes from their perspective, as they do. This is done with LED lights, laser pointers, and sensors with stereoscopic 3D images. The same image from a unique perspective is displayed to the right and left eyes. It creates depth perception, which gives the imaginary world a three-dimensional appearance.

As of 2022, mobile VR headsets like the Samsung Gear VR, Oculus Go, and Daydream View can only do rotational tracking, which means they respond to head movements but not body movements. Future advances will consider complete body movements to create an even more immersive experience.

Field of view. Humans typically see the world in a 200-to-220-degree arc around their heads, with an overlap between the right and left eyes. Currently, VR development works with this overlapped space between the eyes (roughly 114 degrees). In the future, this should improve to 180 degrees and eventually to the entire 220 degrees allowed by the human body.

Frame rate. This rate is the frequency, in frames, that consecutive images are displayed or captured. Modern movies use 24 frames per second (fps) as their standard, although PAL displays at 25fps and the NTSC format for television uses 30fps. *The Hobbit* was filmed at 48fps. To be realistic, VR should aim for a frame rate of at least 30fps, although some believe that a rate of 120fps will cause fewer side effects, such as distortion, headaches, and nausea.

Resolution. This is the number of pixels that can be displayed. Typically, a landscape-oriented monitor is 1920 by 1080 pixels. It might seem that fewer pixels can be used on a small screen (e.g., 3–4 inches across), but using a smaller resolution results in what is known as the screen door effect, where the image seems as if it's being seen through a grid.[11]

HEADSETS

VR headsets are becoming more popular and sophisticated. VR headsets use sensors, including gyroscopes and accelerometers, to track the head movements of the wearer. Headsets also include eye-tracking sensors to understand where a person's eyes are focused.[12]

The most obvious component of a VR headset is the lenses and screens—one for each eye. The headset sends an image through each lens and uses position tracking to understand where a user is located, eventually displaying the correct data for that position.

Many headsets include controllers with two handheld grips, joysticks, and, more recently, haptic controllers that can be used to simulate touch sensitivity.

Several VR headsets are available today. These include:

- *Google Glass.* Google began selling its prototype of Google Glass in April 2014, and it became available to the public in May 2014. In January 2015, the glasses were discontinued, and in 2017 Google released the Google Glass Enterprise edition. Google Glass Enterprise edition 2 was released in 2019. These were eyeglasses, except they had a head-up display instead of a lens. Non-prescription and prescription formats were available.

- *Magic Leap.* This immersive AR headset is designed for enterprises. It has a 70-degree field of vision and headphones.[13]

- *Oculus.* This VR headset supports 1832 × 1920 pixels per eye and has built-in headphones. Two controllers, one for each hand, are included.

- *Samsung Gear VR.* Samsung Gear VR includes a controller that pairs up with the Oculus app on a user's smartphone. The smartphone is inserted into the headset to serve as the display and provide audio.

- *Apple VR.* Apple's VR headset supports mixed reality (i.e., AR and VR), can include a prescription lens, and the screen resolution is 2160 × 2160.

CHALLENGES

There are a few challenges to virtual reality devices:[14]

- The field of view of all VR devices is much smaller than in real life.
- The number of use cases for VR outside of gaming is limited. It is difficult for consumers to justify spending thousands of dollars for a VR headset because they don't understand the value.
- The headsets are somewhat heavy and socially awkward.
- The development of new technology is expensive.
- Supply-chain issues are limiting and will continue to determine the devices that can be manufactured and developed.

FUTURE

As an example of how immersive VR can be, a recent study reported by Nature Scientific Reports described a VR experience called Isness-D that gives four to five users at a time a sense of transcendence. Each group member experienced "energetic coalescence" by gathering in the same space in virtual reality. This, in effect, overlapped their virtual bodies, giving each person a feeling of deep connectedness and ego attenuation.

A self-transcendent experience dissolves a person's self-definition, which defies the line between one's self, others, and the environment, creating a feeling of being united with others or the environment. David Glowicki, the designer of Isness-D, looked to quantum mechanics because that's "where the definition of what's matter and what's energy starts to become blurred." The study measured the emotional response of 75 study participants and found the intensity of their responses matched the intensity of four metrics used in a psychedelics research study—the MEQ30.

This provides us with an early indication of how immersive VR and AR experiences will be.[15]

Mixed Reality

AR overlays images, videos, and other information onto displays (i.e., glasses, contact lenses, smartphones) of the real world; VR immerses people into a simulated environment. Mixed reality (MR) combines physical and virtual worlds into a harmonious whole.

Extended Reality (XR)

VR, MR, and AR are subsets of extended reality. Indeed, someone using AR glasses or contact lenses is using extended reality (XR), and a person immersed in the VR of a video game is also using XR.[16]

Some examples of devices for extended reality include:

Microsoft HoloLens. The Microsoft HoloLens is a holographic device consisting of goggles that wrap around the head. This device is ergonomic, untethered, and self-contained, and displays holographic data for the wearer. It can be used for AR applications for personal use and business applications.

Humans view the world at roughly 210° on average; the HoloLens limited the display to 52°. This smaller view limits the utility of the HoloLens. In the future, a wider angle of coverage will be needed. The other components, such as the processors and batteries, need to be made smaller and lighter.

Google Project Starline. This booth is designed to enhance video conversations so they feel more lifelike. The system consists of two booths at different geographic locations. Users sit in one of the booths and talk to the person or people in the other booth. To everyone involved, it appears they are in the same room speaking over a table.

The product delivers exceptional realism using a fabric-based, multi-dimensional light-field display and spatial audio speakers.

Omnichannel

Omnichannel is a popular term among marketers and advertisers because it enables consumers to have a seamless customer journey. It's easiest to explain by way of example. Suppose a consumer walks into a brick-and-mortar store and browses the merchandise. A salesperson can look up information and help the customer. Later, the customer can use her smartphone to access the store's website to add the products she viewed in the store to a shopping cart. Later, she can jump on her home PC to finalize the sale and order it shipped to her home. After the product is shipped, she can view the progress of her package until it reaches her, then use her smartphone to ask for a return.

In contrast, multichannel describes a branding approach that encourages consumers to use the channel of their choice (e.g., web, catalog, email, brick-and-mortar store) to engage with the brand. Omnichannel evolved from multichannel in that omnichannel blends all the channels into a personalized and cohesive customer experience.[17]

In the metaverse, omnichannel experiences will be enabled by the vast and complex metaverse infrastructure. (It will work the same way as it does for branding in the physical world.) Suppose the same consumer shopped in a virtual store and selected a new pair of virtual shoes. Later, in the physical world, she jumps on the shoe store's website to add that pair of shoes to her shopping cart and makes the purchase, adding an option to the NFT to include an identical pair of shoes to her order in addition to the virtual shoes. Now she can track the shipment of the physical shoes to her house while wearing the virtual shoes in the metaverse.

Omnichannel effectively blends everything so that the virtual and physical worlds become meshed as if they were the same. By using AR, virtual objects could be "seen" and "heard" in the real world. To demonstrate, a virtual comfort animal could be purchased, which the owner could view through their smart contact lenses. The "dog" would act just like a real dog, except that it's not real, and it would "exist" in the real world using AR and in the virtual world as a virtual animal.

Advanced (Emerging) Technology

We've looked at many endpoints that consumers and businesses use to access the internet, games, virtual worlds, and the metaverse. Now, let's look at some technologies that are still evolving but will drive additional adoption of the metaverse.

SMART CLOTHING

If you've seen modern science fiction, you might recall scenes that included clothing or accessories that changed color or shape. To illustrate, in *Ultraviolet*, Violet's main character can change her hair and clothing color on command. The remake of *Total Recall* features a receptionist who changes the colors of her fingernails by touching them with a pin-like device. In *Back to the Future*, Marty McFly puts on shoes that automatically tie themselves.

These are examples of smart clothing and accessories, which are becoming real. In 2021, researchers created a material that looks like chainmail and stiffens on command. In 2016, scientists created self-cleaning clothing. In 2021, engineers at MIT created programmable fibers to support storing data within apparel.[18]

Sensors in clothing can monitor a person's physical activity, heart rate, and blood pressure when they sleep. Of course, clothing can also be created with additional sensors and LEDs. Smart clothing can be designed to connect to the internet and, eventually, the metaverse.

HAPTIC DEVICES

To enable the sense of touch in a virtual environment, haptic devices are used. Gloves can be worn with sensors that allow users to feel objects in their hands. Suits enable touch to extend to every part of the body, which allows users to feel a punch, a caress, or other sensations.

Heather Culbertson, a computer scientist at the University of Southern California, explained:

In the past, haptics has been good at making things noticeable, with vibration in your phone or the rumble packs in gaming controllers. But now there's been a shift toward making things that feel more natural and mimic the feel of natural materials and natural interactions.[19]

Haptic devices fall into three categories: grasping, wearing, and touching. Grasping means using a haptic device to hold something, such as with a joystick or other control. Gloves are worn to send and receive sensations from a virtual world. Haptic sensors can also enable touching, such as modern touchscreens.

These devices will enable users of the metaverse to feel sensations and to use touch to trigger actions to occur in the virtual world.

FACE MAPPING

Modern smartphones and other devices include competent cameras and sensors. Working together, these cameras enable face-mapping technologies that track tens of thousands (or more) precise points on a user's (or player's) face, which allows the software to understand the shape and movements of a person's face in real time. These shapes and movements can be linked to games to show facial shapes and movements on a player's avatar, or to software that understands how to translate facial characteristics into emotions.

This means that people don't have to explain their emotions or use joysticks or keyboard commands to move their heads and faces. Face-mapping applications do the work, and as a result, a person's avatar can accurately reflect his physical world face and facial movements in real time.

APPLE OBJECT CAPTURE

Using their iPhones, Apple's Object Capture lets people quickly scan physical objects to create virtual representations of them. Once scanned, these objects may be used in games, virtual worlds, the metaverse, and even as NFTs.

Modern smartphones, including the iPhone 11 and 12, use ultra-wideband chips that emit half a billion radar pulses per second, which allows the contours of your home, office, street, and everything else you want to be mapped and understood. This technology enables people to quickly create virtual representations of their homes and property in virtual worlds.

Conclusions

Endpoints are required to access the metaverse; they are the interfaces that users will see and use. It's likely that today's smartphones and smartwatches will evolve into the main endpoints, although they will need the faster capabilities of 5G or 6G (see the section about Networking later in this chapter), more powerful processors, more memory, more storage space, and other advances to fully support the metaverse. A smartphone paired with connected contact lenses or glasses and haptic gloves would create the idea endpoint for the metaverse, assuming advances in existing technologies.

Endpoints are inoperable without the services provided by central systems, whether decentralized, cloud, or non-cloud based. The following section goes into detail about these central systems.

Central Systems (Decentralized, Cloud- and Non-Cloud Based)

Now, let's explore the concepts of what we call central systems. These systems are defined as the computing resources that fulfill tasks on behalf of endpoints. When a person plays a multiplayer game, the client (i.e., the game console, personal computer, or smartphone) interfaces with users. The back end (i.e., the central systems) is invisible to users, and its purpose is to store data, route communications between clients, and provide resources to clients. It is entirely possible that endpoints can be used for these purposes; this option will be assessed in this section.

History

Initially, computers were large, bulky machines filled with moving parts and hand-wired components. They were also expensive to purchase and operate, and required climate-controlled rooms, used extreme amounts of power, and were isolated from other computers.

In the late 1970s, a 10MB disk drive was the size of a washing machine and weighed several hundred pounds. The drivers themselves were noisy and required air clean from impurities because any dust on the platters could cause disk crashes. It wasn't just that disks were large and awkward—128kb of memory required a refrigerator-sized cabinet and the CPU required another cabinet all to itself.

In those days, applications ran directly on large mainframes and minicomputers because smaller computers had not yet been invented. Television screens and teletypes were used for output, and input was via punch cards, paper tape, magnetic tape, and keyboards. Personal computers, game consoles, smartphones, and personal assistants such as Alexa were almost half a century away.

As technology improved with smaller and more robust components, more intelligent endpoints (which we reflected on earlier in this chapter) were released. The most revolutionary of these was the personal computer (and later, the gaming console), and not just because it enabled home users to take advantage of computing power. Because of personal computers, the front end (i.e., the parts visible to users) moved to the client (i.e., the personal computer), and the main work of the application remained on the server. This was the birth of a new computing model: the client/server model.

How Servers are Used

Servers have branched into a few distinct models of usage:

Standalone. The client performs all its tasks without the need for servers. The other models can become standalone if they are correctly coded and if the network becomes unavailable.

Thick client. In this case, the application runs entirely on the personal computer (i.e., the client). The applications may communicate with one or more servers to send and receive data.

Thin client. Applications that operate in web browsers are primary examples of thin client applications. The client in the browser contains just enough code to interface with the main application running on the server. Google Apps is an example of a thin client.

Software as a Service (SaaS). This is a subset of the thin client model. The application (software) runs in a browser, but all the work is performed on the servers. SaaS is useful for business applications.

Distributed. In a pure distributed model, the clients contain everything they need to perform their tasks and only communicate with one or more servers to get and receive information.

Mixed. Applications such as Microsoft Office are mixed and run as both thin and thick clients. People can use Word entirely on the web through their browser, for example. They can also edit their documents using a client downloaded to their computer.

Decentralized. In this model, resources like computing time are distributed to various clients on the network. Ultimately, an application may send a compute request to a gaming server, a second request to a personal computer, and still another to a different personal computer in another state. This model allows applications to use more resources as needed rapidly, but latency (i.e., the time it takes to send and receive data across the network) can slow down the process. In the decentralized operations model, endpoints may be used to store data, perform calculations, and do various other tasks as if they were servers.

Of course, applications may mix and match these models as needed. The same application can be decentralized but then change to being a thick client of just a gaming server if that's all that is available.

The applications installed on smartphones, laptops, tablets, personal assistants, and other endpoints all use one or a mixture of these operating models. The metaverse can, and will, take advantage of all or a combination of these models.

Databases

The foundation of the internet, web, and the metaverse is data (i.e., information). Without data, these technologies would not be helpful if they existed at all. Everyone uses data throughout life, even before the internet and computers existed. Your birthday, the current time, or map coordinates are all data types. These individual datums don't need computers or technology, but computers and the internet (and later, the metaverse) allow that data to be used in more creative, complex ways and transmitted more quickly than ever.

Most importantly, technology allows patterns to be discerned from sets of data. These patterns can be interpreted to understand the meaning of the data. Artificial intelligence (AI), machine learning (ML), and computer vision examine data to discover ways to interpret it, then they act upon those patterns.

Data is stored within databases, which are collections of data stored in computer files. Databases are typically stored on dedicated servers for performance and security reasons. Social media platforms typically store several petabytes (i.e., one million gigabytes) per day. Gaming systems store equivalent amounts of information, and the metaverse will hold even more once it is fully realized.

Two types of data are stored in databases: structured and unstructured. Structured data is stored in a standardized format, complies with a data model, and is in a known and understood order, making it easy to access individual items within a record. Unstructured data is the opposite. This data is not stored in neat rows and columns. A video, image, or sound clip are examples of unstructured data. Both data forms have existed since the dawn of the computer age. The content and context of unstructured data are more difficult for computers to understand than structured data. Artificial intelligence (AI) is required to discern and understand the objects and context of anything more than a simple image (an image is unstructured data).

At the beginning of 2020, the amount of data existent in the world was 44 zettabytes (or one trillion terabytes). This means the number of bytes stored worldwide was, in 2020, more than the number of stars that could be observed in the universe. By 2025, it is forecasted that 1,200 petabytes will be stored every single day.[20] Online gaming and the metaverse promise to increase these statistics dramatically.

Of course, all this data must be managed, analyzed, and accessed. Data lakes are central repositories that store structured and unstructured data. Information is kept as it exists without it needing to be modified to fit a structure. This data can then be used for any number of purposes by dashboards, analytics, AI, and ML. The purpose of using a data lake is to be able to gain value from the data that is stored. Data lakes are ideally suited to keeping the information from IoT devices, social media, and web applications.

Databases can be centralized, meaning they are served on one server (or a group of servers known as a *cluster*), or decentralized, which means the data is hosted on several computers. Centralized databases tend to be faster and more secure (because the infrastructure is more isolated and controlled), while decentralized are more expandable.

The Cloud

Since the early 2000s, as the speed of networks improved, a new computing model appeared known as the cloud, which refers to servers in one or more central locations. These servers are accessed over the internet and host applications and databases, which may, in turn, be used by clients all over the world.

As far as the metaverse is concerned, one of the primary advantages of the cloud is that resources—disk space, computation, memory—are allocated "on demand." Meaning that the cloud dynamically allocates resources as needed instead of in advance. For example, during the times of day when few people are playing a multiplayer game or accessing the metaverse, these resources are not used. We must recognize that, as more people use the applications, the cloud can allocate more resources. Companies do not need to purchase enough computing power to fulfill their maximum load because the cloud expands and contracts as required.

To support the metaverse, it's likely that purpose-built clouds will be created just for the metaverse. By specializing in providing metaverse-related services, providers can install hardware and applications optimized for metaverse operations, such as high-power graphics processing units (GPUs).

Quantum Computing

A rapidly growing technology known as *quantum computing*, which uses quantum mechanics to solve complex problems, is emerging. Quantum computers are many times faster than the fastest possible non-quantum computers and overall offer many exciting opportunities in the evolution of the metaverse.[21]

Because of their nature, quantum computers are well-suited for solving highly complex problems such as handling multidimensional spaces, which is beyond the capabilities of traditional computers. Because the metaverse requires immense amounts of computations and simulations, the power of quantum computing can be leveraged to support such requirements.

Additionally, quantum computers support a concept known as quantum randomness. In traditional computers, a truly random number is impossible—they are emulated using various algorithms. In fact, quantum random numbers are truly random. This helps to ensure that people are not able to predict outcomes, and in turn, use the system unscrupulously.

Finally, quantum ML boosts ML to an entirely new level due to the nature of quantum computing. In doing so, it will expand the capabilities of AI to make it more valuable and intelligent.

Conclusions

By central systems, we are referring to the infrastructure on the back end—the systems, whether decentralized, on the cloud, or servers in a compute facility. The metaverse will take advantage of all three methods at the same time. Some data structures, like blockchain and NFTs, might be decentralized; others like images and videos might be stored in the cloud; and still others like secure data might be stored on servers in company facilities. It all depends on the application or the company involved.

But what connects everything? How do endpoints communicate with and use the resources provided by central systems? We'll summarize the connecting tissue and the network in the following section.

Networks

Standalone systems can do many things, but computers must be connected to the internet to access social media, online gaming, cryptocurrency, and YouTube videos. Computers, including desktops, laptops, tablets, smartphones, and IoT devices, are much more valuable when they can communicate with other computer systems. The ability to connect one computer to another is known as *networking*, and it is one of the foundations of modern computing.

History

Until the late 1960s, computers didn't communicate with one another. Believe it or not, each computer stood alone, performing all their processing and tasks without sending or receiving messages from one another, except for what was jokingly referred to as *sneaker net*, which meant walking punch cards, paper tape, and magnetic tape from one computer to another.

In 1969, Defense Advanced Research Projects Agency (DARPA) developed the Advanced Research Projects Agency Network (ARPANET), which implemented TCP/IP as mentioned previously. DARPA developed this network and the associated protocols so that systems could communicate during the war. More specifically, the military financed ARPANET to use in the Cold War. It began as four systems at Stanford, UCLA, UCSB, and the University of Utah and expanded to 40 systems (i.e., nodes) by 1972.

ARPANET relied on phone lines for communication and packet-switching (a revolutionary idea at the time) to route messages between computers instead of directly connecting the computers. Messages were routed from the source to the destination computer because the protocol specified the address of the destination.

In 1973, Bob Metcalfe at Xerox Parc developed Ethernet, and by 1983 it was standardized as IEEE 802.3. Like TCP/IP, Ethernet was open source, which meant anyone could adopt it. This, along with its high flexibility, was the impetus behind its rapid growth. Since its inception, Ethernet has been implemented on a coaxial cable (at first) with speeds of 2.94 mbits/sec. Until now, it's been used in twisted pairs (CAT 5, 5e, 6, 6a, 7, and 8) or fiber optics cables. The speed increased as the quality of cables improved, and now the maximum rates are around 40 gb/sec.

During this time, development proceeded on several competing protocols, such as AppleNet, Token Ring, ARCnet, and DECnet. Fiber Distributed Data Interface (FDDI) and Copper Distributed Interface (CDDI) also gained popularity during the 1990s. Ethernet replaced these two protocols as their speeds improved, and nowadays they have been replaced by Gigabit Ethernet.

Ethernet is a protocol rather than a type of cable or piece of hardware. For this reason, it can be implemented to use twisted pairs (i.e., the standard for most home users), Power-Over-Ethernet (PoE), fiber optics, Wi-Fi, and many other types of cables or media.

What is a Network?

A *network* is a connection between two or more computers. Networks are needed to share resources, messages, files, images, videos, and other things. Connections may be wired (as with a cable from the wall to a computer), via Wi-Fi, satellites, or microwaves.

There are several types of networks:

Wide Area Network (WAN). A WAN is a network over a wide area, such as a city, state, country, or even the planet. WANs are made up of smaller WANs. A city WAN (or a Municipal Area Network [MAN]) is connected to another city WAN in the state, a state WAN (made up of smaller WANs) is connected to other states, and the country WAN is linked to other countries (often over cables deep under the oceans). This is a simplistic view of WANs to make it more understandable—they really are much more complex.

The internet is the consolidation of all the WANs in the world (apart from a few countries that have isolated their internal internets from the greater internet).

Local Area Network (LAN). The network within a home or office building is called a Local Area Network. LANs are the networks most familiar to users (i.e., businesses or homes). They are connected to a

WAN by a modem (i.e., cable, DSL, or broadband), which also isolates the LAN from the WAN. Connections to the LAN can be wired, wireless (i.e., Wi-Fi), or satellite (including the new Starlink satellite systems).

Wired connections—a cable between a computer and a router—are much faster and more stable than Wi-Fi or cellular, although newer standards such as 5G (for cellular) and 802.11 (for Wi-Fi) are quickly closing in on cables for speed and stability.

Wireless Wide Area Network (WWAN). WANs are also known as cellular networks. Smartphones and other cellular devices connect to the internet over these cellular wireless networks. They are owned and operated by telecom providers, such as T-Mobile, Sprint, Verizon, and AT&T (amongst others). When mobile devices access the internet over a WWAN, they do not communicate over a LAN. Instead, the devices connect directly to the WWAN.

Modern mobile devices often have an option to communicate over Wi-Fi because it is far less expensive than the cellular network.

Mobile devices connect to their cellular provider's WWAN using mobile communications technology, such as Worldwide Interoperability for Microwave Access (WIMAX), Universal Mobile Telecom System (UMTS), Code Division Multiple Access (CDMA) 2000, Global System for Mobile (GSM), first generation (1G), 2G, 3G, 4G, 5G, or 6G (coming in 2030).

The speeds of each technology are listed below:[22,23]

- 1G: 2 Kbps (No data support)
- 2G: 14.4–64 kbps (1 Mbps for GSM)
- 3G: 2 Mbps (21.6 Mbps for HSPA)
- 4G: 1–50 Mbps
- 5G: 35.46 Gbps, allows 100 billion devices

There is not a single 3G or 4G technology. Each cellular network is individually developed (and continues to grow) using different interpretations of the specifications.

In a home or business environment, computers connect to routers. The job of a router is to route communications from one place to another. The router communicates to a DSL, broadband, or satellite modem, which then routes the communication to one or more servers or other routers (which then route the communication farther along its way). When the transmission reaches the destination, it goes through another router to one or more servers (which we discussed earlier). In the case of decentralized databases or computing, the communication may be routed to another endpoint instead.

The Internet and the Web

The internet is the global network enabling communications between billions of systems, IoT devices, and other computers. Protocols such as TCP/IP allow computers to connect. These protocols run on top of lower-level standards that support Wi-Fi, Ethernet, and satellite communications. As far as TCP/IP is concerned, it doesn't matter which standard is used for communication—it works the same for Wi-Fi, cellular, or satellite.

The World Wide Web (or web for short) consists of billions of websites accessible using the internet. The http and https (http with security) protocols run on top of TCP/IP, meaning they do not need to be concerned with the mechanics of finding websites—that's taken care of by TCP/IP. Web 1, Web 2, and Web 3 communicate in the same way at this level.

Think of these constructs as an onion. Each onion layer depends on the layer below it. Crucially, the hardware is located at the center of the onion, and we worked our way inward starting at the top layer of the web.

The metaverse (as well as online games, social media platforms, and other virtual constructs) run at this topmost layer. Some argue that the metaverse software doesn't need to be concerned about connecting with your home computer or smartphone, which are handled at a lower level.

DSL, Broadband, and Other Technologies

In the past, people used standard telephone lines to communicate to the internet (before the invention of the web). These connections were terribly slow and were often measured in bytes per second. In fact, they were so slow that image and video compression had to be invented.

As time passed, newer technologies were invented to overcome these speed (and stability) limitations. The Integrated Services Digital Network (ISDN) allows the transmission of voice and data over telephone lines, with the data speed topping out at about 128 Kbps.

Later, telecom providers offered Digital Subscriber Line (DSL), which connects to a standard phone line using a DSL modem and splits the line between voice and data (where voice is not required). DSL offers speeds of up to 500 Mbps, which is suitable for online gaming, streaming, and video conferencing. DSL is less than optimum for many users because everyone must go through the same line.

Broadband is the catch-all term that simply means the connection supports a minimum of 25 Mbps download speed and 3 Mbps upload speed. Broadband can be delivered over fiber optics cable, wireless, copper cable, DSL, and satellite.

Bandwidth, Throughput, and Latency

Many people toss the term *bandwidth* as the line's speed or connection. Bandwidth measures the line's capacity. Throughput measures the amount of data transmitted and received during a specific time. Latency measures the speed of the data.

If we applied these terms to a water hose, bandwidth is the width of the hose, throughput is the amount of water going through the hose, and latency is how long the water requires to reach the end.

Network throughput is measured in bits per second. A bit is a binary 1 or 0—the smallest data unit stored in a computer. (Quantum computers keep data in 1, 0, or both simultaneously.) A byte is typically 8 bits and represents a single character. For example, if a phone line transmitted 8 bits per second, it would send one character per second. (Although, this is not precisely true as there is some overhead involved that uses more bits.)

These measurement terms are used to describe throughput:

- Kbps = Kilo (thousands) of bits per second
- Mbps = Mega (millions) of bits per second
- Gbps = Giga (billions) of bits per second
- Tbps = Tera (trillions) of bits per second

Bandwidth, throughput, and latency determine how much and how quickly data can be transmitted and received. The evolution of the metaverse and Web 3 require substantial amounts of data transfer, and assume that their growth and acceptance are related to how fast businesses and homes can be connected to high-speed networks.

Hotspots

A *hotspot* is simply a wireless access point that allows people to connect to the internet. Many smartphones include built-in hotspots to enable other devices to make those connections. Tethering means wirelessly connecting a smartphone to other devices like tablets. The advantage of hotspots and tethering is that a smartphone can connect over the internet using an available Wi-Fi router or its cellular service network.

Helium is a service based on blockchain, which they call The People's Network, that connects devices and data using a decentralized global network of hotspots, especially 5G. At first, Helium was intended to connect IoT devices to the internet, but now it has expanded to include individuals to earn their native coins, known as Helium Native Tokens (HNTs), to provide devices to the network for connectivity. The purpose is to enable wireless infrastructure to grow more rapidly and take advantage of unused bandwidth for community use. Helium uses LongFi, which combines the LoRaWAN wireless protocol with the Helium blockchain.[24]

The Network and the Metaverse

The metaverse is a layer on top of the network; it expands the capabilities of the internet and requires very high-speed internet service (also known as ultrafast internet). The metaverse does *not* replace the internet. It enhances it like Web 2 enhances Web 1.

The metaverse runs on hardware (i.e., endpoints and central systems) and uses the network to communicate. As we'll review, software is needed to make the metaverse (and everything else in computing) work. We'll go into that in more detail in the next section.

Software

So far in this chapter, we've analyzed endpoints, central systems, and networks. These are important, because the internet, web, and computing would not exist without these foundational elements. Regardless, nothing can operate without software. Hardware, whether a smartphone, server, or router, is built with the capability to perform actions. Software exploits the hardware, enabling devices to perform their functions. In other words, a smartphone is a useless brick without software, servers can't do anything, and networks sit idle.

The History of Software

Before 1946, software didn't exist except as a concept. Instead, early electronic devices were "programmed" by making hardware changes such as moving wires around. The programmers of the first computers, known as the Electronic Numerical Integrator and Computer (ENIAC), consisted of women. Their roles were to examine blueprints of the wiring in ENIAC and determine how to program the machine using patch panels to move wires from terminal to terminal. In 1950, Kathleen Booth created assembly language to make programming the computers at Birkbeck College easier.

Programming between 1948 and 1979 was dominated first by assembly language, followed by early programming languages such as Fortran developed by IBM, and Cobol created by Mary K. Hawes and Grace Hopper. In the 1960s, Jean E. Sammet authored an influential book, *Programming Languages: History and Fundamentals*.

The Apollo moon missions are of note because they depended on software to program the lunar landing modules. The Apollo software would not be recognizable today, because it consisted of wires threaded through magnetic cores. Engineers wrote this code on lunch cards that were later run on a Honeywell mainframe. This simulated the software, and when the programmers were satisfied, the code was woven into magnetic cores.

In the 1970s–1980s, personal computers began hitting the market, and people demanded that these innovative machines do something useful. The computer industry responded with applications such as VisiCalc (i.e., spreadsheet software), AutoCAD, Microsoft Word, and Excel. In 1981, *Time Magazine* featured the personal computer as their Man of the Year.

Open-source software appeared in the 1990s, along with the internet and the early World Wide Web. Linux was released in 1991, Java in 1995, and the source code for Netscape was published in 1998.

Mobile phones began appearing on the scene in 1973, and in 1993 IBM came out with the first smartphone available to the public. Other phones quickly followed suit, with the Blackberry release in 1999 and the Palm OS in 1996. Apple changed the mobile industry in 2007 with the release of the iPhone. Mobile devices use computer languages such as Swift and Java.

In the modern era, software can be found everywhere. It runs in consumer devices such as smart light bulbs and alarms. Software operates smartphones and their applications, in addition to desktop computers and allows businesses of all sizes to work efficiently.

Now that we've presented a very brief history of software, let's examine the purpose of software. What is it and what does it do?

What is Software?

Software is the instructions that operate computers, hardware, and applications. As with networks, software is layered on top of the hardware, and at the bottom is firmware. Above that is the operating system, which uses firmware to perform its functions. Applications sit on top of operating systems to allow people and machines to do something. Let's break these down further:

Firmware. This specialized software operates the hardware itself. Disk drives, CPUs, memory, robots, and every other computing device are used by small (or large) firmware programs. Every component (with few exceptions) needs firmware to enable a device to communicate with an operating system or the real world.

Operating system. An operating system consists of specialized code that "operates" or runs the hardware, applications, network, and everything else. It can be thought of as the controller or brain of the device. Without an operating system, mobile phones, desktops, tablets, and supercomputers are inert, useless sets of components.

Applications. Most people who use smartphones, mobile devices, and desktop computers are familiar with applications. Applications enable users and businesses to perform tasks ranging from accounting to playing games to emailing their friends.

Middleware. These programming tools sit between applications and system software (i.e., operating systems) and often translate data between applications. To this end, middleware is used to submit data on a form on a website and save it into a database.

Drivers. Drivers consist of software that operates devices on computers. They enable communications between the operating system and firmware.

Two-Dimensional Graphics

Most computer games and virtual worlds display in two dimensions on a flat screen, such as a mobile device, desktop PC, or tablet, which limits the immersive feeling of the gaming or virtual world universe because it is not in three dimensions. Two-dimensional graphics plot objects on the x- and y-axis.

To see a simulation of a two-dimensional world, watch the movie *Flatworld*. This delightful, animated movie demonstrates what it would be like to live in a world of only two dimensions.

Three-Dimensional Graphics

To create a truly immersive experience, the metaverse requires three-dimensional graphics in which objects are plotted on x, y, and z coordinates. Objects represented in three dimensions can be twisted, turned, scaled, rotated, and transformed in various ways. This is required for realism because humans view the world in three dimensions.

Persistence

For online games and virtual worlds (and the metaverse), persistence is the concept that the virtual world or game continues to exist and experience the passage of time when a player or user is absent (and even if all players and users are missing).

The real, physical world in which we live is persistent. Time keeps moving when people are asleep, unconscious, and when they die. The world doesn't stand still to wait for people to wake up from their dreams.

The first persistent game was written in 1978 by Rob Trubshaw and Richard Bartle at Essex University, UK. The game ran in 105-minute increments and was reset after each one. During those increments, the game persisted independent of the presence of players.[25]

The first game, introduced in 1989, to be truly persistent was Avalon: The Legend Lives. The game continued operating at all hours of the day, every day of the week, regardless of the presence of players.

The concept of persistence is essential for the metaverse because many people will be coming and going, achieving their tasks or goals, and leaving the real world. The metaverse must be designed to continue operating in real time at all times.

Real Time

Many games let players go back and forth, each taking a turn to perform some actions. The play stops while they consider what to do and only continues when they've made their turn or a timer runs out. This is great for games like chess, checkers, and poker as well as some role-playing adventure games.

In real-time games, one second is equal to one second in the real world. Real time is especially critical for adventure- or action-oriented games because they allow players to show off their skills as if they were that character (i.e., their avatar).

Virtual worlds and the metaverse operate in real time. The metaverse could even simulate the local weather and position of the sun or moon. Therefore, if it is midnight in the area local to the user, they could view their surroundings as if it were nighttime. This will be an option that users could set if desired.

Combining persistence and real time will be essential for the metaverse. The real world doesn't stop just because a user sleeps, so why should the metaverse? Let's look at a couple of platforms that support persistent and real-time experiences in the metaverse.

NVIDIA Omniverse

The NVIDIA Omniverse is a platform that enables 3D design collaboration. It supports scalable CPUs, operates in real time, and contains simulations that are real to reality. This platform accelerates 3D workflows and gives people the tools to visualize, simulate, and program these worlds and their contents. It integrates many technologies into comprehensive tools that support ray tracing, AI, and compute into 3D pipelines and digital twins of people and complex objects. The platform is open, interoperable, scalable, and accessible to everyone.

Universal Scene Description (USD)

USD is a framework that supports the interchange of 3D computer graphics information. It allows collaboration, editing, and multiple views. Initially developed by Pixar, it was released as open-source software in 2016.

How and Why Computing Power Limits What Can be Done

The physical universe enforces constraints on energy usage and how much can be packed into spaces. This limits how small traditional computers and their components can be. Electrical components have actually become so small that designers must sometimes account for quantum *tunneling*, which occurs when the internal barriers in transistors become smaller than a nanometer. Electrons then must start tunneling through the barriers, which causes too much current.

These limits can be overcome (or at least minimized) in several ways, including:

- Running many computers in parallel
- Decentralizing computer functions
- Using new technologies such as quantum computing

How Blockchain and NFTs Fit into the Picture

Blockchain and NFTs are data structures that are implemented in specialized software. There are currently several blockchain implementations, including Ethereum and bitcoin, and they have different advantages and disadvantages. Most blockchain software is open source (at least so far), although nothing prevents a company from developing its proprietary version.

Metaverse-as-a-Service

Software-as-a-Service (SaaS) evolved to free businesses from needing to run their applications. Overall, instead of purchasing servers or using the cloud and then buying software licenses for an application, a company simply needed to connect to an SaaS system to access the software. In particular, by using SaaS, a business pays for the number of users required, instead of purchasing a payroll system and servers and hiring staff to maintain it. Users then connect to the SaaS system using a web browser or local client.

Metaverse-as-a-Service (MaaS) operates the same way. It allows businesses to quickly implement a 3D virtual world solution that enables collaboration, business functions, and cryptocurrency. By using MaaS, a company can set up a virtual world quickly and efficiently without the need for large hardware, licensing, and staffing investments.

Conclusions

The metaverse, like everything else in computing, requires software to operate. Without it, computers are just fancy bricks of metal and rare elements. It's the software that gives computers the ability to perform valuable tasks. This software is in the form of firmware to control devices, operating systems to manage the internals of a computer, applications to provide functions to users, middleware to provide additional connectivity services to applications, and drivers to run hardware.

Now that we've reviewed software, let's look at the role of artificial intelligence (AI) and machine learning (ML) in computing and the metaverse.

Artificial Intelligence and Machine Learning

AI and ML are the final types of technologies needed to support the metaverse. We've already learnt about endpoints, central systems, network, and software. This section presents an overview of AI/ML and focuses on how it will power the functionality of the metaverse.

More detailed information about AI can be found in my other book, *Superhuman Innovation: Transforming Business with Artificial Intelligence*.

History

Believe it or not, a science-fiction concept of AI, *The Grim Game*, was released in 1919, introducing audiences to an AI robot named Q that looked like a human. Other movies, such as *The Wizard of Oz* (with the Tin Man) and *Metropolis* (with a human-like robot that impersonated Maria) continued the trend. By the 1950s, science-fiction books and movies included AI robots and machines. The film *Forbidden Planet*, released in 1956, featured a vast intelligent alien computer complex that almost destroyed the ship from Earth.

In the 1950s, Alan Turing explored the concept using the mathematics of the possibility of AI. He felt that because humans use information and reason to solve programs, it should be possible to build machines that could do the same thing. He created the Turing Test to determine if a computer can think like a human. In the test, one person questions a computer while another person, the questioner, determines which is human and which is a computer. The questioning is repeated, and at the end of the test, the computer is considered to have AI if the questioner gets the answer right 50 percent or less of the time. The computers of that time (and still to this day) did not have the power and capabilities to support these possibilities, and hence, failed the test.

From 1957 to 1974, computers became faster and more capable. Successes, such as the demonstration of Joseph Weizenbaum's ELIZA, showed promising results. Using this and other resources, researchers convinced DARPA to provide funding for AI at a few institutions. The participants were optimistic that they'd have a machine as intelligent as humans within 3 to 8 years. Unfortunately, computer hardware and software didn't exist that could support this thesis.

By the 1980s, funding for AI increased, and the algorithmic toolkits expanded. These two trends allowed experts to pursue research into general AI (i.e., AI that is not explicitly made for a single purpose). The Japanese funded AI development from 1982 to 1990 with an investment of about $400 million; unfortunately, this and other similar projects failed to meet their goals of creating a usable AI system. As a result, funding was reduced and AI research languished.

In the 1990s and 2000s, AI research focused on a more narrowly focused form of AI called, appropriately enough, narrow AI. Instead of attempting to create AI that could simulate or surpass the human brain, narrow AI is focused on creating AI for a specific purpose, such as analyzing speech patterns or playing chess. This narrowed approach was remarkably effective and several breakthroughs resulted.

Additionally, computers became more capable with faster, smaller, and cheaper hardware and more capable software. Disk speeds and throughput increased, memory became inexpensive and fast, and CPU performance increased by several orders of magnitude. In 1997, IBM's Deep Blue chess-playing program beat the reigning world chess champion, Gary Kasparov. In the 2000s, AI became increasingly integrated into smart devices, including cars, alarm systems, and factory robots.

Supervised and Unsupervised Learning

Modern ML and AI are trained using data to perform specific, well-defined tasks. There are several methods for training AI:

- Supervised learning uses labeled datasets to train AI algorithms. There are several different algorithms, but the input data is tagged or identified so that the AI understands the meaning.
- Unsupervised learning means the data is input to algorithms without identification or instructions. The algorithm itself is tasked with the job of determining the structure and meaning of the data.
- A unified model uses a single model for a process or product. In this model, data is pooled together in a single array, which reduces the number of runs from a series to just one.

How AI/ML Apply to the Metaverse

The power of AI and ML is the glue that will tie together all the components of the metaverse to make it immersive, personal, and responsive. AI will process transactions, drive activities, manage chatbots, understand media (i.e., text, images, video, and audio), and respond to users. Additionally, AI will generate and drive 3D animations, create images, formulate responses, and manage the environment and interactions as people move from world to world.

It can be contended that a fully functioning metaverse cannot exist without AI and ML. These technologies will be supported by massive datasets (petabytes or more) of structured and unstructured data. These datasets will be centralized and decentralized, depending on their function, purpose, and the virtual world.

WORLD MODELS

Training AI/ML is one of the difficulties faced by implementers and designers because training usually requires human intervention to set up the parameters and data. World models are an approach that allows AI to be trained within a simulated environment. One way to look at it is that AI uses virtual worlds as "dreams" and uses them for training purposes. By taking this approach, implementation time is reduced and quality is improved.[26]

GENERATIVE AI

People will be experiencing the metaverse in real time, and their actions and needs are not entirely predictable. Generative AI creates the environment and objects needed as people expand through and explore the metaverse. Without generative AI, everything in the metaverse, from the background images to digital people, would need to be created manually. It is impossible to manually design the rooms of a digital house as a person is exploring that digital house. Instead, AI will engage in designing and creating the spaces, complete with the appropriate objects like furniture, as they are encountered.

Another area of importance to generative AI is the generation of images based on textual descriptions. Using this technology, everything from entire worlds to simple objects could be created based on text. Consider a metaverse recreation of the world presented in a novel, using only the novel's text as input. DALL-E 2 is an application that generates images based on text-image pairs. It builds an image from scratch using a data stream of up to 1,280 tokens.[27]

At the Universities of Copenhagen and Helsinki, researchers have discovered how to allow computers to sense thoughts and accept commands based on thought. They used this technology to enable people to edit images with their thoughts. Associate Professor Tuukka Ruotsalo, Department of Computer Science, University of Copenhagen, explained, "We can make a computer edit images entirely based on thoughts generated by human subjects. The computer has no prior information about which features it is supposed to edit or how. Nobody has ever done this before."[28]

VIRTUAL AUDIO

In addition to 3D images and animations, the metaverse AI/ML technology will need to generate and manipulate audio because sound is vital for a completely immersive experience. For example, in a virtual shopping mall, AI will need to generate the appropriate background sounds—footsteps and conversations, among other things. This is audio generative AI—the sounds are generated as needed by AI to provide a personalized, immersive experience. Without those background sounds, the world will seem flat and lifeless.

AI must generate responses from digital people to stimuli in their surroundings. Granting this assumption, if a user asks a digital police officer for directions, the AI must understand the question, interpret what is meant, figure out the directions, and then speak a response.

Another consideration is the room, position of the listener, and type of audio equipment in the physical world. Sound that is not presented properly for the physical environment can ruin an otherwise excellent immersive experience.

Rob Godman, a leader in music at the University of Hertfordshire and an expert in acoustic spaces, summed it up:

> We have to think about how humans perceive sound in their environment. Human beings want to know where sound is coming from, how big a space is, and how small a space is. When listening to sound being created, we listen to several different things. One is the source, but you also listen to what happens to sound when combined with the room—the acoustics.[29]

CONVERSATIONAL AI

Natural language transformers enable spoken language to be transformed and processed by a computer. This allows humans to speak to computers, giving them commands and input instead of typing. Currently, this technology enables chatbots to appear more realistic and provide better results to questions.

The world's largest and most powerful generative language model, created by a collaboration between NVIDIA and Microsoft[30], is trained on 540 billion parameters and shows incredible accuracy in natural language tasks. This is a powerful solution to enable conversational AI in the metaverse.

Named entity recognition is closely related because it detects entities in text to identify those needed to complete a task. This technology extracts such things as medical terms, people, places, and companies, and passes them along so that they may be used for the desired purposes.[31]

Conversational AI is essential for the metaverse to enable people to speak and adequately interpret and understand their spoken words.

Personalized Experiences

Personalization is one of the most crucial features of the modern internet and web experience. A personalized experience can make the difference between the success or failure of an internet e-commerce site.

The metaverse will carry this trend much further. The experience of every user who is engaged in the virtual world must be unique to them. Everything from their avatar, to the view they see of the virtual world, to their interactions with other people and digital people will be seen and experienced by them and them alone.

People won't be attracted to the metaverse if their experiences are the same as everyone else's. Instead, they will demand responsive, personalized experiences. Particularly, they also need to interact with other people in the digital world, each engaged with their customized vision. Two friends attending a virtual concert expect to see the same concert from their unique viewpoint.

AI is required to manage these personalized experiences and the interactions between personalized avatars and physical people.

Cybersecurity

Malicious actors constantly upgrade the tools they use to attack computer infrastructures. In response, defenders must then upgrade their tools to compensate. The almost literal war between malicious entities and defenders goes through this cycle repeatedly, each gaining a short-lived advantage over the other.

AI/ML is a double-edged sword in the world of cybersecurity. Conversely, AI-enabled cybersecurity tools can be highly effective at defending against attacks. Yet, on the other hand, AI-enabled malware presents an exceedingly high potential to breach computer defenses.

Security of the metaverse is of prime importance. The metaverse must be designed and implemented with security at the forefront; it cannot be an afterthought. AI/ML will be essential to not just protecting the metaverse from malicious actors but preventing attacks from occurring in the first place.

Embodiment of Robotics

One of the more promising opportunities for businesses to take advantage of the metaverse is the potential interface between the metaverse and business. Increasingly, new factories or products can be entirely designed and tested in the virtual world and then implemented in the physical world. This capability will allow thorough testing and prototyping before spending the money and resources needed to build the final product.

The metaverse can directly interface to real-world products using IoT sensors and devices. Furthermore, a person could outfit their home with smart lights, a smart alarm, and a smart refrigerator. They could enter the metaverse to program these devices in the virtual world. Technicians for a smart factory could sit within a virtual office, looking at virtual screens showing the status of every device, robot, or process on the factory floor. In this case, physical IoT sensors feed directly into the virtual world to enable these features.

Conclusions

The metaverse requires support from powerful AI and ML. Historically, AI is needed to break down an image into its parts and then understand the meaning and use of each of those parts. When a human looks at a picture of a farm, they see cows, a barn, grass, and a tractor, among other things. A computer "sees" a stream of 0s and 1s. To be useful, the cows, barn, tractor, and grass must be recognized and labeled—only then can they be used.

AI will be needed to generate a virtual world as it is encountered by users, populating that world with digital people, objects, and backgrounds, and then animating it to appear real. This helps create an immersive realtime experience for users.

There are many ways in which AI/ML is needed to implement the metaverse. In this chapter, we've gone over these and many other technologies that enable immersive, persistent, real-time experiences.

Simply put, the metaverse cannot exist without Infrastructure consisting of Endpoints, Central Systems, Network, Software, and AI.

Notes

1 Reality–virtuality continuum, en.wikipedia.org/wiki/ Reality%E2%80%93virtuality_continuum (archived at https://perma.cc/ 59AE-Q9XQ)

2 M Smith, M C Whitton and R Skarbez. Revisiting Milgram and Kishino's Reality-Virtuality Continuum, 24 March 2021. www.frontiersin.org/ articles/10.3389/frvir.2021.647997/full (archived at https://perma.cc/ERU3-WFNC)

3 The Virtuality Spectrum—Understanding AR, MR, VR and XR, creatxr.com/ the-virtuality-spectrum-understanding-ar-mr-vr-and-xr/ (archived at https://perma.cc/3PKL-W7YZ)

4 The Evolution of Augmented Reality, 2017, www.pwc.be/en/news-publications/ insights/2017/the-evolution-of-augmented-reality.html (archived at https://perma.cc/75VE-V6EP)

5   A Lee. The History and Profits of *Pokemon Go*, 2021, moneyinc.com/
    pokemon-go/ (archived at https://perma.cc/3P5C-RU9A)

6   M E P a. J E Heppelmann. How Does Augmented Reality Work?, November–
    December 2017, hbr.org/2017/11/how-does-augmented-reality-work (archived
    at https://perma.cc/JT3Y-8BW7)

7   Mojo, www.mojo.vision/mojo-lens (archived at https://perma.cc/YVG6-
    9M3W)

8   D Barnard. History of VR—Timeline of Events and Tech Development,
    6 August 2019, virtualspeech.com/blog/history-of-vr (archived at https://perma.cc/
    PZF5-DQY5)

9   J Bardi. What Is Virtual Reality: Definitions, Devices, and Examples, 26 March
    2019, www.marxentlabs.com/what-is-virtual-reality/ (archived at
    https://perma.cc/UHV9-HKWC)

10 How Does Virtual Reality Work: The Ultimate 2021 Guide, 15 September
    2021, daglar-cizmeci.com/how-does-virtual-reality-work/ (archived at
    https://perma.cc/DY9L-AG3L)

11 C Hoffman. What Is the "Screen Door Effect" in VR?, 25 January 2022,
    www.howtogeek.com/404491/what-is-the-screen-door-effect-in-vr/ (archived
    at https://perma.cc/F6JQ-AXYK)

12 How Do Virtual Reality Headsets Work?, 10 March 2022, www.xrtoday.com/
    vr/how-do-virtual-reality-headsets-work/ (archived at https://perma.cc/
    QQR7-2HPA)

13 Magic Leap, www.magicleap.com/en-us/ (archived at https://perma.cc/
    XJ3R-MSDQ)

14 A Lewis. 6 Major Challenges Preventing Augmented and Virtual Reality
    Growth, swisscognitive.ch/2021/07/27/6-ar-vr-challenges-in-2021/ (archived at
    https://perma.cc/4J8G-EJJX)

15 H Kiros. VR is as good as psychedelics at helping people reach transcendence,
    MIT Technology Review, 2022

16 T Gerencer. What Is Extended Reality (XR) and How Is it Changing the
    Future?, 3 April 2021, www.hp.com/us-en/shop/tech-takes/what-is-xr-
    changing-world (archived at https://perma.cc/D9CN-8G2Y)

17 S Patel. Omnichannel vs. Multichannel: What Is the Difference?, 11 May 2022,
    www.revechat.com/blog/omnichannel-vs-multichannel/ (archived at
    https://perma.cc/T7RP-B5VY)

18 M Mulko. What Is Smart Clothing Technology and How Does It Work?,
    16 December 2021, interestingengineering.com/what-is-smart-clothing-
    technology-and-how-does-it-work (archived at https://perma.cc/PPG8-TQU3)

19 M Hutson. Here's What the Future of Haptic Technology Looks (Or Rather,
    Feels) Like, 28 December 2018, www.smithsonianmag.com/innovation/
    heres-what-future-haptic-technology-looks-or-rather-feels-180971097/
    (archived at https://perma.cc/FV6N-H6QJ)

20 B Vuleta. How Much Data Is Created Every Day? [27 Staggering Stats], 28 October 2021, seedscientific.com/how-much-data-is-created-every-day/ (archived at https://perma.cc/VAZ6-CYMW)

21 P Sanjay Basu. Exploring the Metaverse and How Quantum Computing Plays a Role, 25 January 2022, medium.com/my-metaverse/exploring-the-metaverse-and-how-quantum-computing-plays-a-role-a1e227f93d2b (archived at https://perma.cc/27Q7-QF54)

22 1G Vs. 2G Vs. 3G Vs. 4G Vs. 5G, net-informations.com/q/diff/generations.html (archived at https://perma.cc/DV2C-JQZ4)

23 Mobile Networks, hpbn.co/mobile-networks/ (archived at https://perma.cc/LK7X-PA8C)

24 A Haleem. Helium Network (HNT): Decentralizing Wireless Networks, 25 October 2021, www.gemini.com/cryptopedia/helium-network-token-map-helium-hotspot-hnt-coin (archived at https://perma.cc/Q7TZ-EK8U)

25 Persistent World, en.wikipedia.org/wiki/Persistent_world (archived at https://perma.cc/2K9L-J6A7)

26 *World Models Explained* [Film], www.youtube.com/watch?v=IZPKohYNri4 (archived at https://perma.cc/7Z85-J4EZ)

27 DALL·E: Creating Images from Text, 5 January 2021, openai.com/blog/dall-e/ (archived at https://perma.cc/9FFA-MB8N)

28 AI Tool Lets Users Edit Images with Their Thoughts, 24 June 2022, www.technologynetworks.com/neuroscience/news/ai-tool-lets-users-edits-images-with-their-thoughts-362995 (archived at https://perma.cc/JYX5-WU5D)

29 R Morrison. Sound of the Metaverse: Meta Creates AI Models to Improve Virtual Audio, 29 June 2022, techmonitor.ai/technology/emerging-technology/meta-audio-ai-metaverse (archived at https://perma.cc/DK3N-JABR)

30 P K Ali Alvi. Using DeepSpeed and Megatron to Train Megatron-Turing NLG 530B, the World's Largest and Most Powerful Generative Language Model, 11 October 2021, www.microsoft.com/en-us/research/blog/using-deepspeed-and-megatron-to-train-megatron-turing-nlg-530b-the-worlds-largest-and-most-powerful-generative-language-model/ (archived at https://perma.cc/245X-4WYC)

31 D Moonat. Fine-Tune BERT Model for Named Entity Recognition in Google Colab, 8 June 2022, www.analyticsvidhya.com/blog/2022/06/fine-tune-bert-model-for-named-entity-recognition-in-google-colab/ (archived at https://perma.cc/L7KK-6NTS)

Part Three
Decoding the Imperative_

11 >Ethics, Privacy and Security, and Standards_

Digital technology is essential for modern civilization to succeed on countless levels. People depend on their computers, whether desktops, laptops, or smartphones, to work from home, buy airplane tickets, order groceries, and do many other tasks. Computers are equally critical for business, military, and medical areas. Businesses depend on the reliability of the web and internet, the cloud, and their applications and equipment to pay employees, process invoices, and manufacture and transport goods. Without reliable computers, business grinds to a halt very quickly.

The metaverse introduces an entire new level of possibilities and uses. Businesses, governments, and individuals will become even more empowered as the metaverse expands worldwide.

The expansion of the internet resulted in many societal changes that affect people daily. Much like the internet, there are, and will be, ethical questions about the impact of the metaverse on individuals and society. The metaverse must be designed to improve collaboration, bring people together, and enrich lives.

Societal considerations also encompass supporting technologies, such as artificial intelligence (AI), internet of things (IoT), and Big Data. How will these disruptive technologies be implemented positively to improve people's lives and society?

The best use of the metaverse is to embrace its potential to improve society and individual freedom (within well-defined limits). In other words, the technology must align with the values and principles that benefit society the most.

Many questions must be examined and resolved as the metaverse is designed and implemented. Some of these include the following:

· How should the technology of the metaverse be deployed?
· How should the metaverse be used?

- How should the metaverse be governed?
- How should children be protected in the metaverse?
- Should there be limitations on free speech in the metaverse?
- What is the right or best approach to governance in the metaverse?
- How should metaverse's security and privacy be enforced?
- How can the metaverse be democratized so it's not just controlled by the powerful and elite?
- Who owns the metaverse's data (e.g., individuals, governments, corporations)?
- Does the government have rights in the metaverse?
  - Does it have the right to subpoena?
  - Does it have law enforcement rights?
  - How shall people and organizations be protected against criminals?

In addition to ethical considerations, the fundamental right to privacy needs to be built in at the foundations of Web3 and the metaverse. People need to know they can use the metaverse as if it was "real life" without being overly concerned about the privacy of their personal information. Security is at the base of privacy because without a secure environment, there can be no privacy.

Finally, just like there is only one internet and web, there will be one metaverse. Certainly, people will find unique worlds, games, and platforms within the metaverse. Getting these worlds to interconnect and work together as a seamless whole requires governance, standards, and regulations. The metaverse must allow people to move from world to world at will with no constraints, and they must be able to transport virtual items from place to place.

The answers to the ethical, security, privacy, and governance questions will determine how technology is used, how risk is defined and mitigated, and what the metaverse means to humanity. In the rest of this chapter, we'll unpack ethics, privacy, security, and standards regarding the metaverse. These essential questions should be addressed as the metaverse technology is being developed and people begin to take advantage of its new capabilities.

Ethics

History demonstrates that the reason humans can function together in society and work towards common goals is based on ethics. With a solid ethical framework, society flourishes. Most obvious, as we discussed earlier, people trust that the money they receive electronically in their bank account can be used in exchange for goods and services. They trust that the bank will not abscond with their money, that their employer will deposit their pay on time, and that their debit cards will work in the supermarket. At its base, ethics translates to trust because trust affects every aspect of the relations between humans—personal, business, governmental, medical, and social.

The modern world is enriched by technology. The metaverse will increase society's dependence on technical solutions. In other words, technology enables the modern age by increasing crop yields, improving transportation, and providing instant communications and usable work-from-home environments. Society would collapse without smartphones, the cloud, fiber optics, undersea cables, and other technical marvels.

Because of this dependence, it behooves us all to collaborate positively, have open and honest dialog about our ethical values, and come to a greater understanding of how these new paradigms and devices will affect people and society in the short and long term.

Eudaimonia, a term dating from the time of Aristotle, means happiness, welfare, and flourishing at the individual and societal levels. By setting our sights on achieving the greatest happiness (or well-being) for the members of society and setting out to meet those goals, we can, as a group, learn to create realistic ethics standards.[1]

Many ethical practices, each with unique viewpoints and philosophies, can help us understand the ethical considerations and maintain intelligent, responsible conversations. Regardless of our ethical backgrounds, the metaverse and its underlining intelligent systems—autonomous or otherwise—should be designed to respect human rights and dignity, help people flourish and prosper, and sustain the environment.

General Ethical Principles

The concept of ethics has been a theme of interest for millennia, even if humans have existed. *Ethics* is the study of values, principles, and rules of morality. It's a branch of philosophy that recommends concepts of right and wrong, creates systems for those, and recommends resultant behavior. As such, the goal of ethics is to help define:

- Good and evil
- Right and wrong
- Virtue and vice
- Justice and crime

Related fields include value theory, moral philosophy, and descriptive ethics.

In the context of ethics, here are some of the core terms that will help bring alignment to conversations about ethics in the metaverse:

Values. Subjective beliefs that people hold

Virtues. A trait or quality is considered to be morally good

Ethics. The philosophy of determining the difference between right and wrong

Norm. Standard ways for conduct and behavior

Business ethics is a relatively new sub-set field that attempts to create guidelines for ethical behavior by business entities. Some of the questions considered by business ethics (and these apply to business in the metaverse as well) include:

- What kinds of products and services should and shouldn't be sold?
- What methods can be used to sell, advertise, and market them?
- What is the responsibility of a business towards its stakeholders, employees, managers, and others?

- Is it the place of business to address social concerns?
- Should businesses be involved in politics?

These are just a few of the many questions that business ethics attempts to answer.

To support ethical- and value-based implementations of the metaverse and its supporting technologies (such as artificial intelligence [AI], cryptocurrencies, blockchain, and so on), the following general ethical principles should be followed:

Human rights. The design and implementation of the metaverse and its parts should respect human rights recognized internationally.

Well-being. The metaverse should be aimed at enhancing the well-being of humans.

Data agency. Individuals should be empowered to access and securely share their data and to be in control of their identity.

Effectiveness. Evidence of the effectiveness and fitness should be recorded and available.

Transparency. Any decision should be discoverable.

Accountability. An unambiguous rationale for any decisions should be created and available.

Awareness of misuse. The designers and implementers should be responsible for guarding against risks and negatives of the metaverse and its parts during operation.

Competence. Individuals responsible for implementation and design should have the knowledge and skills to perform their tasks safely and effectively.

Let's take a moment to examine several leading theories of ethics as a reference point for building an ethical metaverse.

Ethical Foundations

In the Western tradition, beginning with Plato and Aristotle, ethics focused on the individual, the family, and the polis (i.e., city or public). The individual is related to these and to the administrative duties within the family, which then expands to the public. In our evaluation about the ethical considerations of information systems, these three focus areas must be considered because individual morality is often isolated from economics and politics in the modern world. Many thinkers have explored the reasons behind this disconnection. Undoubtedly, this discourse is vital because it helps understand the subject of ethics for the metaverse.

Classical Ethics. The Institute of Electrical and Electronics Engineers' (IEEEs) Ethically Aligned Design accessed over 2,500 years of data about ethics and researches scientific and religious approaches, including secular philosophy, to help understand digital age morality. This work reviews autonomy and ontology and explores the potential for autonomous systems (AS) and how morals apply to amoral systems. Their work proceeds to explore moral decisions made by amoral systems and the moral consequences of those decisions.

Virtue Ethics. As previously mentioned, Aristotle argued that the goal of people is eudaimonia, which means to flourish. This is achieved by balancing the social environment, material things, family, friends, and self, by using habituation, which is using virtuous actions to achieve the "golden mean," a principle of rationality. This requires that extremes of excess and deficiency be balanced. For the metaverse, this means to provide a model of iterative learning and moral values, adjusted by contact and practice as opposed to a static set of rules. Virtue ethics also gives the people who design and implement technology an ethical framework that they can use as a counter to the tendency to lean towards excess.

Deontological ethics. Immanuel Kant, an eighteenth-century philosopher, developed this system of duty-based ethics. Deontological ethics states that rules that produce duties are valuable and don't require justification by comparing them to the greater good. These rules are fundamental because they are a foundation for self-worth and create an environment where people can coexist and interact. It is based on the categorical imperative stating, "Act only on that maxim through which you can at the same time will that it should become a universal law." In other words, the rule must be desirable, achievable, valuable, and able to be understood by others. Hence, rules created by personal choice cannot be universal unless they are more universally accepted.

Utilitarian (consequentialist ethics). This focuses on the consequences of decisions and actions, meaning the correct course of action is to maximize the utility (i.e., utilitarianism) or pleasure (i.e., hedonism) of the most significant number of people, except for superficial and short-term utilities or pleasures. According to this ethics, technology developers must consider long-term effects, including social justice (will the project help or harm humanity, among other things). All stakeholders should understand the benefits.

Ethics of care. In this approach (usually thought of as a branch of feminist ethics), stress is placed on context-bound relationships, and caring for other people is foundational for humans.

In many ways, people's personal perspectives and viewpoints in the physical world surface in dialogs about the metaverse, including the ideal economic, political, and social systems for the digital world. The ethical approaches that we surveyed previously can be used to help address these concerns and guide future dialogs.

Impact of Ethics

The ubiquitous and affordable internet gives access to the metaverse and related technology to people who live anywhere in the world. Using these technologies, institutions should lead change in improving the human condition, including goals such as sustainable living. By using the ethical foundations presented previously, organizations can guide the metaverse forward; businesses can contribute to the further advancement of culture, art, collaboration, and communication, in addition to making a responsible profit for their stakeholders.

These are complex topics and subjects, but if ethics is at the center of these conversations, the metaverse will be more additive to society.

Privacy/Security

The designers of the early internet and web didn't include security and privacy in their specifications, at least not to any great extent. The underlying architecture and protocols (i.e., TCP/IPv4, HTTP) were not designed with security and privacy concepts in mind. Passwords were often stored in plaintext, and routers and system accounts remained set to the factory default settings. Operating systems and applications were designed and implemented without security concerns, and even today the domain name system suffers from poor security practices by its design.

However, this situation wouldn't work in the age of internet-connected personal computers and mainframes. E-commerce requires a minimum level of security to protect credit card and consumer information. Malicious actors (i.e., hackers, hacking groups, and even nation states) broke into phone switches (which in those days were used for the internet), compromised routers, and penetrated military, e-commerce, and infrastructure systems.

While a significant purpose of TCP/IPv6 was mostly to solve the problem of TCP/IPv4's limitations on the number of addresses, it also introduced a much-needed layer of security into the protocol. Computer operating systems and applications are patched regularly to resolve security vulnerabilities, encryption of communications and data became the norm instead of the exception, and strong passwords, combined with biometrics, are now enforced.

Along with security, privacy has grown in importance. Consumers trust social media, e-commerce, and their hospitals and banks with their confidential information. Malicious actors seek to penetrate the defenses of these and other institutions to gain massive databases filled with sensitive personal information, which can then be used for nefarious purposes or even sold to the highest bidder. Keeping these malicious actors out is so important that many businesses are creating an executive, c-level position with the responsibility for privacy.

Many other books, courses, and university programs detail computer security and privacy subjects. Correspondingly, this section will evaluate security and privacy concepts specific to the metaverse and is intended to open a dialog about these subjects.

Metaverse Security

The primary intention of the metaverse is to create an immersive environment complete with an economy, system of governance, ownership of items, and social connections. People need to feel safe and have peace of mind that their private information is protected. Security and privacy must be at the forefront of the metaverse to ensure that users are not reticent about visiting, engaging in commerce, and being involved in social interactions.

The metaverse will consist of virtual worlds sponsored by organizations, businesses, governments, and individuals. These worlds will often be hosted either in the cloud or on-premises, which means it's up to the provider to ensure their platforms are secure by following best practices, including those listed here:

- Educate their team members about security practices, policies, and procedures.
- Enforce complex passwords and take advantage of biometrics for logins.
- Secure their networking, including Wi-Fi.
- Create a sound and tested backup policy that is followed.
- Install anti-malware and anti-virus software.
- Secure any physical devices.
- Perform regular security updates on their operating systems, firmware, and applications.
- Create, publish, and test an incident response plan.
- Data, especially personal consumer data, must be encrypted at all points in the network.

AUGMENTED AND VIRTUAL REALITY

Augmented reality (AR) and virtual reality (VR) is essential to providing a quality, engaging, immersive experience. AR collects and receives data that is stored in either centralized or decentralized databases, depending on the application. This data may be compromised during transmission and receipt (i.e., in flight), or on the database and the AR/VR device itself. Each represents a potential security concern and presents an avenue for attack.

Some questions associated with these devices involve the following:

- What are the security and privacy concerns when the AR/VR device is compromised?
- How will the data be protected in flight and in databases?
- How will the user be protected from spoofing?
- How will identity be verified in a virtual setting, considering that avatars do not prove identity the same way as a fingerprint or retina scan?
- Will the data be shared with third parties? How will consumers control this sharing?
- How will AR/VR devices receive firmware and security updates?

SOCIAL ENGINEERING

In the real world, identity is proved by providing documentation, such as a driver's license, social security card, or passport. Determining identity is often based on recognizing a person's face or other physical characteristics. In the virtual world, how shall people prove their identity accordingly? People can create an avatar with desired features, which includes mimicking another identity. Without a solution, malicious entities can use social engineering to trick people into giving up personal information and invest in scams.

MARKETPLACES

Marketplaces are used to buy, sell, and trade cybercurrencies and NFTs (among other things). By their nature, these marketplaces must store financial and other personal information (usually in a person's online wallet). This raises the bar for the security concerns associated with marketplaces; their security requirements are equivalent to those of banks and other financial institutions.

BLOCKCHAIN SECURITY

Back when it was first implemented, blockchains were commonly believed to be unhackable, primarily because they would require at least 51 percent of the network resources. So the thinking went, with that kind of computing power why not just use it to mine new coins? Unfortunately, in 2019, an attacker gained control of over 50 percent of the computing power available to Coinbase and used it to rewrite transaction history, which made it possible to spend the cryptocurrency more than once. The attackers then stole $1.1 million. Another exchange, Gate.Io, lost roughly $200,000 to this attacker.[2]

Therefore, blockchain security is not inviolate and it can be hacked. Another concern is whether the underlying encryption methods used to encrypt blockchain blocks can become vulnerable. Hackers have cracked encryption before, most notably with network security protocols such as wired equivalency privacy (WEP). The same possibility exists for the encryption used for blocks. How will entire blockchains be updated with newer, more secure encryption if it becomes vulnerable?

IDENTITY THEFT

Stealing identities means using various means to acquire a person's personal data, then using it to mimic a person. Often, this is done by gaining access to sensitive information like social security numbers. With that information, a nefarious person could apply for credit in another's name without their permission or knowledge. Protections must be included in the metaverse to prevent or reduce this.

DATA SECURITY

The metaverse will require an immense amount of data—on the order of dozens or hundreds of petabytes per day. Some of this information will be stored in a decentralized manner, which means it will be duplicated on all (or many) nodes on a network. Most will be held in large, centralized databases. A significant concern of implementing the metaverse is how this vast volume of data will be kept secure. It will be necessary to encrypt all this data or at least the parts of it that contain personally identifiable information (PII) data. Additionally, it will need to be protected with security best practices.

Metaverse Privacy

As consumers become more dependent on the metaverse in their daily lives., they will use it for banking, shopping, playing games, investing, going to concerts, and a virtually infinite number of other things. As with the internet, they will be genuinely concerned with keeping their personal information private. Equally, a security breach resulting in releasing personal data into the wild could severely damage a business's reputation.

> *It is vital to understand that security is senior to privacy. Without good security practices, privacy cannot be maintained.*

Personal information (PI), also known as personally identifiable information (PII), is any data that can be used to identify, locate, or contact someone. This data is considered personal if it can be used alone or in combination with other data.[3] Some examples of PII data include a person's name, address, email address, password numbers, license IDs, and credit card numbers. Other less obvious PII includes geolocation (i.e., GPS) data, a TCP/IP address, or a screen name. PII data is any data that can be used to identify an individual.

Various standards and regulations exist at the state, provincial, national, or international levels. The California Consumer Privacy Act (CCPA) and General Data Protection Regulation (GDPR) set the standards and law for protecting personal information. Organizations must understand the privacy requirements for their location and where they do business (importantly a US business must be GDPR compliant if it does business in Europe).

Numerous techniques are used to protect PII data. It is common to reduce the identifiability of the data, which involves masking the data (such as overprinting a password with asterisks), removing it (shortening a name from Joe Smith to J. Smith), or aggregating it (8 out of 10 enjoyed this movie).

Some areas of primary concern for data privacy (among others) include the following:

- Healthcare
- Religious data
- Political information
- Intimate or highly personal data
- Genetic information

Sometimes, the determination of the sensitivity of information is not as simple as it might seem on the surface. The context of the information must be considered as well. An email address on its own may not be considered sensitive unless it is associated with something else that is sensitive.

The companies with access to personal information must be determined and limited to those who need to know and only when they need to know it. For instance, PCS DSS states credit card numbers must be encrypted. Needless to say, the fraud department might need to look at those numbers occasionally to settle cases. In this instance, only those employees who need to know that information can decrypt and view credit card numbers.

Organizations must care about and enforce good security and privacy. It's in the best interests of consumers, employees, stakeholders, and the organization. The ideal way to do this is to ensure that best practices infuse the entire organization. Everyone must understand security and privacy and must practice it. This involves everyone from every department, including contracts and developers.

Data undergoes a particular lifecycle, which is outlined here:

- The data is collected.
- This information is encrypted and stored. Encryption might occur as the data is being collected.
- The information is used as necessary.
- The data might be shared as outlined in the organization's privacy policy.
- The data might be archived or destroyed. Note, decentralized data in blockchains are not customarily archived or destroyed.

Protecting the privacy and integrity of data must be an integral part of the design of any system or application from beginning to end. It's the best way to ensure that data remains private.

Standards, Governance, and Regulations

Standards, governance, and regulations are the foundation of the modern digital world and they allow systems to work together as a harmonious whole. We must also consider that the TCP/IP standard defines how communication works on the internet, which means that people can connect and do their business without worrying about how to connect their computers. Web 1.0, 2.0, and 3.0 work in much the same way, by enabling anyone to use their web browser and applications to interoperate with servers and systems across the planet. No one needs to worry about whether a website will work in a browser because standards require that all browsers accept HTML, JavaScript, and other web-based languages.

For the metaverse to operate in the same transparent manner, standards, governance, and regulations are required. With standards, people can transfer their virtual possessions between worlds at will, without concern for how that transfer occurs. They will be able to travel into a world, then leave and move on to the next one in much the same way that people currently traverse the web, moving from website to website.

Some examples of well-known standards include the following:

Industry Standards. These are a few standards that apply to the industry to ensure equipment and software work seamlessly together:

- IEC 60038 Standard voltages
- IEC 60228 Conductors of insulated cables
- IEC 60269 Low-voltage power fuses
- IEC 60320 C13 Connectors and C14 inlets
- IEC 60884 Household plugs and socket-outlets
- IEC 61970 APIs for energy management

Multiple Standards. Hardware and software standards work together to support a wide range of technology needs:

- Bluetooth
- USB

- HDMI
- SCSI
- Ethernet
- TCP/IP
- HTTPS
- Wi-Fi
- Display port

Constellation of Standards

Many standards organizations will and are contributing to an open and inclusive metaverse:

- W3C
- IEEE
- Web3d
- Khronos

One group, the metaverse Standards Forum, is helping create the standards needed for this next level of interoperability in the same way that W3C defines the standards for the web. Neil Travett, Khronos Group President, explained:

> The metaverse will bring together diverse technologies, requiring a constellation of interoperability standards, created, and maintained by many standards organizations. The metaverse Standards Forum is a unique venue for coordination between standards organizations and industry, with a mission to foster the pragmatic and timely standardization essential to an open and inclusive metaverse.[4]

In 2022, the metaverse Standards Forum was created to unite companies, businesses, and organizations to develop the interoperability standards needed to build the open metaverse. One of the group's primary goals is to determine gaps in interoperability standards that might be delaying the development and deployment of the metaverse. The Forum is open at no cost to any organization.

Many industry leaders agree that a foundation of open standards is the best way to ensure that the full potential of the metaverse is realized. Many interoperability standards will be needed and are led by Standards Developing Organizations (SDOs) such as The Khronos Group, The World Wide Web Consortium, The Open Geospatial Consortium, The Open AR Cloud, The Spatial Web Foundation, and so forth.

Why are Standards Needed?

Standards are the reason that technology and the digital age function. One way to think about it is that web pages follow specific standards. They are written in a markup language called HTML defined by a series of standards. Browsers consistently depend on web pages following those standards to interpret and display billions of web pages. This would not be possible without these standards.

Images work in much the same way. Each image format follows a standard. Without this standard, an image file would just contain a series of random characters and numbers. It wouldn't make any sense. The standard explains how those files should be interpreted to produce visible images and metadata.

The metaverse will involve many different components, from images and text to videos to 3D animations, blockchain, NFTs, and DAOs. All these require standards, so applications understand how to create, modify, display, and secure them. While many standards are already defined (images, for example), others are either in progress or have yet to be designed.

In other words, standards are agreements that define how something operates across industries. Once a standard is accepted, companies can use it to design and build so that their products can interoperate smoothly.

The Vision

Businesses and organizations of all sizes have collaborated to create the standards to design, implement, and deploy the metaverse.

According to the metaverse Standards Forum, a few of the technologies that require standardization include the following:[5]

- Synthetic visual reality
- Practical XR optics
- Real-time environment scanning and semantic understanding
- End-user 3D content creation tooling
- Physical simulations
- Remote social interactions
- Supporting millions of simultaneous users
- Streaming of large geospatial data sets
- Persistent real-world geo-anchoring
- Universal digital twins
- Online personas and social connections
- Realistic avatars
- Sharable consumer assets
- Security and privacy
- Online economies and currencies

Because of the standards, proven technologies can be deployed, which allows businesses to create opportunities that benefit all consumers.

Open Standards

The Forum encourages open standards as these lead to consistency between different implementations. These open standards will meet the needs of diverse markets and use cases. Open source will be used for implementations, tools, samples, and validators.

Summary

A solid underpinning for the metaverse is built on industry-accepted open standards. Open standards support the transfer of virtual items between virtual worlds, the usability of various cryptocurrencies throughout all worlds, and the ability to maintain the same avatar anywhere. Governance and regulations will enforce these standards, so they are accepted and used anywhere.

The creation and acceptance of open standards drove the creation and acceptance of the internet, World Wide Web, browsers, hardware, applications, and anything related to technology. Even the fact that electricity works the same in every home and business is due to the creation of standards.

With ethics, security, and standards in place, we can now focus on defining the principles of a metaverse designed to connect and unite people from all levels of society so they can collaborate, prosper, and live better lives.

Notes

1   C Moore. What Is Eudaimonia? Aristotle and Eudaimonic Wellbeing, 8 April 2019, positivepsychology.com/eudaimonia/ (archived at https://perma.cc/A4PV-F6YQ)

2   M O Page. Once Hailed as Unhackable, Blockchains Are Now Getting Hacked, 19 February 2019 www.technologyreview.com/2019/02/19/239592/once-hailed-as-unhackable-blockchains-are-now-getting-hacked/ (archived at https://perma.cc/EYT7-LDAG)

3   Personal Information, content.next.westlaw.com/practical-law/document/I03f4d9aaeee311e28578f7ccc38dcbee/Personal-Information (archived at https://perma.cc/NZ5E-L8M3)

4   Metaverse Standards Forum, metaverse-standards.org/ (archived at https://perma.cc/PFM6-XE2T)

5   The Metaverse Standards Forum, metaverse-standards.org/ (archived at https://perma.cc/PFM6-XE2T)

12 >Connection, Unity, and Community_

What conditions are required for a person to be happy and healthy as they experience life? Is there a pattern common to people who are happy and missing from those who typically aren't?

Remember *It's a Wonderful Life*? In this holiday-time favorite, George Bailey (James Stewart) believes his life is hopeless. A guardian angel intercedes and shows him what his town and its inhabitants would have been like if he hadn't been around. George realizes that life is more than money or possessions—happiness is about relationships with family and friends.

Inside Out, a Pixar movie released in 2015, followed the adventures of Riley, a young woman, and her five animated emotions: Joy, Sadness, Anger, Fear, and Disgust. During the film, we follow the feelings as they attempt to help Riley navigate a series of personal dangers. She learns each emotion serves a purpose, and by being able to experience all of them, she learns how to be happy. An unstated undercurrent of the movie is that the value of friendship and family adds to the quality of Riley's life.

Sister Act is another movie about the human experience. Deloris, played by Whoopi Goldberg, is placed in a convent by witness protection. She leads the choir and shakes up the sisters' world in the convent with her boisterous personality. By the movie's end, Deloris learns the value of friendship and that she is a loving, caring person.

Each of these movies endeavors to illustrate a story of personal happiness and fulfillment through creative storytelling. George Bailey, Riley, and Deloris each overcome challenges and learn their lives feel more complete because of their social connections, family, and friends. They were able to overcome obstacles and find happiness with the help of their friends and family.

Everyone has known individuals who are happy much of the time. Speaking to them, it seems that very little phases them. They don't suffer much from stress, anxiety, and depression. Instead, they move throughout life with their health intact, prosper in their careers, and have a fulfilling family life. On the other side of the coin, many lives are, to a greater or lesser degree, not proceeding.

As most proceed through life, they focus first on building the skills they need to earn a living and perhaps raise a family. This has been the way of the world for ages, and regardless of our technical advancements, this basic paradigm has remained unchanged. Many would argue that the key to happiness is productivity. In other words, the more a person produces or earns, the happier they are. But is this true? Do we become happier as we earn more money and gain more material things?

A study known as the Study of Adult Development by Grant & Glueck attempted to find an answer. The Grant Group comprised of 268 males, all of whom were Harvard graduates between 1939 and 1944. The Glueck group consisted of 456 men, all of which were lower-income men from the inner cities of Boston. This study has followed these two distinctly different groups of men for over 80 years. The purpose was to find out if any identifiable factors could be used to predict people's health and well-being as they grew older.[1]

The Power of Connections

The study found that the key to happiness and fulfillment in life is relationships (in other words, connections), especially those of high quality. In contrast, many claimed they aspire to get rich, famous, and own material things. A recent study reported that 49 percent of millennials wanted to get rich, in comparison to 40 percent for baby boomers, and 55 percent for Gen-X.[2] Their aspirations are not much different than those of the men in the Study of Adult Development. Typically, over time it has been found that those with successful careers and lives were deeply invested in relationships and connections with family, friends, and their community.

Dr. Robert Waldinger, a psychiatrist, psychoanalyst, and Zen priest presented the study and its finding about happiness in a TED talk on January 25, 2016. Doctor Waldinger authored scientific papers and two books and teaches psychiatry residents and medical students at the Massachusetts General Hospital in Boston.

In his TED talk, Dr. Waldinger contemplates what makes a good life. He references lessons from the Study of Adult Development (the most comprehensive study about happiness) and the behaviors and attitudes that result in long-term happiness and health. He points out that our upbringing constantly reinforces that we must focus on getting ahead, earning a living, and focusing on work; in many people's minds, this makes for a good life.

Of course, getting educated, finding a fitting job, and being competitive are all reasonable goals and should be pursued as they will aid in the creation of a stable, healthy, and happy life. Although, doing these actions to the exclusion of a social life, family, and friends leads away from the path to happiness and fulfillment.

Dr. Waldinger explained there are three big lessons to be understood about relationships. Humans crave social connections, and a lack of those connections, leading to loneliness, is a killer. Being socially connected leads to happiness, health, and longevity. Being alone without those connections reduces happiness, causes health problems, shortens lives, and even reduces the functioning of the brain.

He said, "Good relationships keep our bodies healthier and help us live longer."

We've all experienced moments of loneliness in our lives. Individuals can be lonely in the middle of a crowd of friends. Sometimes, the loneliest moments are those spent in relationships that are not fulfilling or even toxic. Even those who appear very social and well connected might be lonelier than they let on. The quality of relationships is far more critical than the number of social interactions or connections.

Another lesson is that mental health declines in the face of conflict. Toxic friendships, bad marriages, and unfulfilling workplaces will cause people to feel miserable, which may lead to poor physical health, a decline in cognitive abilities, and unhappiness. In other words, even though there are connections, bad connections cause unfortunate side effects to mental health.

The study also determines that healthy relationships lead to better brains, which means it's good for human beings to be attached to another person as they get older. Being able to count on someone else to step up when the going gets tough leads to sharper memories for a longer time. Conversely, those who cannot depend on another person experience a decline in memory at an earlier age. In this case, it's not so much the quality of the relationship that matters. It's the fact that the individuals involved could count on one another to help when needed.

Waldinger explained, "Those good relationships don't have to be smooth all the time. Some of our octogenarian couples could bicker day in and day out. But if they felt they could count on the other when the going got tough, those arguments didn't take a toll on their memories."[3]

He concludes with the observation that the main reason people live long, happy lives is related to the quality of their connections. Happy people experience quality relationships with friends, family, coworkers, and others. Therefore, the most significant factor in experiencing happiness is social connections.

"We figured that if you have good relationships," Dr. Waldinger said, "you're likely to be happier, but we did not believe at first the data showing us that good relationships keep our bodies healthier and help us live longer. And then other studies began to find the same thing."[4]

Connections

Jon Levy echoes this in his book *You're Invited: The Art and Science of Connection, Trust, and Belonging*, where he talks about the need for trust, connection, and community.

Jon states, "Bringing people together in a unique way produces contagious results." He continues, "Ultimately, the people around you matter. Who you surround yourself with defines your success (whatever that means for you personally) and has the potential to change the direction of your life and society?"

He goes on to say, "The most universal strategy for success is creating meaningful connections with those who can impact you, your life, and the things you care about." He finishes up, with, "Nothing is more universal than our need to connect, it is what has allowed us to survive as a species. We aren't loners like tigers or sea turtles."[5]

Given that meaningful connections are one of the keys to a happy, healthy, and meaningful life, how can the metaverse play a role in constructing and encouraging connections? The internet certainly changed society for the better in many ways, including allowing employees to work from home, communicate with smartphones, and give society the ability to order products from all over the world.

UNINTENDED CONSEQUENCES OF THE INTERNET

Consider unintended consequences associated with the internet and technological advances have profoundly affected individuals, businesses, society, governments, and even the world. An unintended consequence happens because of an action that was not anticipated. The Law of Unintended Consequences is often cited by economists and social scientists and doesn't differentiate between good and bad consequences—it means the consequences, good or bad, were not anticipated or planned.

As a society, we must be prepared to talk about these issues honestly, which allows us to find better solutions. The following overview of unintended consequences is an attempt to reframe the future in a beneficial, efficient, and effective way to create a positive metaverse that supports a super organism feeding off the inspiration of everyone. Let's look at a few of the unintended consequences associated with the internet and technology.

DOES THE INTERNET POLARIZE PEOPLE?

According to *Scientific American*, digital platforms do not necessarily polarize people; researchers found that the opposite was true. A somewhat obvious contrast, they did discover something different: digital platforms amplify influencers, who can use their power over millions to radicalize or polarize large groups. Egalitarian groups (where ideas can come from anyone in the group) further ideas based on quality; centralized groups (which are run by one or a small group of influencers) can amplify bias due to their influence over their followers.[6]

Compounding factors, the internet has increased the velocity and volume of data that individuals and groups view. Messaging can spread to millions of individuals in seconds, and that can be shared and reshared countless times. Subsequently, false or inaccurate data created by an influencer (or a group of influencers) can spread quickly and be accepted by a sizable group without fact-checking.

Jolynna Sinanan, University of Sydney, suggested an alternative view, "All the sorts of extremes we've seen this year [in America] is very much the externalization of the 'I matter as an individual.'"[7]

Thus, an unanticipated consequence of the internet is that it allows people to be more forceful about their identity and beliefs because it gives them a channel to communicate quickly, easily, and usually without consequence.

DOES THE INTERNET CREATE ECHO CHAMBERS?

An *echo chamber* is created when the opinions of people in a group constantly receive the same opinions over and over. Essentially their own opinions are echoed back to them, which reinforces their opinions, creates a belief system, and isolates them from other contrary or conflicting opinions. The effect is to reinforce confirmation bias, which means the people in the group consistently see their opinions mirrored back to them, and this confirms, in their minds, that they are correct.

Echo chambers are a byproduct of digital platforms, search engines, and online social groups. Because digital platforms allow people to quickly find and socialize with people with the same opinions and beliefs, echo chambers tend to form. This is reinforced by search engine and digital platform algorithms.

Essentially, the nature of the fast communication and the ability to form groups of like-minded people, combined with search engine and digital platform algorithms, tends to create and reinforce echo chambers. This effect was certainly not anticipated when the internet was first envisioned.

DOES THE INTERNET AMPLIFY EMOTIONAL, ANGRY, OR FALSE POSTS OR INFORMATION?

The internet allowed humanity to communicate with others all over the planet, individually and as part of groups. This, in turn, enabled people to easily share their ideas, feelings, and thoughts at will. Studies have found that online posts trend toward what's known as a *positivity bias*, which means most posts are of positive content.[8] Equally important, according to a 2016 study by FiveThirtyEight. com, commenters often feel they are experts on a subject, and possibly their responses tend to be impassioned, emotional, and hostile. This, combined with the anonymity of the internet and the provocative nature of headlines on the internet, leads to angry posts.[9]

Thus, the internet and digital platforms tend to amplify emotions such as anger and tend to cause the spread of false information. This was not anticipated when the internet was first designed and implemented.

DOES THE INTERNET INCREASE THE LIKELIHOOD OF VIOLENCE?

According to a report produced by the CDC[10], electronic aggression is an emerging public health problem. They cite data that indicates that internet harassment is becoming more common. In 2000, 6 percent of internet users in the age range 10 to 17 stated they were a victim of online harassment; in 2005, this had increased to 9 percent. The research into aggression and violence that occurs or is facilitated by digital platforms and the internet is in its initial stages, so the data is incomplete. Notwithstanding, early results support the premise that harassment and violence have increased because of the internet. This increase in violence was not anticipated by the creators of the web and internet.

DOES THE INTERNET HELP FOREIGN GOVERNMENTS TO SOW DISCORD?

A study backed by the United Nations found that, "Rather than being initiators or causes of violent behaviors, the Internet and digital platforms can be facilitators within wider processes of violent radicalization."[11] To this end, the researchers also found that digital platforms are used to create fear and polarize societies. They recommended that the news media "refrain from fearmongering, stereotyping, confirmation bias, fake news, and the creation of 'media panics,' and to reassert the importance of media ethics in the face of radicalization of young people; for violent extremism."

Additionally, a RAND paper called Combating Foreign Disinformation on Social Media[12] states that several foreign governments have funded disinformation campaigns on digital platforms. Vinton Cerf, co-inventor of the Internet Protocol, summed it up, "We didn't focus on how you could wreck this system intentionally."[13]

Considering that the protocols and standards designed for the early internet didn't include much in the way of security, it can be concluded that using the internet to sow discord was not something they anticipated.

DOES THE INTERNET REDUCE TRUST BETWEEN PEOPLE?

The internet was not designed with trust or security in mind. Digital platforms and the ability to communicate quickly have resulted in quandary about trusting people even though they might be strangers.

Vinton Cerf, Vice President and Chief Internet Evangelist at Google, the co-inventor of the Internet Protocol and a member of the Internet Hall of Fame stated:

> Trust is rapidly leaking out of the internet environment. Unless we strengthen the ability of content and service suppliers to protect users and their information, trust will continue to erode. Strong authentication to counter hijacking of accounts is vital.[13]

Because the internet and digital platforms were not designed to address trust, it is true that the reduction in trust, as a result, was not anticipated.

DOES THE INTERNET RESULT IN STRONGER POPULIST MOVEMENTS?

According to the National Library of Medicine, digital platforms and the internet act as a force multiplier that allows individuals or groups to disseminate information to others quickly. Digital platforms give populists or other movements a method where they can reach mass audiences much more quickly and efficiently than in the past. The designers of the internet did not anticipate this.

HOW DOES THIS APPLY TO THE METAVERSE?

The metaverse will be a ubiquitous and fast communication method for the population of nations and the world. The effects of this on people, groups, and society must be considered as the technology behind the metaverse is designed and implemented. Otherwise, these same issues might proceed forward into the metaverse. By building good security, privacy, and trust, the metaverse will be a safe place for businesses and individuals to be entertained, informed, and engage in business.

Connections: The Solution

Now let's examine seven select focus areas to help ensure we have a productive and inclusive metaverse that will be additive to the world.

User Authentication

Currently, user authentication involves creating an account with an associated email address, password, and a two-factor code or biometric. Platforms generally require users to enter their age and other data, but this is not validated. Once an account is created, a user can perform read, post, and edit and connect to other participants on the platform.

To tighten up authentication, users could be required to prove their identity via a third party not affiliated with the platform. Here are the levels of authentication:

1 No authentication. This is the current method used. Anyone can create accounts, fake or not.

2 Add a captcha that users must pass to prove they are human and not a bot. This may prevent bots, but it doesn't help users create thousands of spam accounts by hand.

3 Authenticate the user's unique identity once without storing the information. Users must prove their identity via a third party not affiliated with a platform. This step is only performed on account creation. Additionally, users would be allowed to create only one account.

4 Authenticate to a third party who stores the information.

5 Authenticate everyone and require them to post with their real name.

Special considerations would have to be made for dissidents in repressive countries and whistleblowers to protect their identity.

Age Restrictions and Age-Appropriate Design

People can generally post whatever they want to digital platforms (and, by extension, the metaverse). Some digital media restrict some subjects (such as pornography and false information about COVID and vaccines). Although, it's difficult and resource-intensive to scan images and videos (and other media) for compliance with these restrictions.

Currently, most digital platforms (and websites) ask the user for their age without verification. A method must be created to validate the age so that age-sensitive content is not displayed to minors. This would require user authentication via a third party (i.e., options 3, 4, and 5 above).

Platform Accountability and Transparency

Because digital platforms are now an integral part of the lives of the general population worldwide, it is essential that the platforms be transparent in their practices and held accountable:

- The Platform Accountability and Transparency Act allows independent researchers to propose access to platform information by submitting it to the NSF.
- The Algorithmic Accountability Act of 2022 is intended to enhance the powers of the Federal Trade Commission (FTC) to oversee and guide the private sector on the impact of algorithms.

Architectural Changes to Reduce Virality

Every digital influencer desires their content go viral, which means their post is seen by thousands or even millions of people within a short time. We can also observe, there is a downside because propaganda, malicious messages, and other undesired content can reach many people within a noticeably brief time. This can be alleviated by limiting the number of individuals who can join a group within a set time or by modifying the share feature to limit or slow down how quickly posts can be shared.

Changing Incentives to Reduce Trolling and Antisocial Behavior

Trolls, or individuals who harass others online by stirring up emotional responses, have been a problem since the beginning of the internet and message boards. Requiring user authentication as described in options 3, 4, and 5 under user authentication would reduce the number and reach of trolls.

Changing Parameters to Reduce the Noise/Signal Ratio

The signal means information that is truthful and supports the democratic process. Noise consists of misinformation, propaganda, and other untruthful content that undermines positive discourse. A high ratio of signal to noise means truthful, accurate content prevails. Conversely, a low ratio indicates untruthful content overpowers truthful content. A higher ratio of signal to noise is the most desirable state.[14]

Platforms need to include, as part of their design, the ability to detect and counter false, malicious, and untruthful content in a manner that doesn't get in the way of freedom of speech. The United States is particularly reluctant to limit freedom of speech and leans towards allowing the "marketplace" to regulate the noise. In general, truth is expected to outshine lies and false information.

Individuals can be manipulated into sharing malicious or false information if they do not know who is communicating with them. They cannot know if the message was posted by a malicious foreign actor attempting to undermine an election or an innocent person talking about their opinions. Increasing the transparency of authorship (which requires better user authentication) is one method to alleviate this. Some laws that are proposed include the following:

- The Bot Disclosure and Accountability Act would prevent candidates, their campaigns, and political groups from using bots for political advertisements.
- The Honest Ads Act proposes maintaining a list of all political advertisers who spent more than $500 on sponsored ads.
- The California Disclose Act requires advertisers of political campaigns to list the top three contributors.
- The New York State Democracy Protection Act says that information identifying the source of the ad be available.

Other laws and guidelines are being proposed to make it more evident that a bot was used for posting.

Deepfakes are a method of creating realistic fake videos, images, and audio that misrepresent the truth. The Deepfake Accountability Act would require the addition of an irremovable watermark to any deepfake.

Algorithmic noise is another problem. As Julie Cohen outlined in *Law for the Platform Economy*:

Algorithmic mediation of information flows intended to target controversial material to receptive audiences ... inculcating resistance to facts that contradict preferred narratives, and encouraging demonization and abuse... New data harvesting techniques designed to detect users' moods and emotions... exacerbate these problems; increasingly, today's networked information flows are optimized for subconscious, affective appeal.[15]

Regulators and industry will need to co-produce and develop standards and regulations to counter these tendencies.

The Need for and Legitimacy of Federal Regulation

With great power comes great responsibility. Digital platforms impact billions of people throughout the world. People and businesses depend on them for social connections, physical and mental health, e-commerce, and information. Does their importance over the well-being of so many people and businesses need more regulatory oversight?[16]

Regulators need to recognize the importance of digital platforms to the economy and social well-being of the population. Thereby, using the regulations of Dodd-Frank as a model, they should state which of the companies are of systemic importance. Regulators must also establish a forum or council to discuss technology risks.[17]

In many ways, the goal is to curb attention-grabbing manipulative practices and provide billions of users with greater agency. Although many platforms are free to use, they can produce a dopamine response, causing users to stay online for prolonged periods. The average American spends 40 percent (60 percent for teens) of the time they are awake online. Because of this, digital platforms need to be designated as systemically important platforms. This means they legally will be required to open their platforms to middleware, which is intended to let users curate their experience.[17]

Finally, what happens to user data if a Big Data company fails or closes? Existing governance frameworks don't address this contingency. An agenda needs to be set for research and policymaking to account for these possibilities.[18]

Unity: Swarm Intelligence

Individuals are more powerful together than alone. You can see this unity in nature. Scientists have observed how insects and animals work together in swarms to achieve a greater chance of survival for the group. Like connections positively impact individuals, this concept of unity can be leveraged to improve business opportunities, efficiencies, and outcomes.

As noted by *Harvard Business Review*, Southwest Airlines noticed that cargo flights into some airports couldn't schedule their freight loads despite the average plane only using 7 percent of its cargo space fleetwide. This presented a conundrum: why was this problem happening, and how could it be solved?

Southwest looked to nature for answers to help solve this problem. Insects such as bees and ants forage for food efficiently to feed their hives or colonies. How do these insects find the most efficient routes to food? Looking at nature's examples, Southwest applied the lessons to its problem. Counterintuitively, they realized it might be better to leave cargo on planes, even if it appeared to be better to unload them immediately. Sometimes, this meant leaving the cargo onboard going in the wrong direction. Once they applied this approach to their problem, their freight transfer rates dropped by as much as 80 percent and were reduced by roughly $10 million per year.[19]

This brings us to the subject of Swarm Intelligence. *Swarm intelligence* is the collective behavior of a decentralized or self-organized system. These systems consist of numerous individuals with limited intelligence interacting with each other based on simple principles.[20]

Approaches founded on mathematical models describe how social insects behave. These approaches have moved from the theoretical to the practical and may be applied directly to business issues and problems.

In the *Harvard Business Review* article, the authors state that insects use swarm intelligence to succeed using three characteristics:

1 Colonies are flexible so that they can adapt as the environment changes.

2 The group can continue to perform its tasks even after individuals fail.

3 Individuals self-organize without central control or local supervision.

This approach helps address many different problems facing businesses every day. For example, several large telecom companies (i.e., France Télécom, British Telecom, and MCI WorldCom) included the concepts of swarm intelligence in their solutions for the extraordinarily complex task of routing internet traffic. They believe their algorithms will outperform every existing method used to route traffic by simulating this technique.

Swarm intelligence enables complex behaviors based on individuals following simple rules. Evolution worked to create insect-based social patterns that serve as rules that optimize efficiency, flexibility, and robustness. Can these concepts be utilized to solve business problems by replacing organizational hierarchies and their associated command structures with swarm intelligence?

The authors of the *Harvard Business Review* article stated: "We believe these findings have implications for companies because the size of an organization, the characteristics of a marketplace, and the competitive environment are similarly intertwined in the business world. When markets are volatile and short-lived but sufficiently large, and when competition can emerge from anywhere, the ideal enterprise, we suggest, would be of medium size (a business unit within a larger conglomerate). More important, we believe, the organization would do well to possess strong internal mechanisms that enable—if not encourage."[19]

Taking advantage of the concept of swarm intelligence applies directly to helping businesses succeed and prosper with the metaverse. The metaverse, if built correctly, will connect and unite people for individual and business benefits to form communities for the betterment of society.

Community

In previous chapters, we've already showcased the idea that many participants attend virtual social events and play virtual games for friendship and a feeling of belonging to a social group or community (i.e., a sense of fellowship with others). Socializing with friends is the most powerful motivator for engaging with the virtual world and the metaverse.

If you've used any social media, you know that connections are of primary importance. Without connections (or friends as they are often called), the experience isn't as meaningful. You can post photos, videos, and messages, but no one will see them, like them, share them, or comment on them. That's an exercise in futility in most cases. Members join social media to connect with friends and others they know.

This is true even for gaming or social events. In the physical world, most games are played with one or more other gamers (except in the case of Solitaire). Playing Monopoly, Battleship, or Chess alone is somewhat pointless and unfulfilling. This carries over into the gaming world. Playing games with online or offline friends is far more engaging and interesting because of the connections that already exist or form in the virtual world.

A significant component of socializing is to connect and unite with friends and people in social groups, resulting in a feeling of community. Most social media platforms support the concepts of groups, which serve to unite people into communities. During the days of the early internet, message boards served this purpose. The sense of unity or belonging could become very profound. It's common for moderators and members to become very protective of their group, much like the fans of a soccer game will have an intense sense of belonging and defend their teams. Metaverse communities will become even more immersive, engaging, and meaningful.

Summary

We've established that connections have enormous benefits to personal health and well-being. For the metaverse to be a maximum multiplier of success, connections must be at the center of the metaverse's core value proposition. Metaverse's second value proposition can be seen with unity on a business and organizational level. For instance, the power of unity is represented in nature through a phenomenon known as swarm intelligence, also described as collective intelligence. Metaverse's third value proposition is community, resulting in shared immersive experiences.

The metaverse, when comprised of Connections + Unity + Community = Empowerment. This equation will usher in a new world of business expansion and social advancement.

Notes

1 Study of Adult Development, www.adultdevelopmentstudy.org/grantandglueckstudy (archived at https://perma.cc/9ZRQ-5GMM)

2 Millennial Millionaires Just Want to Get Rich, 28 March 2014, www.nbcnews.com/business/business-news/millennial-millionaires-just-want-get-rich-n66286 (archived at https://perma.cc/347H-UPKE)

3 Anahad O'Connor. The Secrets to a Happy Life, from a Harvard Study. 23 March 2016, archive.nytimes.com/well.blogs.nytimes.com/2016/03/23/the-secrets-to-a-happy-life-from-a-harvard-study/ (archived at https://perma.cc/PWJ2-KARA)

4 Alison DeNiscoRayome. How to Be Happier, According to Science, 11 July 2022, www.cnet.com/culture/how-to-be-happier-according-to-science/ (archived at https://perma.cc/QQ87-4EMK)

5 Jon Levy (2021) *You're Invited: The Art and Science of Connection, Trust, and Belonging.* Harper Business

6 Damon Centola. Why Social Media Makes Us More Polarized and How to Fix It, 15 October 2020, www.scientificamerican.com/article/why-social-media-makes-us-more-polarized-and-how-to-fix-it/ (archived at https://perma.cc/PMD8-GYWM)

7   Tyler Sonnemaker. 11 Experts Explain How Our Digital World Is Fueling Polarization, 28 December 2020, www.businessinsider.com/how-internet-social-media-fuel-polarization-america-facebook-twitter-youtube-2020-12 (archived at https://perma.cc/Z825-NRU6)

8   Sophie F Waterloo, Susanne E Baumgartner, Jochen Peter, and Patti M Valkenburg. Norms of online expressions of emotion: Comparing Facebook, Twitter, Instagram, and WhatsApp, 23 May 2017, journals.sagepub.com/doi/10.1177/1461444817707349# (archived at https://perma.cc/R5RP-2347)

9   Adam P Stern MD. The Psychology of Internet Rage. 17 May 2018, www.health.harvard.edu/blog/the-psychology-of-internet-rage-2018051713852 (archived at https://perma.cc/PQY6-H4LN)

10 C David-Ferdon C. Electronic Media and Youth Violence: A CDC Issue Brief for Researchers, www.cdc.gov/violenceprevention/pdf/electronic_aggression_researcher_brief-a.pdf (archived at https://perma.cc/ML3X-7GJ2)

11 'No clear Evidence' Social Media Leads to More Violent Behavior, UN-Backed Study Reports, news.un.org/en/story/2017/12/640702-no-clear-evidence-social-media-leads-more-violent-behavior-un-backed-study (archived at https://perma.cc/E8X6-C5HX)

12 Raphael S Cohen, Nathan Beauchamp-Mustafaga, Joe Cheravitch, Alyssa Demus, Scott W Harold, Jeffrey W Hornung, Jenny Jun, Michael Schwille, Elina Treyger, and Nathan Vest. Combating Foreign Disinformation on Social Media, www.rand.org/content/dam/rand/pubs/research_reports/RR4300/RR4373z1/RAND_RR4373z1.pdf (archived at https://perma.cc/4GTS-N22P)

13 The Fate of Online Trust in the Next Decade, 10 August 2017, www.pewresearch.org/internet/2017/08/10/the-fate-of-online-trust-in-the-next-decade/ (archived at https://perma.cc/2N82-5Q92)

14 Elen P Goodman. Digital Information Fidelity and Friction. 26 February 2020, knightcolumbia.org/content/digital-fidelity-and-friction (archived at https://perma.cc/P89K-N6A3)

15 Julie E Cohen. Law for the Platform Economy. https://lawreview.law.ucdavis.edu/issues/51/1/symposium/51-1_Cohen.pdf (archived at https://perma.cc/Z97Q-CQJK)

16 Lindsay Sain Jones and Tim Samples. On the Systemic Importance of Digital Platforms, 1 June 2022, papers.ssrn.com/sol3/papers.cfm?abstract_id=4040269 (archived at https://perma.cc/X67K-S8EV)

17 Caleb N Griffin. Systemically Important Platforms, 19 March 2021, papers.ssrn.com/sol3/papers.cfm?abstract_id=3807723 (archived at https://perma.cc/2FFM-DMGE)

18 Carl Öhman and Nikita Aggarwal. What if Facebook Goes Down? Ethical and legal Considerations for the Demise of Big Tech, 11 August 2020, policyreview. info/articles/analysis/what-if-facebook-goes-down-ethical-and-legal-considerations-demise-big-tech (archived at https://perma.cc/Q6AE-JACD)

19 Eric Bonabeau and ChristopherMeyer. Swarm Intelligence: A Whole New Way to Think about Business, hbr.org/2001/05/swarm-intelligence-a-whole-new-way-to-think-about-business (archived at https://perma.cc/5MP8-U85F)

20 Aboul Ella Hassanien and Ashraf Darwish. *Swarm Intelligence as a Solution for technological Problems Associated with Internet of Things*, www.sciencedirect.com/topics/engineering/swarm-intelligence (archived at https://perma.cc/DB75-42HL)

13 >Conclusion: World of Empowerment_

According to geopolitical analyst Peter Zeihan, the world is experiencing unpredicted change. Supply chains are breaking down; demographics are collapsing; and climate emergency, recent wars, and fears of inflation and economic troubles are rising. He sums it up, stating, "Just as geopolitics tells us that the free trade era is closing, demography tells us that the era of consumption-driven growth that has been the economic norm for seventy years is coming to an unceremonious end."[1]

These challenges cause forward-looking visibility to be incredibly challenging, which makes it difficult, if not impossible, to produce workable solutions using the current economic tools. The world needs an entirely new way of approaching the problem.

Jamie Damion, the Chairman of the Board and Chief Executive Officer of JPMorgan Chase & Company, reinforced the challenges present in the world:

> Geopolitical tension, high inflation, waning consumer confidence, the uncertainty about how high rates have to go and the never-before-seen quantitative tightening and their effects on global liquidity, combined with the war in Ukraine and its harmful effect on global energy and food prices are very likely to have negative consequences on the global economy sometime down the road.[2]

Yet, in numerous ways, this is a tale of two worlds. According to Scott Galloway, from a macro standpoint, the world is much wealthier, has more freedoms, and is better educated than ever:

- In 1980, 40 percent of the people in the world lived in extreme poverty; in 2022, that number was less than 20 percent.

- In 1980, 44 percent of people didn't have democratic rights; in 2022, that number dropped to 25 percent.
- Children born in 1980 could expect to live 63 years, and now that number has increased by a decade.
- In 1980, 30 percent of people over 15 years old were not formally educated; today, that number is down 50 percent.

The one undeniable aspect about the world is, it's increasingly dynamic. Herein lies the opportunity for businesses to invest in the metaverse by applying Persistent Utility, a strategic methodology and mindset for providing an ongoing service loop across three audiences:

1 Those who build the metaverse.
2 Consumers who benefit from the metaverse.
3 Businesses that are expanding.

Charles Darwin pointed out that it is not the strongest of the species that survives, nor the most intelligent that survives. It is the one that is the most adaptable to change. This philosophy applies to businesses as they adjust to the current marketplace disruption and accelerate their metaverse transformation (i.e., adoption of the metaverse into their business models).

Mark Read, the Chief Executive Officer at WPP, emphasized, "I think growth is the most important thing for companies and people. Are we living up to our purpose as best we can, and are we leaving something behind that we're all proud of?"[3]

The metaverse has the potential to increase bottom lines by an order of magnitude, impacting social return on investment (SROI) and other capital models, including Environmental, Social, and Governance (ESG) models.

Economic and Social Value

As expounded throughout the book, the metaverse is a persistent, interconnected environment with social and economic outcomes that mirrors reality and creates an intersection between the physical and virtual worlds.

To underscore the importance of the metaverse, the World Economic Forum is working on a metaverse strategy:

> ... together, leading voices from the private sector, civil society, academia, and policy are coming together to define the parameters of an economically viable, interoperable, safe, and inclusive metaverse, focusing on two core areas: governance, and economic and social value creation.[4]

The metaverse will be a driver to provide businesses and society the command to drive growth and, in the process, resolve the 17 major sustainable development goals as outlined by the United Nations:

1 Goal 1: No poverty
2 Goal 2: Zero hunger
3 Goal 3: Good health and well-being
4 Goal 4: Quality education
5 Goal 5: Gender equality
6 Goal 6: Clean water and sanitation
7 Goal 7: Affordable and clean energy
8 Goal 8: Decent work and economic growth
9 Goal 9: Industry, innovation, and infrastructure
10 Goal 10: Reduced inequalities
11 Goal 11: Sustainable cities and communities
12 Goal 12: Responsible consumption and production
13 Goal 13: Climate action
14 Goal 14: Life below water
15 Goal 15: Life on land
16 Goal 16: Peace, justice, and strong institutions
17 Goal 17: Partnership for the Goals

Business Growth

According to the latest McKinsey Global Survey[5], 55 percent of companies rank building new business growth and expansion as a top three priority. This is almost doubled from a few years ago. McKinsey found that the key factor for a company's expansion is to go where the revenue growth will be coming from. The metaverse is a source for near future revenue growth. A different business model will be required to unlock these growth areas.

Citigroup Investment Bank stated in a report issued in early 2022[6], the total addressable market for the metaverse economy is between $8 trillion and $13 trillion. Goldman Sachs puts it at $12.5 trillion in this space, assuming one-third of the digital economy shifts into virtual worlds and then expands by 25 percent.[7] To put this in context, the total global GDP in 2021 was $96.2 trillion.

These prospects are a rallying cry for professionals, researchers, artists, and others to create socioeconomic and cultural dynamism. New business models will be needed to address more evolved consumer expectations for Persistent Utility.

Creativity and Innovation

The metaverse generates an entirely new nonlinear type of economy. Firms worldwide are getting ready for a metaverse where people can play, shop, socialize, be entertained, and work. Many people will spend increasingly significant portions of their lives in the metaverse. They will join ever larger communities, filling them with content they generate. This virtual space will be decentralized and will unite the currently disparate siloed ecosystems.

The on-demand economy of the metaverse creates a new economic dynamic and model that will require a leadership mindset that places the customer first with utility at the core. This will usher in a new age where creativity powers economic prosperity. People will expand their skills because of this new metaverse approach.

Scott Belsky underscored, "If there's anything we learn from exiting a boom cycle and returning to one of constraint and innovation (vs. valuation optimization): too much/easy money delays meritocracy amongst products and is a distraction from building for the right reasons."[8]

The metaverse is a new engagement model through virtual communities to increase business expansion and customer value, forging a new era of the need for creative, technical, and soft skills.

There are still many unknowns with regards to the metaverse, but as Adam Grant, organizational psychologist at Wharton, identified, we need to build growth mindsets, "I don't know what I'm doing yet. It's only a matter of time until I figure it out. The highest form of self-confidence is believing in your ability to learn."[9]

Strategy

Implementing the metaverse is not a mere matter of flipping the script. Instead, it is the creation of an entirely new economy and economic model to unite people, businesses, and society. The metaverse serves as an economic multiplier.

Joseph Schumpeter's theory of creativity states: Creative Destruction is the "process of industrial mutation that incessantly revolutionizes the economic structure from within, incessantly destroying the old one, incessantly creating a new one."[10] This implies that regulating existing technology may hinder future innovation, so it's essential to be very thoughtful about the metaverse regulation approach.

We can be confident the metaverse will be an evolution consisting of multiple technologies where the mission is to put human utility first.

World of Empowerment

As we move from the Age of Information to the Age of Creativity in the metaverse, our decisions will shape our future. Granting this assumption, if we relinquish decisions to others, we give away our ability to design the lives we want to live.

When designed thoughtfully, the metaverse will facilitate a world of empowerment inclusive across gender empowerment, social empowerment, educational empowerment, economic empowerment, political empowerment, psychological empowerment, physical empowerment, and individual empowerment.

The metaverse will place individual people in control of their destiny and acts as a call to action to businesses that it's not about brands at the center of the universe. It's about people. According to Jim Kennedy, Senior Vice President for Strategy at The Associated Press:

> It may be more useful, and certainly more exciting, to think of the metaverse not as virtual reality but as a new reality itself. Things created there, and things we will choose to do there will be, in a very true sense, real. And in that context, it can become a realm for both work and play."[11]

Led Zepplin seemingly prophesied the metaverse in a line from their song "Kashmir": *I'm a traveler of both time and space.*

As the metaverse becomes a reality, we all will be empowered travelers in this newfound dimension.

See you in the metaverse!

Notes

1 Peter Zeihan (2016) *The Accidental Superpower: The Next Generation of American Preeminence and the Coming Global Disorder.* Twelve

2 Hugh Son. JPMorgan Chase Earnings Fell 28% After Building Reserves for Bad Loans, Bank Suspends Buybacks. 14 July 2022, www.cnbc.com/2022/07/14/jpmorgan-jpm-2q-2022-earnings.html (archived at https://perma.cc/Z3FG-T9A9)

3 Mark Read. LinkedIn Post, August 2022, www.linkedin.com/posts/michaelwright_361-mark-read-the-pragmatic-leader-activity-6953691693657337856-OiXs (archived at https://perma.cc/QT7P-XGTJ)

4 World Economic Forum. Defining and Building the Metaverse, initiatives. weforum.org/defining-and-building-the-metaverse (archived at https://perma.cc/8CUN-4GN6)

5 2021 Global Report: The State of New-Business Building, 6 December 2021, www.mckinsey.com/business-functions/mckinsey-digital/our-insights/2021-global-report-the-state-of-new-business-building (archived at https://perma.cc/8XVT-7WGN)

6 Metaverse and Money, March 2022, ir.citi.com/gps/x5%2BFQJT3BoHXVu9M sqVRoMdiws3RhL4yhF6Fr8us8oHaOe1W9smOy1%2B8aaAgT3SPuQVtwC 5B2%2Fc%3D (archived at https://perma.cc/NP68-5ZHF)

7 Jack Denton. Metaverse May Be Worth $13 Trillion, Citi Says. What's Behind the Bullish Take on Web3, 31 March 2022, www.barrons.com/amp/articles/metaverse-web3-internet-virtual-reality-gaming-nvidia-51648744930 (archived at https://perma.cc/CZ75-HDCB)

8 Scott Bellsky. August 2022, www.linkedin.com/in/scottbelsky (archived at https://perma.cc/Z4A9-AQK9)

9 Adam Grant. Adam Grant Twitter Feed. 25 July 2022, twitter.com/AdamMGrant/status/1551584622420672513 (archived at https://perma.cc/3V92-9PKF)

10 Carol M Kopp. Creative Destruction, 23 June 2021, www.investopedia.com/terms/c/creativedestruction.asp (archived at https://perma.cc/GR3A-UQ5X)

11 Janna Anderson and Lee Rainie. The Metaverse Will Fully Emerge as Its Advocates Predict, 30 June 2022, www.pewresearch.org/internet/2022/06/30/the-metaverse-will-fully-emerge-as-its-advocates-predict (archived at https://perma.cc/X3GA-GJYF)

Index_

Page numbers in *italic* indicate figures.

CPSIA information can be obtained
at www.ICGtesting.com
Printed in the USA
BVHW090107090223
658149BV00009B/40

9 781398 609044